Job Surfing:
Freelancing

The Princeton Review

Job Surfing:
Freelancing

Using the Internet
to Find a Job and Get Hired

Robert Anthony and Jim Blau

Random House, Inc.
New York
www.review.com

Princeton Review Publishing, L. L. C.
2315 Broadway
New York, NY 10024
E-mail: comments@review.com

ISBN 0-375-76235-3

Editors: Anton Malko, Jennifer Mallozzi, and Russell Kahn
Designer: Scott Harris
Production Editor: Julieanna Lambert
Production Coordinator: Greta Englert

Manufactured in the United States of America.

9 8 7 6 5 4 3 2 1

Acknowledgments

The history of freelance work is a daunting and nebulous subject. Independent, free-agent, or freelance work is by its nature an unorganized and random industry, scattered pell-mell across the panorama of time and geography. Little specific information is available on the subject that is composed in a standardized, understandable, or organized manner. A significant amount of information in this book was, therefore, extrapolated from unrelated texts, research studies, and websites.

In compiling the information within this book, special acknowledgment should be given to the work of self-employment experts Paul and Sarah Edwards, who have made significant contributions to the study of online commerce and employment. Also to the library of Michigan State University (go Spartans!), where historic information is kept safe and sound so that books such as this one can be accurately written.

I would also like to acknowledge the efforts of independent freelance workers throughout the world for their imaginative, enterprising, and independent free spirits, which, through the Internet, are transporting our work lives into a new age.

Last, and most importantly, I acknowledge my awesome wife and children, Amy Rose, Jonathan, Zoey, and Keeley, who have encouraged me, sometimes pulled me, through an ever-rewarding freelance career and have kept me stocked up on dictionaries.

Robert Anthony

Thanks to Julieanna, Anton, and Russ for giving me this opportunity; to Greta for providing the hardware, time, patience, and support; and to our landlord for not locking the door to the roof.

Jim Blau

Contents

Part One: Introduction 1

    Chapter 1: Wake Up and Smell the Opportunities 3

    Chapter 2: Who's a Freelancer? 9

    Chapter 3: Keys to a Career in Freelancing 21

Part Two: The History of Freelancing: Past, Present, and Future 25

    Chapter 4: How We Got Here 27

    Chapter 5: What It's Like Now 49

    Chapter 6: Virtual Recruitment: *Inter*netting a Job 63

    Chapter 7: It Takes an E-village: Collaborating Online 85

    Chapter 8: Online Theft: Identity Crises 95

    Chapter 9: Down the Line: What the Future Holds 105

Part Three: Online Tips, Tools, and Tricks 115

    Chapter 10: Be Prepared: Computer Skills You Will Need 117

    Chapter 11: Past, Present, and Future: The History of the Internet 123

    Chapter 12: Getting Wired: Obtaining Internet Access 129

    Chapter 13: Sharpening Your Tools: Basic Internet Software and Skills ... 155

    Chapter 14: Online Résumés 165

    Chapter 15: Creating an Online Portfolio 183

    Chapter 16: Attracting Employers' Attention 197

    Chapter 17: Internet Job-Hunting Resources 201

    Chapter 18: Moving Forward 205

Part Four: The Sites 207

Index 303

Chart of Freelance Websites 318

About the Authors 321

Part One
Introduction

Chapter 1
Wake Up and Smell the Opportunities

Imagine that you awoke this morning from a nap that had lasted twenty years, the modern-day incarnation of Rip Van Winkle.

The world that greeted you is a radically different place than it was in the early 1980s. When you fell asleep, Ronald Reagan was president, and the letters I, B, and M were associated with typewriters, calculators, and keypunch machines. Michael Jordan had just entered college at the University of North Carolina at Chapel Hill, and personal computers with 8080 processors had only begun to sneak their way onto the American business scene. Microsoft Corporation was an upstart software firm owned by a young computer whiz kid named Bill Gates, who had just cut a deal with IBM on something called the Disk Operating System.

Wake up, Rip Van Winkle, for today there are technologies and everyday tools that you could not have dreamed of twenty years ago. And every tool and technology has borne an industry of professionals who build, maintain, and utilize each one. In the short span of two decades, human innovation has developed the unprecedented ability to move and sustain huge, instantaneous, and continual transfers of raw data and information in an electronic, digital format. Real information is transmitted across phone lines, fiber-optic wires, and satellite signals. Personal electronic organizers and cell phones with wireless Internet access dangle casually from the belts and purses of those who pass, issuing reports on the weather, traffic, and stock markets in bits and bytes to their hurried and harried owners. Coworkers now bounce information and documents impetuously around the globe using e-mail or cell phones. Stolen cars can be tracked from satellites in space. Computers are as prolific as televisions, and televisions have three-figure channel capabilities. It seems that human discourse moves at the same speed as the electrons that comprise the heavens and the earth. Ultimately, the development that impacts all others in the most profound ways, and opens the biggest range of possibilities for professionals, has been the rise of the Internet.

Together with the Internet—including the World Wide Web, newsgroups, and Usenet—computers have become the ultimate tools for connectivity and productivity. Dynamically driven websites, intranets, e-mail, instant messaging, and wireless networks have replaced typewriters, Dictaphones, and answering machines. Everywhere you turn, life gets faster and the world gets smaller.

The extraordinary aspect of these technological advancements in recent world history is the relatively small amount of time that it has taken for us to assimilate these new tools into everyday life. Alexander Graham Bell invented the telephone in 1876, but it wasn't until halfway through the following century that it became a common and affordable household appliance. Television as we know it was developed in 1923 but didn't become a common fixture until the mid-1950s. The Internet has not been so languid. The first graphical Web browser, called Mosaic, was invented in 1993. The eventual basis for many popular Web browsers, it was rudimentary and simple, supporting only basic HTML forms. All it could do was display simple text and images. A sizzling year and a half later, by the release of its second version in October 1995, you could order pizza delivery online. Five years later you could visit Apple.com and watch movie trailers on a QuickTime Web browser plug-in. The speed at which communication technology has progressed in the last two decades has been breathtaking. The ability for an individual to communicate simultaneously and instantaneously with all parts of our global society plugs us directly into each other and electrifies life as never before. People now enjoy the physical ability to access a computer terminal from home, office, or other domicile that tangibly connects them to every cranny, crook, and corner of our Web-spun planet. We are truly connected in ways that weren't imaginable just a few years ago. The implications that these capabilities can have on your life as a freelance professional are absolutely revolutionary. There is more opportunity on this very day, Rip Van Winkle, than there was in your entire lifetime.

At its current growth rate, the Internet has become a global phenomenon that is expected to bloat by 70 percent in the next ten years. Even at that breakneck pace, it will still take that long before it exceeds the size of the world's current telecommunication (telephone) network. ("Is Globalization Right for You?" *Webtechniques Magazine*, September 2000). As of January 1, 2001, more than 400 million people were online worldwide (see Computer Industry Almanac: www.c-i-a.com/). Thirty percent, or 134 million, of them were located in the United States. That's more than 65 percent of the adult population. These statistics include

@ 4.6 million African American households

@ 3.8 million Hispanic American households

@ 2.2 million Asian American households

@ 14 million kids two to twelve years old

@ 13 million teens thirteen to eighteen

@ 12 million college students

@ 23 million American households with people age fifty and over

"Seeing the Internet become a part of everyday life for Americans of varying backgrounds solidifies its potential as a medium for content, communication, and commerce," reports CyberAtlas.com. ("Internet Use Continues to Pervade U.S." http://cyberatlas.internet.com/big_picture/demographics/article/ 0,,5901_775401,00.html). The Internet, it seems, has become the kernel of the world's great equalizer, placing all corners of our terrestrial sphere on equal footing. Behind the kinetic veil of fiber-optically transmitted electrons, there is no gender, race, age, economic difference, religion, creed, or national origin. Logging on from behind a keyboard, all presence is equal.

The avenues the Net opens to freelance employment are infinite for both the types of work and the types of people who can access the work opportunities. Consider, for example, the predicament of the physically disabled. Homebound individuals with disabilities are often hindered in finding gainful work because of their inability to physically go on job interviews, attend training events, or otherwise attain access to the workplace. A 1994 survey of Massachusetts vocational rehabilitation workers found that 12 percent of those who were disabled could accept a wider range of active work if they were able to work independently from their own location or home. On a national basis, that's more than 150,000 disabled Americans who could enter the workforce more productively by procuring independent freelance work online. These same workers, who can now earn more online than they could in previous work history, will add to the number of gainfully employed, thus increasing economic productivity and the number of active taxpayers. Nearly all employers who currently use this telework approach to hiring the disabled report a positive result, with 57 percent concluding that their workforce has become more productive. The far-reaching social, political, and economic impact of this new, independent, and decentralized freelance workforce is jolting.

What's in a Domain?

At this writing, there are more than 28,869,097 registered commercial Web domains on the Internet. This figure is composed of

@ 21,940,515 .com registrations

@ 4,330,364 .net registrations

@ 2,598,218 .org registrations

Sixty percent of all Web domain owners report that their online endeavors will comprise a significant portion of their business strategy in the coming decade.

The ability to transmit megabytes of information and data simultaneously and worldwide at an insignificant expense has tremendous implications for your future as a freelance professional. Like science fiction come to life, time and distance are no longer a factor in a world of markets and commerce that is inextricably linked in a virtual actuality. The e-commerce revolution offers tremendous opportunities for low-cost interaction and communication.

Improvements to distribution, business-to-business communication, supplier organization, and other e-commerce methods will revolutionize the manner in which you do business and provide dramatically new and ever-efficient models from which to operate. Competition will increase as freelance professionals improve their abilities to go virtual with little or no significance to geographic separation. Competitive edges such as the resources made available in this book are the keys to getting the work you seek and deserve.

Taking the E-way to Work

A tremendous amount of everyday work activity is being performed online. More than 48 percent of American employers surveyed in 2000, reports Jobsonline.com, prefer to receive job applications by e-mail, which is becoming the predominant form of "regular" mail. Compare that to 21 percent who want to receive them by snail mail. Half of all North American CEOs cite the impact of technology in effecting business as their main agenda over the next three years. Seventy-eight percent say that the role of Internet technology is extremely important to the overall success of their companies.

In order to gain the specialized knowledge they seek, businesses, academic institutions, and governmental employers must often outsource or contract freelance professionals. The geographical relocation and decentralization of the workforce has been recognized for more than thirty years. The introduction of technology to the workforce over that same period, and the subsequent systematization of work processes and methods that it has facilitated as a result, continues to increase the need for outsourced freelance work at an exponential pace. The Bureau of Labor Statistics' *Occupational Outlook Handbook* (http://stats.bls/gov/oco/ocos092.htm) reports that the need for freelance visual artists, for example, will grow at a significantly faster pace in the next decade than it did in the previous decade. Technological advancements in the entertainment industry and continued expansion of the Internet will provide many opportunities for visual-arts freelance workers. Vast opportunity is also expected for people in a wide range of related freelance fields, including the following:

Animators
Broadcast and sound technicians
Business consultants
Cartoonists
Copywriters
Court reporters and medical transcriptionists
Designers
Financial planners

Grant writers
Graphic artists
Illustrators
Interpreters
Marketing consultants and researchers
Network engineers
Packagers
Photographers
Programmers
Proofreaders

Proposal developers
Public relations professionals
Scriptwriters
Web page designers and developers
Word processing professionals
Writers and editors (especially for online content)

The Internet has become the single largest spending catalyst ever developed, and it will forever change the way you do business. The nature of business today is a collaborative effort, where many of the traditional barriers of workforce integration simply don't exist. The digital age, with its abilities for hypercommunication, has ushered us into an era when you can effortlessly network and "Web" your creative, organizational, and productive intelligence. The possibilities for innovative approaches to business organization and problem solving are endless. Freelance professionals moving to online venues will find ever-increasing opportunities for work.

As a freelancer, you will find "Internet integration" to be a fundamental factor to your business success and competitive superiority in coming years. The future of freelance work online may indeed be synonymous with the very nature and future of most work. "In a knowledge economy," writes Don Tapscott, author of *The Digital Economy*, "the wealth creation shifts from being the corporate hierarchy to the networked individual—like a molecule."

Chapter 2
Who's a Freelancer?

Most people associate freelance work with writers and editors, and although it is true that freelance professionals permeate the publishing trade, there are many other industries and areas of business in which freelancers operate, such as photography, public relations, accounting, financial planning, wedding planning, computer programming, graphic designing, and more. As independently contracted professionals who are self-employed, they are often confused with business owners. Every freelancer is indeed a business owner, but that doesn't mean that every business owner is a freelancer. Business owners are usually people who are engaged in commerce for commercial reasons. They are the Sam Walton types of the world. Entrepreneurs build business dreams—the storefront, company, or corporation. They build standardized operations and concerns for their commercial exploitation. Freelancers, on the other hand, are politically unorganized, sovereign free agents who work autonomously. Usually avoiding and sometimes rejecting authority, they enjoy the freedom of self-employment, offering a wide range of services on a temporary, one-person/one-business basis to a diversified class of clients. They have the ability to set their own hours, take breaks and vacations whenever they want, and be their own boss. And they love what they do for a living. Eighty-seven percent of them assert, when polled, that they are eminently satisfied with the nature of their work.

Freelance professionals are people who get paid to do what they would pay for an opportunity to do. Many of them hold down private offices, but most prefer to work from their homes. The ability to avoid the hassle of commuting, to work whenever they choose, full-time or part-time, and to work in their pajamas is what attracts most people to freelance work. But don't get the wrong idea. They are predominantly educated professionals who sometimes command colossal hourly rates, fees, or retainers. They may just as well be homemakers who wish only to earn a little extra money in their spare time. Regardless of their educational background, socioeconomic circumstance, or demeanor, there is one attribute among them that is common: independence. Freelancers are free-agent workers, an independent lot in the true sense of the word. Tell a freelancer what to do and you'll instantly understand, because freelancers don't like to be told what to do. They are entrepreneurs who organize, manage, and assume the risks of their own enterprise.

"I think that a great many people seek independent business venture as a freelancer," says Jack Jesse, Ph.D., owner of Miracles Unlimited Counseling Center and a freelance author. He believes freelancers fall into three major categories.

1. Those who have tried many conventional routes of employment without much success, so they think, in desperation, "If I'm going to make it, I will have to do it myself." This is true with many people who have been victims of corporate downsizing.

2. Those who have trouble sustaining attention to one or two major tasks within a set span of time. Freelancers can set their own schedules and create the variety of tasks necessary to satisfy their creative appetites.

3. There is also a set of people who researchers have defined as thrill seekers (those with low levels of the neurotransmitter MAO). They seem to be driven, more adventurous, and definitely risk takers. They appear a little manic and may become addicted to their own adrenaline.

Although some may be physiologically or psychologically predisposed to the lifestyle, most freelancers are driven and disciplined, independent professionals. Perched at the edge of a technological revolution, they are highly focused people determined to succeed. "More so," says Dr. Jesse, "the adventurous spirit of the new Internet freelancer is very much like that of the frontiersman who saddled up the horse and hitched the wagon in 1842, setting out for the Gold Rush. 'There's gold in them thar hills.' And there's gold to be mined on the Internet. In part, it's the search for the American Dream all over again. It's those single-minded, persevering individuals who have a tenacious grip on their dream and a vision for what's possible. They are seeking opportunities, and many are finding their own little gold mine inside the technology of their home computers."

There are a lot of people mining for gold in the cyberworld. The U.S. Department of Labor reports that more than 3 percent of those employed in the United States today, or roughly 8 million people, are independent contractors, and there are more online freelancers entering the ranks of the self-employed every day. Some reports project that there will be more than 20 million by the turn of the decade. The Bureau of Labor Statistics reports the following statistics about independent, self-employed freelance workers:

Average age	35
Average income	$36,000
Average length of workweek	50 hours
Percent satisfied with their work	84%
Average length of self-employment	8 years

"Other sources say that the real number of total freelancers could be as high as 25 to 30 million," writes Diana Fell in her column, "The Future Is Now! Free Agenting," for About.com. Regardless of the numbers, this is a movement that will continue to gain ground as wage slaves revolt toward increased independence and more control over their own work life. The average worker in 2002 demands far more power and authority over his or her career. One in four Americans told a Gallup poll in 1997 that they would like to fire their boss, and in this new work world many of them are doing it. *American Demographics* magazine reports that more than 2 million people start freelance businesses each year, not by necessity but by personal choice. Eighty-four percent of these newly declared freelance professionals state that they prefer being independent to their previous role as a traditional wage slave. Why wouldn't they when on a national average they earn 15 percent more than those who work for someone else? PBS Career Center for Teens reports that half of all Americans will be in some form of freelance job by 2010. It is evident that the United States is quickly becoming a nation of freelance workers.

Freedom's Just Another Word For . . .

"Simplify! Simplify!" said Henry David Thoreau. "Let the affairs of your life measure one, and two." That's why many people go freelance—for the simplicity. Drop a freelancer from a plane with nothing but a PDA (personal digital assistant) and he or she is still in business. The lifestyle can be that simple and flexible.

There are many other advantages to going freelance. Being self-employed offers flexibility and simplicity. Versatility in setting your own hours and the kind of work you enjoy is a prime reason. Freelancers work with a diversified range of people in differing industries and can quickly change their area of focus without significant consequence on their abilities to earn a living. Seeking the more adventurous side to life, they get the opportunity to see how other individuals and/or organizations operate. If you are willing to work hard, you may well be rewarded with substantially greater returns than those who choose to "work for the man." A look at salary ranges for a few freelance jobs in the Internet industry may offer a peek to earnings potential nationwide for independent, free-agent workers.

Animator	$55,000–$75,000
Financial planner	$55,000–$80,000
Graphic designer	$38,000–$47,000
HTML programmer	$40,400–$50,000
Photographer	$25,000–$40,000
Technical writer	$47,000–$55,000

There's a lot of entitlement and freedom to being a freelancer. The varied projects and shifting demands of independent freelance work can be challenging and inspiring. Freelancers enjoy flexibility in their work, but it's not all lavish luxury. It takes discipline, a warriorlike, blood-and-guts attitude, and an intensely competitive, winner-take-all mentality to be successful in the freelance markets.

@ Aggressiveness: You can be your own boss and run your own business. Self-confidence and decisiveness are important traits for successful work as an independent contractor. Opportunities rise quickly, and you must be able to act quickly in order to capitalize on them.

@ Self-discipline: Distraction is the worst enemy of the freelancer, especially if you work from your home. "Stick-to-it-iveness" and iron-willed determination are absolute requirements for freelancers. The freedom to set your own hours and work schedule can encourage procrastination. Good freelance professionals are not distracted from their work.

@ Passion: The success of your freelance business relies on your ability to sell your services to others. You must convince your prospects of your capabilities and character for completing the job satisfactorily. A good attitude, a positive demeanor, and passion for what you do goes far in persuading potential clients of your freelance value.

@ Talent and skill: Even the best idea will fail miserably if it isn't carried forth adeptly. Your personality, aptitude, and abilities should befit the kind of work you profess.

Traditionally, freelance professionals have had to "hit the streets" to find paying jobs, taking the spaghetti-on-the-wall approach to find work and spending many anxious hours prospecting for accounts. Pass out enough brochures and business cards, make enough cold calls, and send enough prospecting letters—that is, throw enough spaghetti against the wall—and some of it will stick. It can be a life, at times, of anxious uncertainty that requires iron-willed resolve, antacids in the medicine cabinet, and the ability to perform occasional financial gymnastics.

Wondering when the next paycheck will arrive and where it will come from is not a lifestyle for everyone, let alone having to worry about the taxes that must be self-deducted from the pay once it does arrive, or about the pension, health insurance, and social security expenses. There are long, grueling hours involved in independent contract work. There is record keeping, tax work, and many financial risks in addition to complete liability and accountability in all business affairs. But if you have freelance blood and adrenaline pounding through your veins and brain, it's a life of rich and enriching rewards.

To: Freelancers

From: An anonymous e-mail source on the Internet

Subject: The difference between working in-house and as a freelancer

	In-house	**Freelance**
Attire	Business casual	Socks
Office space	Small office cube	The kitchen table
Benefits	HMO/PPO	SOL
Vacation time	Two weeks	Fifty-two weeks
Office politics	Ignoring people who gossip behind your back	Ignoring strange voices in the back of your head
Rules	No smoking	No smoking in bed
Bending rules	Wasting company money	Trying not to spend too much on personal phone calls on 1-900 phone lines
Best advantage	Steady income/paid benefits	No need to shower daily
Lunch	Three-course lunch on company expense account	Slim-Fast and a donut
3:00 appt.	With the vice president	With Jerry Springer

Getting Trendy

Why would employers be willing to hire you as an online freelance worker? *Because good help is hard to find these days.* A recent McKinsey & Company report found that 75 percent of top corporate executives surveyed said that their companies were chronically short of good talent. Hiring U.S. firms predicted a shortage of almost 850,000 skilled technology workers in 2002 alone, according to a survey released by the Information Technology Association of America. The survey found that more than 1.6 million new technology workers would be needed to satisfy demand by 2002 in addition to the existing workforce of 10 million. In a study sponsored by Cisco Systems Inc., Microsoft Corporation, Oracle Corporation, and other corporations, it was estimated that companies would seek to fill more than 600,000 technical support positions alone. Positions that were held in most demand included technical support, database developers, network administrators, programmers, software developers, and Internet site developers. Average annual earnings for those same workers as reported by Salary.com ranges from $42,000 to $77,000. Such expectations have, of course, gone largely unfulfilled in the face of 2001's economic downturns and America's war on terrorism. They are, however, an important indication of an underlying, long-term movement in the workforce—a movement being driven by a fundamental shift toward a digital economy. So, in the long run, prospects for you as an independent freelancer should remain very promising. More promising, perhaps, than future work possibilities for the average wage slave. Now, it seems, is a good time to be an independent contractor or freelancer.

In coming years, productive companies will find it necessary to adapt to an ever-savvy online workforce if they are to remain competitive. Many companies are already retaining and hiring workers to suit their immediate work needs, contracting independent workers to complete project work. Contracting workers as free agents saves these firms the conventional expenses of benefits such as health insurance, retirement, and disability plans. Workers of the future will be expected to take larger portions of responsibility for their own careers.

In order to adapt more quickly to these changing trends in the workforce, many American companies are finding it necessary to procure the services of outsourcing agencies such as Outsource International or Technisource. Freelance independents signed up with such outsourcing or temporary employment firms receive work assignments or contract work through the agency. If the number of workers using such outsourcing firms were included in the total figures of those considered freelance workers, the total number of independent workers in the United States alone would exceed 25 million.

Even in a soft employment market, the demands for freelance talent remains high. A McKinsey quarterly report in 2000 titled *The War for Talent* confirmed that, even in a tight job market, American employers desperately need freelance talent. Interviews with 8,900 managers confirmed that 89 percent of those surveyed felt it was harder to acquire talented people for work than it has been in previous years, and even more difficult to retain them.

When asked what he found most beneficial about using freelance workers, Jay Heinrichs, deputy editor of *Outside* magazine, stated, "We get a variety of the best writing; the writers we go after generally don't have full-time jobs on a magazine staff, and they have the time to write exceptional stories." Because freelancers are independent contractors, they are often more motivated than wage workers. In a competitive work environment, independents must work hard to please their contracting employers and turn in quality work. The best way for competitive companies to maintain productivity while keeping expenses low is to retain freelance talent. So, even in a poor work economy, your chances of successful free-agent work remain high.

It's a new work world with a new organizational structure. Regular jobs are becoming project work, and the outsourcing and contracting of freelance workers is becoming a standard practice. That's opportunity knocking at your computer monitor. The new millennium means contract work and lots of it. Today's careers are becoming portable, paid-by-the-job professions, take-it-with-you jobs driven by the need for independent free-agent workers, and there's an endless line of buyers waiting to contract their services. As a freelancer, you will find it necessary to get familiar with these new organizational work models and to acquire the tools and skills needed to maintain your competitive edge in this new world economy.

Get Connected

In 1842, "Go west, young man" was the call to fortune. It's "Go online" right now, especially for freelance workers. There are thousands of outstanding online resources designed to help you as an online "e-lance" professional. Increasing numbers of independents are discovering the ease and convenience of landing work, managing projects, and meeting deadlines using the Internet. Wired into the Web, a growing number of sites such as Freelance.com, Guru.com, and eLance.com are offering openly posted professional-service marketplaces to help you meet your working needs. Plugged in, you can find it profitable to work on projects and proposals made possible through high-speed computer connectivity. Sites like eLance.com offer you an opportunity to auction off your professional services to the highest bidder in an electronic public sale. By posting your résumé and pertinent information on your expertise and skills online, you can attract potential clients in need of your services in exchange for professional fees. You can find the jobs you like, place competitive bids on the work, and get paid, all in a one-stop-shopping online marketplace. Need to prospect for new clients, send a newsletter to existing clients, or send direct e-mail? That's no problem with online mail centers such as Roving.com, an online e-mail-marketing manager for your freelance business. The Web-based service makes it easy for independent business owners and freelancers to realize the benefits of mass e-mail marketing by helping build their customer databases. You can create great looking newsletters for clients, send mass-marketing appeals to prospects, and track your results efficiently. Costing as little as ten dollars per month, online services such as these can be a highly effective way to reduce your overhead and increase profitability.

The advancement of the Internet also offers some awesome ways to search for, find, and collaborate on projects, jobs, and contracts. You can virtually expand your staff by tapping into today's vast online community and working together with other freelancers and contractors to collaborate on and complete projects. With just a few moments of time, a computer, and a modem, collaborators can mutually view résumés, request work samples, and obtain references on potential project partners. In this digital age, freelancers can find it possible to work on contracts for clients to whom they've never even spoken. "I work for a company located in California," says Kristen

Keets, a freelance writer in Michigan. "That's almost 3,000 miles away. We've never met, but he's become one of my best and steadiest customers." Kristen's relationship with her client was initiated and has been facilitated entirely by e-mail and over the World Wide Web. Her rate of pay for contract work is $65 to $150 per hour, depending on the kind of work she's hired to complete.

Finding online freelance work can be an exhilarating experience, offering exposure to new faces and clients from around the world with a click. Even in the face of the recent economic downturn for many of the large dot-coms, there's still a digital rush in process—a Web boon that offers ways and means to the wired way to get hired, without ever leaving the privacy of your own home! Using the Internet, you can significantly reduce the amount of time spent in search of the next paying engagement, and spend more time making money, without ever making a single cold call.

They're Looking for You

Ninety percent of all companies seeking to fill contract employment vacancies in 2002 employ online methods for conducting their search, affirming low cost and speed as their primary reasons. It is predicted that 98 percent of all companies seeking contract work will have their job postings online by the end of 2002. Indeed, many of the world's large online recruitment tools offer employers the option of freely posting contract needs to their open audiences. By posting recruitment petitions selectively, companies can more effectively target the freelance market to which they hope to appeal. By alleviating the traditional paper costs of placing newspaper advertisements, managing the receipt of hard-copy résumés, and limiting interviews to an online agenda, companies can save a bundle in recruitment expenses. In 2000, companies spent their recruiting dollars in the following percentages:

Newspaper ads	49%
Online recruiting	25%
Outside recruiters	20%

Sheer numbers play a significant part in the savings. Monster.com, for example, America's largest job site on the Web, holds a total database of more than 400,000 résumés alone, a task impossible without the electronic advantage of the Internet.

Using channels such as the World Wide Web, Usenet, and newsgroups, employers can post their freelance contract needs immediately, with little concern for turnaround time in their advertising. Job listings can be posted live online, ready to be viewed by millions of potential candidates who can instantly reply via e-mail, fax, or phone. Specialty sites constructed by many industry associations offer job-posting capabilities within specialized fields of endeavor, for a digitally articulated approach to recruiting contract candidates for specialty tasks. Your candidacy as a virtual freelance worker depends upon the kind of professional responsibilities you perform, but the list most often includes those who produce information or documents that can be transmitted electronically by modem or fax. If you are a professional who performs his or her duties on a personal computer, you can certainly be a virtual freelancer or e-lancer. There are many tangible benefits that make this kind of work arrangement a winning situation for you, your contractor, and society as a whole.

Contracting firms or companies benefit from the value of increased productivity and reduced absenteeism. Their independent workers are also free of the nonessential responsibilities that must be performed by traditional wage slaves, such as staff meetings, office parties, and unscheduled work interruptions. E-lance workers do not require office space, another significant savings to the corporate client, who will find it necessary to provide an average of 120 square feet of space to traditional payroll employees. There are potential tax savings, reduced benefit costs, and greater flexibility in the use of facilities and resources to be considered. Finally, there is the impact of improved performance and accuracy in job completion on the firm's bottom line.

As an e-lance worker, you also benefit. Alleviating the cost of commuting provides immediate savings in both time and out-of-pocket expenses. Flexibility in job schedules can reduce your costs for day care and other domestic expenses that would otherwise be required in a traditional work or business environment. Savings in meals, wardrobe expenses (a lot of freelancers really do work in their pajamas), and mortgage expenses can be considerable.

Finally, there are the larger benefits to society that come about as a result of your working freelance online. Fewer vehicles over the road saves precious fossil fuels and preserves a clean environment. The decentralization of the work population can lower demand for parking, reduce the need for highway maintenance, and diminish the negative effects of large numbers of people crowded inside urban areas.

Good News

It doesn't require a lot of resources to find freelance work online. This book, a personal computer, a modem, the proper software, and an online connection are all you need. Finding work online doesn't necessarily mean working virtually or telecommuting, because there are also a lot of traditional work situations that can be procured using regional online search mechanisms. The work world today is ever-changing and constantly looking for new ways to use online capabilities for making operations more efficient and cost-effective. That makes your world a happier place, for with the help of technology, you are freed to succeed at high speed.

Supreme Court Favors Freelancers

Because of the decision in *New York Times v. Tasini* in June 2001, several freelance writers were successful in protecting their ownership rights to electronic copies of their articles as written from *The New York Times*, *Newsday*, and *Time* magazine.

The case resulted in a 7–2 decision, with the Supreme Court holding that the freelancers, as independent contractors who had allowed their publishers to use their work in print publications, did not forfeit their electronic rights to the material. The publishers had licensed the rights to a third-party computerized database, which planned to duplicate and market the freelancers' work.

In upholding Section 201(c) of the Copyright Act, the Court stated, "Essentially, Section 201(c) adjusts a publisher's copyright in its collective work to accommodate a freelancer's copyright in his/her contribution. If there is demand for a freelance article standing alone or in a new collection, the Copyright Act allows the freelancer to benefit from that demand; after authorizing initial publication the freelancer may also sell the article to others."

Chapter 3

Keys to a Career in Freelancing

Abundant and electrifying opportunity awaits you in this new millennium as a freelance worker. The best way to predict your future is to take a positive approach and create that future for yourself. You can determine where you want to go in life and what you can accomplish.

> *"The worlds of thought and action have a way of overlapping. What you think has a way of becoming true."*
>
> —*Robert von Oech, Ph.D.*

Planning a career in freelance work is a process that involves four important steps.

Step One

Discover your expertise and interests, and clarify your wants and needs.

Before you can get wired to find freelance work, you should understand yourself. Although you are undoubtedly a complicated person, the process to self-discovery is simple. Ask yourself these important questions:

@ What do you like to do? What are you passionate about?

@ At what do you excel? (Everyone is really good at something.)

@ What personality traits do you have that will affect your freelance career choices?

@ How much money would you like to earn?

@ Do you want to live in the city or in the country?

@ Are you willing to move around the country or the world?

@ How much training are you willing to participate in?

@ Will you have the necessary skills to complete the work?

Your answers to these questions will have a large effect on your freelance career choice, because everything about you is interrelated.

"By focusing on your preferences, you can begin to determine the ideal job that would make you happy."

—*Gary Joseph Grappo,* author of
Get the Job You Want in Thirty Days

Step Two

Explore different career alternatives that may match your skills and interests, and realistically assess them against your wants and needs.

Once you have discovered what kind of freelance work really excites you and have identified your desired lifestyle, you can explore realistic options. Do you enjoy writing? If so, examine freelance careers that require your writing skills. When you explore freelance career options, it is important to assess as much information about yourself as you can. Ask yourself more questions, such as

- @ What specific duties does the freelance career require?

- @ What are the working conditions?

- @ What skills and/or education will be required?

- @ What is the long-range outlook for this career?

- @ Will it still be in demand in ten years? Twenty years?

- @ What kind of rates can I charge for this kind of work?

Step Three

Choose a defined career course and implement your plan.

This is where your planning is set in motion. Most important, it is time to establish your goals and determine what specific actions you can take toward their accomplishment. Stormy times will arise. Life changes and things can go wrong. Rarely does anything go exactly the way you want and prefer, but choosing smart goals will keep you moving forward and in the right direction.

The career you choose for yourself will largely determine your lifestyle. Your lifestyle is the way you live, the clothes you wear, the house you live in, the money you earn, the car you drive. It is also a culmination of your attitudes, income, and education, as well as your political and spiritual beliefs. In the freelance career planning process, it is extremely important to determine what kind of lifestyle you want. This requires that you establish effective goals for yourself.

Once you have established realistic goals, outline the specific actions that will be necessary in order for you to accomplish them, for without action, even the wisest of plans is destined to fail.

"One who strides confidently in the direction of his dreams, will be met with a success unexpected in common hours."

—*Henry David Thoreau*

Step Four

Whenever the need arises, go back and revise your plan.

Even the best-laid of plans can get short-circuited. There is no assurance that your freelance career plan will last a lifetime, especially in this ever-changing, technologically new millennium. The average life cycle of a career decision can last as few as one to seven years or as many as forty years. Most people switch careers at least once during their lifetime. Freelance work offers the flexibility to make changes in career direction, especially in this age of online employment. The world is ever-changing, and you are, too. Whatever happens, once you reach a freelance career goal, it is important to keep learning and improving yourself, striving for satisfaction. Periodic assessment and revision of your career plan will be necessary if you want to remain happy. Freelance is an ongoing cycle, not a final destination. Don't worry too much about your destination. Enjoy the journey—the destination will come soon enough.

Part Two

The History of Freelancing: Past, Present, and Future

Chapter 4
How We Got Here

A thousand years ago, everyone was a freelance worker—that is, anyone who could enjoy working for free. Back then, society was dominated by a feudal system of economics, actually a form of freelance agricultural economy. In a feudalistic society, those who worked were largely required to do so for the sake of fulfilling the necessary requirements of operating a functional kingdom. In ninth-century Europe, for example, workers were primarily required to serve as civil or military personnel. Those who pledged their allegiance to the reigning king, and served him well in the service of carrying forth the daily operations of the kingdom, could have confidence that their lives would be spared. People, most of them peasants, were required to attend to their own needs. They grew gardens or slaughtered cattle for food, built their own domiciles for shelter, bartered with other folk for the exchange of specific items or services, or stole what they needed. It was a fierce, brutal, and ruthlessly barbarous life. (Some say that about today's capitalistic economy.) It was a working system of economics and employment nonetheless. Indeed, most of the world's great societies—Japanese, Chinese, Russian, Spanish, Italian—have passed through an economic and employment system based on feudalism.

Due to attacks from independent rival forces, which you could easily call the first supporters of independent freelance work, feudalism began losing its grip on the masses in the twelfth century. A new form of economy was sweeping the European continent, built upon the concepts of a free society, safe existence, and public order. The relationship between serf and sire, aristocrat and plebian, king and slave changed. Spearheaded, sometimes literally, by the Romans, a new public order replaced the feudalistic ways of secular lords and royal powers. Gradually local kingdoms became independent, free-trade societies, often becoming territories or states in themselves. The basis for a new and well-ordered society economy was laid. Towns flourished as they developed their own independent economic structures based on free trade and exchange. By undermining the monarch's economic power, this new form of free market weakened the last feudal kingdoms and caused them to finally collapse in the twelfth and thirteenth centuries. By the fourteenth century, the feudal way of life (you could call it a "futile" way) was entirely eliminated. An infantile form of capitalism and the crafts were born, dominated by the freewheeling ways of independent craftsmen.

The feudal experience, however, left a lasting influence on economy and government. Resentment and revolt against taxes and defiant attitudes toward government left an enduring impression in the souls and psyches of the common worker. Although the new world order of free trade, free exchange, and freelance independence proved eminently more effective than its feudal predecessor, negative attitudes toward economic authority continued.

Getting Commercialized . . . Go to Commercial

After several hundreds of years of successful economic growth, the aristocratic stratum, which by this time had successfully laminated itself above the dense layers of common workers, began to commercialize its economic power. These pedigreed noblemen basically became money-grubbing, power-hungry, rapacious profiteers. The problem was that the Roman Empire was crumbling, and as it tumbled, so did the noblemen's power and prestige. Spiteful as they were, these princely, silk-stockinged, blue-blooded bandits began tossing their peasant farmworkers and laborers off their farms. Forced to scour the countryside in search of an honest day's wage in exchange for their labor, peasants and commoners were forced out of necessity to develop an increased economic prowess. They became responsible for their own labor. So was born the first free-labor movement and, most probably, the first class of freelance, independent workers. This independent movement of the labor pool primed the creation of an attendant system for the production and disbursement of products and services, and for the first time provided the necessary and suitable environment for the creation of an effective marketplace. The mechanisms of an efficient marketing network took shape, and commercial institutions flourished. So did the notion of freedom for each worker and the condition of payment in exchange for work, both important precursors to the rise of an independent and free workforce.

"Ironing Out" the Workforce

In the eighteenth century, a series of scientific developments occurred that had a monumental impact on society and labor. In 1709, the development of iron as a building material fueled gargantuan expansions of organized industry. The construction of metal bridges, buildings, ships, trains, and other metallic structures required massive numbers of employed people. Social structures previously dominated by the bourgeoisie gave way to a new entrepreneurial spirit. The upsurge of scientific knowledge called for new skills, and the trades emerged in response to the overwhelming needs of industry. The building sciences also broadened the need for more educated workers. Architects were needed to envision suitable structures, designers were needed to plan them, and engineers were needed to supervise their construction. So constant was the demand for educated professional services that several of the first organized work societies were founded during this period of time. A more educated worker, however, is a more skilled worker, and in a market-driven economy those with more skills can command larger wages. As a result, the professions grew, as did the organization of professional societies, associations, and fellowships. Organizations such as the Royal Institute of British Architects and the American Institute of Architects were created at this time.

Career Profile: Freelance Architect

If you dream of turning your creative inspiration into concrete reality, you might consider building a career as freelance architect.

Architects plan and design buildings of all types, including residential homes, office buildings, or shopping malls. They may also scheme and design large buildings and structures such as factories, hospitals, libraries, or municipal complexes for cities, states, or the federal government. In construction projects for buildings, it is the responsibility of the architect to design the project to see that it is constructed safely and in a manner that is aesthetically pleasing within its surroundings.

The job of an architect "doesn't involve as much artistic design as most beginners think," says Katie McDonnough, a freelance architect from Detroit, Michigan. Most of her time is spent communicating ideas and concepts—selling—to clients and talking with other independent contract workers, such as surveyors and construction workers, about construction plans. She also coordinates project activities with government agencies to assure that compliance regulations are met. "There's frustratingly little time to run away with artistic expression," she says. "But that makes me more appreciative of the times when I can do design work, drawing new ideas, taking pictures of building sites, or making model elevations to present to a new client."

There are many occupations related to architectural work, which can also be a good freelance career possibility. You may find it helpful to investigate the following career alternatives:

- @ Drafter
- @ Surveyor
- @ Landscape architect
- @ Civil engineer
- @ Mechanical engineer
- @ Painter and sculptor
- @ Industrial designer
- @ Marine engineer and architect

Employment Outlook: Next Ten Years

The Bureau of Labor Statistics reports that there will be a 19 percent increase in the need for architects in the next decade. "There's really more demand than people to satisfy it," says McDonnough. "You can pretty much pick and choose the clients you'd like to do work for."

Number of Architects	
Total architects as of 2000	99,000
Total needed by 2010	118,000
Need for new architects each year	8,000*

*due to the need for growth and total replacement

Annual Earnings	
Starting salary	$25,000
After 5 years	$38,900
After 10 to 15 years	$80,000

Education and Training

Beyond high school, candidates must obtain a Bachelor of Architecture degree from an accredited university. Due to the technical importance of this position, many employers now require a master's degree from a two-year, accredited Master of Architecture program. Those enrolled in architectural curricula will undergo course work in architectural history, architectural design, building design, mathematics, physical science, and architectural theory. Currently, there are approximately 105 accredited schools of architecture in the United States. States impose a three-year junior associate internship and an examination requirement upon newly hired architects before they can become licensed. Most states have adopted a formal training standard based upon the Intern Development Program of the American Institute of Architects or the National Architectural Registration Board.

For More Information

@ www.aiaonline.com: the website for the American Institute of Architects, with resources and information about careers in architecture

@ www.acsa-arch.org: the website for the Association of Collegiate Schools of Architecture, with educational information, links, and resources for students of architecture

@ http://arts.searchbeat.com/architect.htm: an architectural Web guide, with job listings, career resources, and links to universities, journals, and teachings

@ www.thinkjobs.com: a search engine for technical careers, including architectural- and architectural design–related jobs throughout the United States

Full site reviews appear in Part Four of this book.

The Industrial Age and Work Responsibilities

The industrial age was an effective catalyst in the evolution of employment and work. With the explosion of industry, and mountains of wealth for industrialists, came some pretty nasty effects on those who worked for the industrialists. Large numbers of workers were jammed into dark, hot, and dangerous environments (ever smelt iron?). Tyrannical, money-hungry tycoons who demanded long, grueling hours of work ran most of these places. Needless to say, this created oppressive and outright dangerous places for workers. Before the industrial age, workers were independent free agents who managed personal relationships with their employers on a one-on-one basis. The boss was visible, and although he may not have always been approachable (employers were mostly bourgeois types), he was accessible. Work life was an intimate affair carried forth on a day-to-day basis in direct contact with the boss in an assumed agreement for labor, a you-work-today-and-you'll-get-paid-today kind of arrangement. All that changed, however, with the developments of electricity for power and steel for improved industrial and structural strength, which created the need for even larger numbers of workers. As populations grew in urbanized areas, the need to supply them grew along with the demand for products. This is how the age of mass production was born. But, as you undoubtedly already know, people can be a revolutionary lot. As workers toiled, breaking their lower-class backs and succumbing to the humiliation and shame of sweatshops and industrial labor dungeons, they began to organize against their employers. By 1866, an action for better work conditions and wages had developed, culminating in the formation of the National Labor Union in 1866. Arguably the very first successful U.S.-based labor union, the National Labor Union was created to collect and organize workers from all backgrounds. Workers now combined in solidarity demanded fair wages, healthy work hours, and humane treatment. The continued organization of labor movements throughout the late nineteenth and early twentieth centuries advanced the outgrowth of effective labor representation. By the mid-twentieth century, labor unions had firmly knit their existence into the social, economic, and political fabric of America and the world. Their fending for workers' rights gained them valuable bargaining power in the trade of wages and benefits for labor services. Using their power of unity, labor unions had in effect become the watchdogs of free agency and independent contracting, albeit with a mass-worker twist.

Dollars and Sense: It's All About the Benjamins

So what does all this have to do with your ability to conduct freelance work? A lot, actually. You see, the labor force overall includes everyone who works for wages in whatever capacity they work. It also includes those who are unemployed and those who are looking for work, whether it is full-time employment, part-time employment, independent contract work, or freelance work. To understand where we are going in the world of freelance work, you must have a clear understanding of where it has come from. When you live in an industrialized nation such as the United States, most of the workforce is employed for someone else. The general condition of the workforce, however, is largely dependent upon the economic conditions that surround it. Circumstances and conditions such as educational levels, wage controls (the effect of labor unions), demand, and so forth contribute significantly to the vim and vigor of the workforce. History also substantiates the experience that wage levels in a unionized, industrial society tend to be higher. But higher wages also mean a more educated and mobile workforce. These two conditions, higher wages and a more educated workforce, working in tandem, lead to a more mobile labor pool for those who contract work. It was this development of an increasingly mobilized workforce through the middle of the twentieth century—the 1930s through the 1970s—that has created a general direction in labor economics that shines the lights fantastic for modern-day and future freelancers.

Oh, The Tangled Work Web We Weave

Working life continued rather smoothly during the early and mid-twentieth century without much fanfare or ado, at least in comparison to previous centuries. Relative equality had developed between workforce and industry. Improvements in the economic condition and educational level of the workforce, and the technological advances made during this period of time, cultivated a significant number of opportunities for workers, both independent and organized. There were several critical developments during this time that also fostered a pathway toward an even more independent and mobile workforce. The most notable was the development of an independent highway system in 1956.

Originally intended for national defense (like the Internet—details back in part one), the Federal Aid Highway Act of 1956 was a major advance in the building of an interstate highway system—a development, believe it or not, that has had a monumental impact on your ability to conduct freelance work today. In fact, the extended effects of the then-new highway system benefited the American worker to a much greater extent than its original benefactors, those in national defense (like the Internet). The intricate system of interstate highways offered the national workforce an unprecedented mobility in their work life (like the Internet). Not only did the construction of the highways provide an immense number of jobs, but it also gave workers a far greater level of mobility in their work life. Industrial centers that were located in urban areas in order to reap the benefits of reduced business costs became accessible to workers traveling from rural areas. This increased mobility of the working population greatly simplified the interchange of economic activity. That gave the overall economy a terrific boost, like an economic steroid (like the Internet has done for our modern economy). You need think about it for only a moment to understand the far-reaching implications that the interstate highway system has had on the capabilities of the nation as a whole and on the independent workforce. The key factor to consider here is that a more mobile workforce is a higher-paid workforce. As the workforce becomes higher paid, it becomes more independent. As it becomes more independent, it becomes more educated, which increases its ability to command higher wages. Higher wages improve its capabilities to become even more independent. See any trends? If not, read on. You're going to get excited, especially if you're planning a career in freelance work.

The "Information" Highways

Three additional technological developments in the twentieth century further propelled the mobility and effectiveness of the workforce. All of them, in fact, have occurred during your lifetime—that is, if you're twenty to thirty years old or older.

The first of these three developments was the facsimile machine, now commonly called a fax machine. The technology for faxing has actually been around since the 1840s. The first commercial use of a fax machine, in fact, occurred in 1902 when German-born Arthur Korn demonstrated his selenium photocell transmitter. It wasn't until the 1960s, however, that the technology became cost-effective enough for widespread use. Early fax machines were cylinder-based, and the process for using the ancient method of faxing was so messy that you wouldn't even want to hear about it.

"Oh my God, I hated those old things," says Delores Wallace, an analyst for a Michigan-based securities firm. "You had to place a sheet of paper over a cylinder and it took fifteen minutes to fax each page. Then you had to call to see if it was received at the receiving end because the machine wasn't very reliable. It could take hours to make sure that an important document made it intact to its destination."

Even though it was difficult and time-consuming to operate, this device was the precursor to the analog telephone fax machine that is widely used today. The explosive use of fax machines did not occur until 1974, when the International Telegraph and Telephone Consultative Committee issued the first world standard for fax communications. Adopting the new Group 1 fax standards, fax-machine manufacturers were able to produce intercommunicating machines that could send and receive documents worldwide over ordinary telephone lines. It was still a slow method of transmission, sending a one-page document in about six or seven minutes.

"I'll never forget the first facsimile machine I ever saw," says veteran life insurance agent Joseph Rodriguez. "Back in 1977 or 1978 and it was incredible to me. The only comparison we had to it was the copy machine. It seemed miraculous that you could put a piece of paper into it and that the facsimile would seemingly photocopy it at another location across the country."

Because of reduced cost and improved technology, the use of fax machines grew considerably through the 1970s. Eventually, there were millions of them in business and personal use throughout the world. Their impact and contribution toward a more mobile and independent workforce and business climate cannot be underestimated. Group 1 machines gave way to Group 2, 3, and 4 machines. Fax machines today are much more expedient, transmitting a full-page document in less than ten seconds. Capable of transmitting data at a rate exceeding 60,000 bits per second, the fax machine has become a staple in business offices and residences.

The second major technological development to contribute toward independent work abilities was the modem. Modems were also developed largely for the benefit of national defense. Although they had been around since the 1930s and in use on telephotography equipment, their widespread use for digital communications was not made available for commercial use until 1962, when American Telephone and Telegraph (AT&T) released its Bell 103 modem for use on conventional telephone circuits. The first generation of data communication units, they transmitted at a pokey rate of 300 bits per second. But here, too, commercial developments by 1970 had moved the technology along to the speed of kilobits per second. Improvements in frequency modulation, telephone circuits, and data transmission lines eventually advanced the technology to the point that it could be made available for high-speed data communications within the general workforce.

Last but by no means least in this list of twentieth-century technological developments toward an independent workforce was the manufacturing of the personal computer in 1974. Engineered by a relatively obscure little firm named MITS, the first PC was built around Intel Corporation's 8080 microprocessor. It wasn't until Steve Jobs's creation of the Apple computer in 1977 that a mass-produced and affordable computer was available to the general population. Within the year, Radio Shack and Commodore Business Machines had released their own models. Constructed with puny eight-bit processors, these machines were little more than large calculators with limited amounts of internal memory. Usually built with one or two floppy drives (there were no hard drives), the scarcity of applicable software programs prevented the machines from being used for much more than basic spreadsheet applications and word processing. Then International Business Machines (IBM) rocked the world (if you can believe that) with the introduction of the IBM PC. Housing an 8088 processor that was only slightly faster than that of its competitors, the machine built for personal computing held ten times more internal memory than any other available PC. Stocked with Lotus 1-2-3 software and whiz kid Bill Gates's operating system, called DOS, IBM laid its 1-2-3 punch into the computer market, and its PC quickly became the world's most popular computer system. It wasn't until 1984, though, that personal computing would prove to become an effective tool for the routine use of the general population and, more important, the independent worker. That's when the graphical user interface (GUI) was developed to aid and speed the use of the PC.

And You Should Care Because . . .

What does this have to do with freelance work in America? Tons, because the GUI turned the personal computer into a plug-and-play machine—a ready-made, take-it-out-of-the-box, compact production utensil that could be unpacked and put to use immediately. With the GUI, pictures, symbols, and pull-down menus standardized the use of software programs and applications so that their use was simplified and accelerated. This was not only an effective approach to personal computer operations, especially for an increasingly impatient, increasingly wired, have-it-your-way-and-have-it-now workforce, but it was also extremely productive.

"The first computer I ever saw," says Pat Kenrick, a freelance financial services professional and insurance agent, "sat on top of the biggest desk in the middle of the office. All the agents walked around it like it was something out of science fiction, like it was some kind of a monolithic structure or something. It was new and nobody understood it, but we quickly learned how to do things with it in minutes that would have taken weeks to accomplish before we had it."

Career Profile: Freelance Computer Programmer

If you're into computers and ways to help people put these machines into practical use, then a career as a freelance computer programmer may speak your language.

"Most people think of computer programmers as techno-geeks who make up video games," says Sylvia Kirsch, an IT professional and freelance computer programmer." But that's far from reality. What programmers do is develop formulas in a coded computer language that is bundled into what we call a piece of software or 'computer program.' We write the stuff that manipulates computers into accomplishing what their users want them to do. Basically, I tell computers what to do."

There are many types of freelance computer programmers, most of them specializing in their own area of expertise. In addition to those who write business programs, such as Sylvia, there are programmers who write engineering and scientific programs for these applications; system programmers who test, maintain, and modify operating-system software; and program analysts who develop, test, and document computer programs for specific uses by individual users. "Regardless of the kind of programmer, we all pretty much do the same thing," Kirsch says. "We construct systems and step-by-step instructions that tell computers what kinds of problems to solve and how to solve them."

There are many occupations related to a freelance computer programming career. You may find it helpful to investigate the following career alternatives:

@ Computer systems analyst

@ Telecommunications specialist

@ Computer engineer

- @ Information systems manager

- @ Computer security professional

- @ Microcomputer specialist

- @ Software engineer

- @ Network engineer

Employment Outlook: Next Ten Years

The Bureau of Labor Statistics reports that there will be a 30 percent increase in the need for computer programmers in the next decade. About 5 percent of all freelance computer programmers in the United States today are self-employed.

Number of Computer Programmers	
Total programmers as of 2000	32,400
Total needed by 2010	41,950
Need for new programmers each year	955

Annual Earnings	
Starting salary	$42,500
After 5 years	$66,200
After 10 to 15 years	$89,000

Necessary Skills

It takes good logic and analytical skills to be a computer programmer. The ability to make quick assessments and accurate mathematical calculations is necessary. "But it's not all programming," adds Kirsch. Good verbal and written communication skills are important to computer programmers. "You really have to know how to communicate with people because they're the ones using the software programs that you develop. If you can't understand others, or if they can't understand you, then your job becomes impossible."

Education and Training

As suggested by Kirsch, potential contractors place a heavy emphasis on experience when seeking freelance candidates for computer programming work. Beyond high school, employers generally require a bachelor's degree. Those who have an educational background in accounting, business, mathematics, or computer programming will significantly increase their ability to find freelance work in this career category. Educational requirements for this profession are expected to rise as technology becomes more accessible to small and medium-size employers. Many community colleges offer two-year computer programming curricula. Approved vocational and/or adult educational programs in computer programming also help prepare students for active employment in this career category.

For More Information

@ www.siia.net: the website for the Software Information Industry Association, with links and information on software and computer programming careers

@ www.iccp.org: the website for the Institute for Certification of Computing Professionals, with educational information and resources for pursuing a computer-related career

@ www.awc-hq.org: the website for the Association of Women in Computing

@ www.doaproject.com: a referral service that connects companies looking for outsourced services with individuals and firms seeking contract-based work

Full site reviews appear in Part Four of this book.

Workers Declare Independence: Teleworking

The movement toward a mobile, independent workforce was advanced considerably by the telework movement of the 1970s. With the aid of 1970s technology, workers discovered the ability to complete their jobs at home and deliver their work to their employer electronically. For the first time, with the benefit of advanced computers and telecommunications equipment, it was possible to work for an employer who was located at a distance. Workers could undertake the daily responsibilities of employment from a home-based office and never set foot upon the employer's site of operations. Savvy employers who quickly realized the savings in such an arrangement began organizing all manners of new working operations. They developed satellite work centers where independently located workers (often in their homes) were integrated into the overall company scheme. Although ineffective in an industrial setting, this form of telework became increasingly successful within an economy moving quickly toward an information standard. Increasingly dominated by information, the workplace began a fundamental shift toward a communications-based environment. New innovations such as teleconferencing, computer networking, and cellular radio communications further improved the ability for workers and their employers to operate independently. Emerging technologies continued to outmode the centralized form of business operations as more and more companies and corporations moved toward an external workforce, seeking savings and bold-typed dollar signs in their annual reports to shareholders. "The very idea of providing an office to workers," suggests Paul J. Jackson in his book *Teleworking: International Perspectives,* "may give way to the notion of it being provided only as an employee benefit or perk."

Think Pink

By 1980 a fundamental pivot had occurred in the way work was organized, and it became evident that the age of employment—the age of industrialization—was quickly losing its steam. The trend toward a decentralized workforce was further catapulted into the forefront of American work life when millions of workers, many of them white-collar professionals, became unemployed in the downsizing and corporate restructuring tragedies of the mid- to late 1980s. The Bureau of Labor Statistics reports that during the 1980s, one worker in twenty-five lost his or her employment during any twenty-four-month period. Job dislocation spread like wildfire and to every sector of the economy. By 1989 more than 75 percent of all U.S. firms had downsized, many of them using automated technologies as replacements for people. In spite of a growing economy, the trend continued throughout the decade, peaking at an all-time job loss of more than 3 million workers.

Downsizing, 1985–1991	
Financial	40%
Manufacturing	60%
Professional	45%
Wholesale/retail	40%

"I was downsized in 1986 by a Des Moines, Iowa–based insurance company," says Bob R., a midwestern-based insurance executive who prefers to remain anonymous. "They showed me the pink slip with a three-hour notice. One day I was their top producer—the fair-haired golden boy—the next day I was unemployed. The vice president of the company flew in, met me at the airport, collected my company car keys and expense account credit cards, and flew out. It was a real hatchet job. Seagull management where they fly in, dump on everything in sight, and fly off. One of the most traumatic experiences I've ever had."

IT Phone Work

During the 1980s many American firms began adopting telework as a cost-saving method for doing business, with companies reporting a savings of 30 percent or more. They also experienced a 40 percent increase in productivity within certain kinds of working environments. The improvements in productivity and reduced costs of doing business proved that teleworking was a viable workforce alternative. Lower costs for recruitment, less staff turnover, reduced overhead expenses, and better skill retention were strong motivations for employers. Furthermore, employers found that when employed in a teleworking environment, workers responded well and could adjust their working hours to develop peak workloads with minimal interruption for nonproductive activities such as road travel. Companies with teleworking structures also discovered that their decentralized workforce buffered them from outside agitation of their workforce. With production being delivered electronically, workers were unaffected by the work strikes of trucking personnel or shutdowns in other distribution systems. These benefits allowed many American corporations to focus their efforts more highly upon their management and communication activities versus the fixed costs of rent, real estate, and fixtures. Business objectives could very often be accomplished with the minimal investment of equipment and technology such as a phone line, modem, fax machine, and personal computer. E-mail and wide area networks offered even quicker, more effective integration of the teleworker into everyday business operations.

Essentially, teleworking is good for business, and the statistics prove it. In 1980, for the first time the census accounted for the numbers of Americans that were teleworking. At that time 1.2 million people were employed in home-based occupations or were teleworkers. By 1983, a study issued by the Internal Revenue Service estimated the numbers of teleworkers at 5.3 million. By the end of the decade, as many as 12 million workers were telecommuting or teleworking on a regular basis. With the benefits of technology, the original need to separate the employee's place of work from his or her home no longer existed. Old stereotypical attitudes about home-based work and self-employment began to erode while individual productivity in teleworking environments rose.

Teleworkers in the United States

	Year	Number of teleworkers
	1980	1.2 million
	1983	5.3 million
	1985	7.3 million
	1990	12 million

Norma Rae, or Take This Job and Shove It!

There's no question that, by the mid-1980s, workers began pushing away the depersonalized nature of employment in an industrial age in favor of a more personalized method of earning wages. For most of human history, work has comprised the primary portion of a person's life. In order to survive, the average person was forced to undergo grueling and laborious work in exchange for poor or inhumane treatment and meager wages. At the turn of the twentieth century, the average workweek exceeded sixty hours. But attitudes toward work and employment changed. Through the 1970s and 1980s a new workforce emerged, with new philosophies, beliefs, and opinions about working life. As workers today spend more time in educational pursuits and leisure, they are less willing to toil and travail "working for the man." Today workers average only thirty-five to forty hours per workweek, and more workers, a significant number of which are men, elect to work part-time or from home as society's attitudes toward male participation in the home become more liberalized.

Family and Medical Leave Act of 1993

 The Family Medical Leave Act was passed by Congress in 1993 to provide U.S. workers with up to twelve weeks of unpaid, job-protected leave for qualifying family or medical reasons, including:

@ The care of the employee's child after birth

@ The care of the employee's spouse, child, or parent who has become seriously ill

@ A serious health condition that prevents the employee from performing his or her job

Employees are eligible for family medical leave if they have worked for a covered employer for at least one year and for 1,250 hours over the previous twelve months, and if there are at least fifty employees within 75 miles.

Source: U.S. Department of Labor Employment Standards Administration, Wage and Hour Division of Washington, D.C.

The Clean and Green Way to Work

Teleworking provides some rather considerable benefits to the environment as well as to employers and their employees. With millions of people taking the information highway to work, there is a significant reduction in fossil fuel emissions. A 1994 study conducted by the U.S. Department of Energy estimated that if workers in American urbanized areas telecommuted rather than drove to work, they could reduce the emission of greenhouse gases by twenty pounds of carbon dioxide for every gallon of gas they saved. More than 10,000 miles of highway would be eliminated. Other studies indicate that each telecommuter would remove more than 3,000 pounds of carbon emissions per year from the environment. There is no question that a significant number of people teleworking has a worthwhile effect on the environment—so worth the effort that President Bill Clinton signed the Clean Air Act in 1995, which included the encouragement for companies with 100 employees or more to look for alternative options to traditional employee commuting

Technological Value for Those with Disabilities

Telework is an ideal circumstance for a wide range of people with disabilities because it allows people to complete their work irrespective of how far they are from their employer. That can be a terrific way to provide income-generating opportunities for those with disabilities, an option that not only enriches their lives as individuals but can also reduce their dependence upon public assistance programs. In 1994, the United Nations released official statistics estimating that 10 percent of the world's population is disabled. When the *dis*abled are *en*abled with the ability to work from their homes, they have the benefit of working within a work-friendly environment that meets their physical needs. By using advanced technologies in computing and communications to extend working relations beyond the immediate workplace and into the domains of the disabled, a majority of those with disabilities can become productive members of the global workforce.

The resulting feelings of autonomy and self-control extended to the disabled and physically challenged under such teleworking arrangements can have a positive and profound impact on their psychological and emotional well-being and can be a liberating experience. Teleworking can serve to alleviate the negative, stereotypical, and prejudiced attitudes associated with disablement. Using electronic equipment to perform and deliver their information-based work, those with speech impediments need not talk, people with visual impairments need not see, those in wheelchairs need not walk, and those with physical deformities need not concern themselves with the psychological barriers of communication with other people. Online, there is no stigma attached to the special disposition of disabled workers.

The Downside to Teleworking

For every action, there is an equal and opposite reaction, and that truth applies to teleworking. There are some inherent disadvantages to teleworking that should not be ignored by either the hiring party or the hired.

Hitting Employers' Pocketbooks

Employers on occasion have found difficulty tracking the productivity of offsite personnel working online. Even though it is tempting to believe that a teleworking workforce would be easier to supervise and organize, the reverse is true. The lack of onsite supervision and guidance in many situations can elevate the need for direct supervision of teleworking personnel, an added cost that employers will consider in their plans to go virtual in their workplace. Working online, employees may not be as accessible or otherwise accountable as they would be in physical attendance under the watchful eye of a qualified supervisor or manager. It's not so easy to escape the boss when you're sitting in a cubicle within a controlled office environment. It's far easier to evade unwanted contact when it requires that the employee only flip a switch on a computer or turn off e-mail software. Even when they are available, workers may live and work outside reasonable time zones for suitable business transactions with company personnel and customers. Companies adopting teleworking programs must also absorb the added expense of establishing the technology necessary to organize a teleworking delivery system to their place of business. Additional outlay for information technology such as dedicated lines, local area networks, wide area networks, and Internet sites are often required. The costs can be considerable—

enough to prevent otherwise accommodating firms from adopting a telework program.

Downsides for Workers

Isolation is the largest complaint of those who telework, telecommute, or telecompute. The separation of the individual from his or her centralized workplace can have negative psychological effects. Those who telework must tolerate the long-term effects of separation and isolation from their coworkers and supervisors. Teleworking can also be disruptive to family life. When workers occupy portions of the family domicile for work-related purposes, day-to-day work activity in a home environment can become distracting and nonproductive. This is especially true if there are children in the household. There are increased costs for workers who must invest in the technology necessary to implement a teleworking approach to earning a living. Even with the latest available equipment and technology, there is no guarantee against glitches or technical problems. When such occasions arise, it can be detrimental to the work relationship that is dependent upon the necessity to deliver work on time. Oftentimes, contract employers already expect too much productivity in too little time from workers not under their direct supervision and control. So, as with anything else, the benefits of teleworking can also become its disadvantages.

Chapter 5
What It's Like Now

We've examined the history leading to the current state of freelance work. But where are we now, you ask? What's up with freelance markets today, and where is it all headed? You'll want to start that investigation by taking a good look at your computer. If you don't have one, get one.

Computers are everywhere: in the marketplace, in the workplace, in the home, and even in the palm of your hand. If you don't believe that, take thirty seconds to look around. Today computers are used for every process and function, including word processing, accounting, filing, graphic design and layout, audio editing, architectural design, medical transcribing, pharmaceutical disbursement, auto repair, road maintenance, child care, home and commercial security—the list goes on and on.

Computers have enabled us to automate our lives. Essentially, they complete many of the processes and operations that used to be completed by human beings. ATMs dispense cash and automate bank accounts where human tellers used to work; robots construct automobiles where humans once did; and high-tech closed-circuit televisions monitor nighttime corridors that at one time were monitored by night watchmen. In many environments, such as industrial, service, and retail, machines have been used to replace humans entirely. For example, in the spring of 2001, NFO WorldGroup discovered that 93 percent of leisure air travelers in the United States were using online means to find travel information and to book airline flights, as opposed to the 66 percent who did so in the year 2000. The study also concluded that the number of travelers using a travel agent decreased between 2000 and 2001. There's no question that the automation of travel accommodations over the Internet has significantly impacted the number of employed travel agents in the United States. Computers will also minimize our role in traditional, labor-intensive industries such as manufacturing. Computer-integrated manufacturing (CIM) and computer numerically controlled (CNC) systems are becoming widespread applications for computers. Engineers who design automobiles in this new millennium will create their designs on a computer-aided design (CAD) system, which will be tied into a central network that links into the engineering department where the new design is inspected and parts are fabricated. Once completed, those parts will operate efficiently on computer-controlled devices that will automate the assembly process. As it is rolled onto the showroom floor, the unit will be tracked for sales statistics, which will be tied into the primary computer network of the manufacturing plant for complete inventory and sales analysis. This complete computerization of the manufacturing process will keep down manufacturing costs and hopefully the ultimate price that you will pay for your automobile at the dealership. Human workers will maintain, direct, and supervise the process.

Current office environments are even more automated, as computers and their peripheral devices control and manage almost every basic daily operation, from word processing and desktop publishing to faxing and accounting to answering telephones. Today's office environment houses armies of workers at computerized workstations where printers, faxes, and scanners drone the hum of modern-day productivity. It was widely held in previous decades that the computer's ability to automate the office would eventually do away with hard-copy documents and usher the human species into the age of the paperless society. That, of course, hasn't happened. Another pattern has instead emerged. The more we automate the office, the more paperwork we actually create. But the more paperwork we create, the more we innovate machines to automate the processing of that paperwork. We are innovative-process freaks.

The Structure of Computer Networks: Know Your Stuff

See Part Three for a comprehensive primer to the skills needed to optimize your freelance opportunities using computers, the Internet, and the World Wide Web.

Network

A computer network is the connection of two or more computers, personal or mainframe, that are in some way connected for the purpose of data communication. The physical connections of computers through cable or telephone lines and the use of specialized software allow the seamless exchange and transfer of data between computers. Although you may find it valuable to acquaint yourself with the variety of major networks used in business applications (Novell or Windows NT, for example), network use is not usually a required ability for you to complete online freelance work.

Local Area Network (LAN)

Local area networks (LANs) connect two or more computers and their peripheral devices such as printers and external drives within a specific confined area like a business office, building, educational institution, or government institution. Computers within the LAN are physically connected by cables, fiber-optic lines, or wires that provide the capability of transferring and exchanging data between computers and their peripheral devices. As with the basic network, you may want to acquaint yourself with the operations of LANs so that you are aware of the nuances in the operation of possible client systems. It is not, however, a usual requirement in a freelance work environment.

Wide Area Network (WAN)

A wide area network (WAN) connects two or more LANs and other smaller networks to systems spanning large geographical areas. Many WANs span entire states. They can even cross entire continents. Computers and networks within a WAN can be linked physically through cables, wires, or fiber-optic lines, or wirelessly through satellite transmission. Users of a WAN generally gain access through a modem. The Internet itself is the world's largest example of a WAN. As with the basic network and the LAN, you may want to acquaint yourself with the operations of a WAN so that you are aware of the nuances in the operation of possible client systems. Unless you are speaking to the Internet itself, however, it is not a usual requirement in a freelance work environment.

Internet

The original purpose of the Internet was for military defense in a program called ARPANET (Advanced Research Projects Agency Network), which was created in the 1960s. ARPANET's purpose was to develop a resilient network of computers that could survive a nuclear attack and instantly reroute messages through a dense lacework of computer links that stretched coast to coast. By 1983, the Internet had expanded well beyond the confines of military use and employed the Transmission Control Protocol/Internet Protocol (TCP/IP) communications standard for freely linking computer communications worldwide. (See Part Three for more information.)

World Wide Web

Tim Berners-Lee, with the help of several colleagues, created the hypertext transfer protocol (http), a programming-based, digital system that facilitated communication between computers over the Internet. It became the World Wide Web in 1989. The further development of a text-based Web browser provided a standardized system of communication between Web servers and browsers and was available to the general public by 1992. The release of the Mosaic Web browser in 1993 made available a convenient, Web-based graphical user interface that offered users point-and-click ease and simplicity.

For More Information . . . or FYI

It's all about information. In past industrialized times, raw materials and natural resources were the commodities of trade. But today's commodity isn't raw materials; it's information. Once acquired (a timely and valuable but costly process in itself), that information must be managed or processed. It must be categorically organized and archived so that it can be networked, retrieved, and displayed for optimal use. There is more knowledge and information—data, facts, expressions, theories, and experiences—managed on Earth on this very day than what could have been dreamed of in the last decade. Most of it is transmitted over the Internet. It could be said that the Internet is quickly becoming the mass of accumulated and accrued information for the entire human species: the accumulated consciousness of mankind. That's a lot of information.

Man's interest in acquiring knowledge in all disciplines—religious, educational, social, economic, and political—is not, as you might think, on the wane whatsoever. The ever-improving ways to accumulate and manage information have actually served to heighten and encourage the human acquisition of more knowledge—more information. Another one of those wily patterns emerges. In other words, the more knowledge we gain, the more we thirst for additional information, for every science, profession, and thought. You might even say that we're obsessed and absorbed with information, certainly immersed in it. This is not a new phenomenon by any means. The volume of accumulated information has almost doubled every decade since the seventeenth century. It's our ability in the twentieth and twenty-first centuries to automate the accrual and collection of information that sets us apart from previous generations.

As we acquire and manage this information, we discern and discover newer and better ways to automate. More automation provides even more time for the pursuit of knowledge, which creates even more information. See any more patterns? The more knowledge we gain, the more we automate, but the more we automate, the more information we are able to acquire. Like the industrial age and the feudalistic agricultural age before it, the information age is an endless upward spiral with no end in sight—as far as we can foresee, anyway.

The New Ivory Tower

Corporate management in the new millennium is completely different than it was fifty years ago. Computerized networks and information-processing systems have become the central focus of corporate management in America and around the world. The traditional power structures and pyramidal-shaped organizational charts of corporate institutions are quickly giving way to team-based networking units that communicate directly and openly with upper management. Business today is managed in small units knit tightly together that are integrated into the larger scheme with highly structured systems of communication. Yesterday's ivory palace corporation has been replaced with highly sensitive work groups that are piloted toward their goals using leadership by consensus decision-making, a common consent and wisdom made possible only through the flexibility of educated workers using high-speed communications and document exchange. The ability to effect such energetic and expansive levels of communication through means of networking—whether it is an internal network, a LAN, a WAN, the Internet, or the World Wide Web—is the very catalyst for such dynamic changes within the world's workplace.

"It's just not possible any longer to figure it out from the top and have everyone else follow the orders of the grand strategist," writes Peter M. Senge of MIT in his book *The Fifth Discipline: The Art and Practice of the Learning Organization* (Currency Doubleday, 1994). "The organizations which will truly excel in the future will be the organizations that discover how to tap people's commitment and capacity to learn at all levels in an organization."

The key element to consider in this new-millennium corporate model is that information—the collection, storage, and retrieval of it and the ability to manipulate it—has become the nucleus for effective business management. Information processing is at the heart of business today, and slowdowns in economic growth will not change that modern truth.

These profound changes within the infrastructure of the world's corporate framework are changing the very essence and nature of the economy. Information management and the tools used for that management have become the fulcrum on which rests the cost efficiency and productiveness of our society. Above all, more important than inventory, sales, competition, material costs, and human resources is the acquisition of information. Information is power, and today it is more powerful than money, politics, or social standing. "The transformation to a new economic engine of prosperity and growth," writes Blake Harris, editor at large for *Government Technology* magazine, "began decades before the Internet, when knowledge, rather than capital or physical resources, became the key to generating new wealth."

This shift away from the industrialized age and toward an information age is greatly influencing the world's distribution of labor. Management positions have been particularly affected, with millions of wage earners permanently removed from the labor force. The continued expansion of information technologies and information-based management structures will undoubtedly continue the toppling of old and outmoded economic structures. In other words, the world has been stalwartly thrust into the information age. It's an odious process but one that will bode well for you if you're planning a freelance career.

Stat Attack

 CyberAtlas reported in June 2001 that worldwide use of online recruiting rose from 29 percent of the Global 500 companies in 1998 to more than 88 percent in 2001. European and Asian companies led the increase.

The AOL/Roper Study of 2000 indicated that e-commerce, although on a temporary slump, would not be slowing anytime soon. Online retail purchasing had more than doubled since 1998. Within ten years, the study projected, the average home will not only be wired for access but will also be online-ready in every room.

The American Society of Association Executives reported in July 2001 that, on average, 4 percent of new members in American associations were recruited using the Internet. Two percent of American association suppliers and vendors were recruited online.

In 2001, Ispos-Reid concluded in a study of thirty countries that 98 percent of survey respondents owned a television, 51 percent owned cellular phones, and 48 percent owned a computer, but only 36 percent were online.

Europemedia reported that Internet users in the Ukraine rose from 120,000 in 1999 to more than 750,000 in 2000.

> In February 2001, the Kelsey Group reported that only 25 percent of American small businesses were on the Internet. Only 10 percent used e-mail.
>
> "American small businesses have been entering the world of electronic commerce in large numbers, as both developers and beneficiaries of the systems that are revolutionizing business practices. 'Connectivity' is the watchword of this new era—and small firms are connecting rapidly."
> —U.S. Small Business Administration, Office of Advocacy, June 2000

Small Business Is Big Business

Look to small business for big-time opportunity in the next several decades. Why? Because cyberbusiness is becoming the backbone of small firms (those with two to one hundred employees). By the end of the last decade, small business was earning more than $3 billion annually in e-commerce. E-commerce, however, is not the primary purpose for small businesses going online. Less than 5 percent of them use the Internet for e-commerce purposes. Advertising, external communication to customers via e-mail, internal communication to employees via networking and e-messaging, and information research are the biggest reasons small businesses are using the Net. E-mail is the number one reason why most companies are getting wired. The Local Commerce Monitor, an ongoing study of 600 small businesses conducted by the Kelsey Group of Princeton, New Jersey, concluded in February 2001 that 10 percent of all small businesses were using e-mail to deliver their marketing appeals. "What we're seeing now is that because small businesses are being encouraged to conduct business with their suppliers online and over the Internet, they're realizing that they can use the same technologies and applications to interact with their customers," said Neal Polochek, a senior vice president for the firm. "While e-commerce retains the spotlight as far as Internet-related business operations, it's clear that the larger goal of most small businesses is to leverage the Internet to enhance operational efficiencies rather than to simply grow revenues."

Research is the second largest reason, with the accumulation of customer-related information as the motive. These technological developments are proving effective and profitable as companies in all sectors show higher revenues and profits when they use the Internet in their business operations. Only 30 to 35 percent of all small companies have a website, but 80 percent of those that do claim they've found it an effective way to communicate to their key public, such as shareholders, consumers, the media, customers, and employees. The primary focus of the average website is to expand business markets by attracting new customers *and new employees*. Small businesses are going online, not necessarily to make sales but to attract people to their firms, freelancers included. (You will be encouraged to know that more than half of American freelancers are currently employed or contracted by small businesses.)

The explosive growth in small-business use of information technology shows no signs of a slowdown in the foreseeable future. Spending tells the story. American firms are spending lots of money on the expansion of their technology, mostly for Internet access and networking capabilities. In June 2000, the Office of Advocacy for the U.S. Small Business Administration predicted in its report "Small Business Expansion in Electronic Commerce" that more than $28 billion was spent in 2000 for small-business Internet technologies and services. Small, independent, or home-based offices called Small Offices/Home Offices, or SOHOs, are also moving toward automation and virtual operations and are projected to spend more than $70 billion on information technology products in 2002.

With the world of commerce quickly shifting toward an e-business model, the value in business-to-business transactions will rely more on the information being exchanged than the product or service being rendered. The Internet will function as the primary exchange conduit for such transactions, an electrifying transformation for the future of small enterprise.

If You Build It, They Will Come. Unless . . .

A significant number of challenges must be overcome before freelance commerce can be useful for the average company. Information technologies within the firm must be fully integrated with Internet access, and the company must have the ability to manage a massive volume of information. Even when they do have the resources and personnel to develop information technology, small businesses are often left with concerns about their abilities to manage it on an ongoing basis. Costs can also be prohibitive, with the average price tag for website development alone exceeding $10,000. Business operations will in many ways be more complex than in previous eras. These complexities, however, will create terrific opportunities for contractors and freelancers as small businesses wrestle with the demands of new technology and the need for personnel to manage it. Indeed, the necessity for additional manpower will rise considerably in the next five years as computers and information technologies become less costly for small firms entering the information age.

More than 5 million high-tech jobs were added to the U.S. economy between 1990 and 2000, and it is projected that more than six out of every ten new jobs will be associated with an information technology. The information technology sector will grow at 8 percent annually, with average earnings per worker of more than $52,000.

The Internet is quickly becoming the very infrastructure upon which small business is built and maintained, and that's creating a big demand for freelance services. The robust job growth created by the scramble for qualified personnel with high-tech expertise is creating a serious shortage in the labor markets. As a result, hundreds of thousands of jobs were left vacant throughout the 1990s, even though the percentage of adults with jobs remained at the highest rate in history. The U.S. Department of Labor has projected that the computer industry alone will add more than 1.6 million new skilled jobs to the U.S. economy within the next ten years. Some projections expect a shortage of more than 2 million workers by or before the end of 2002. Surveys in recent years conducted by the Electronic Recruiting Index have shown that more than half of the survey respondents outside the information technology fields also indicated a serious shortage of qualified workers. In order to address their immediate needs for skilled labor, a significant number of companies are turning to the Internet to attract and recruit independent contractors and freelance workers. So, you'll want to be sure to have your cyber hard hat ready to take maximum advantage of these explosive realities.

Career Profile: Website Designer

Needed: website designer for project work to design our firm's Web-based applications.

Large financial firm seeks freelance website and graphics designer proficient with Web page creation software and various browsers.

These are just a couple of the classified advertisements appearing in newspapers across the country for website designers, one of the fastest-growing freelance fields in the nation. With more than $250 billion worth of goods and services sold over the Web each year, the increasing need for talented website designers is expected to grow well into the new millennium. Some statistics project growth to be as much as 68 percent each year for the next ten years! If that holds true, freelance Web design is an occupational category that can provide unlimited promise for you.

Website designers are essentially considered a new breed of graphic designers. Their artistic input and creative ability for developing the appearance and functionality of websites and Web pages provide the framework for delivering the content that appears on the Web. This is done through the manipulation of electronic graphics with hypertext machine language, or HTML, a computer programming language used by website designers for constructing Web pages. The text that is produced by writers, marketing professionals, or corporate managers is transferred to the designer with an indication of where to place material in the finished format. The designer then structures and organizes the material into an efficient visual presentation for Web browsers. This is accomplished through the use of "links," or hyperlinks, that are used to navigate viewers from page to page in an effort to communicate and present information in a stimulating, creative, and effective manner. Being a good website designer requires not only technical know-how and ability but also strong artistic talent.

"Providing advanced websites today can be challenging," says David Robinson, a freelance website designer. "Anyone can throw together a few simple Web pages using popular design software. The trick to building a professional website for your customer is providing a site with functionality. A retailer, for example, may want to allow his customers to view their complete order history online. This type of site requires programming experience beyond HTML. It's rare that any one person has the ability to complete every aspect of an advanced website. For the individual freelance designer, it's best to build on your strengths and form strategic partnerships with other contractors for assistance in your weak areas."

There are many occupations related to a freelance website designer career. You may find it helpful to investigate the following career alternatives:

@ Graphic designer

@ Computer programmer

@ Multimedia designer

@ Advertising professional

@ Sales professional

@ Marketing professional

Employment Outlook: Next Ten Years

The Bureau of Labor Statistics reports that there will be a 30 percent increase in the need for website designers in the next decade. Of the 647,000 or more website designers currently employed in the United States, approximately 68 percent of them are self-employed freelance workers. Most operate from their homes or in small offices, working long and quiet hours in front of computer terminals attending to detail work and intricate computer programming.

Number of Website Designers	
Total website designers as of 2000	647,000
Total needed by 2008	838,000
Need for new website designers each year	23,875*

*Due to the need for growth and total replacement

Annual Earnings	
Starting salary	$40,000
After 5 years	$50,000
After 10 to 15 years	$70,000 (projected)

Independent, self-employed Web design specialists generally charge from $80 to $150 per hour for their project work services.

Necessary Skills

Each website designer has his or her own method for design work. Good communication skills are first and foremost in order to effectively execute the will and desire of clients for their websites. A good designer will listen carefully to the needs of his or her clients, editors, writers, programmers, and marketing personnel to create and implement an effective website for communicating the ideas and concepts that are important to the customers. Thus, the ability to participate in a team is essential.

Designers must also be familiar with the application programs for design work such as imaging programs, 3D modeling, drawing programs, HTML editors, and compilers. If this weren't enough, they must also be aware of programming systems and protocols such as UNIX, Windows and Windows NT, TCP/IP, FTP, and http, as well as Internet-related technology such as bandwidth abilities, T1 lines, and modem technology.

"The best investment for a Web designer," says Robinson, "is to invest in the best computer equipment he or she can buy, with the absolute best high-speed modem they can find. Work with it, study it, and learn it until you know it like the back of your hand. It's such a new technology, there's no other way to learn it."

Education and Training

Although the number of formal educational programs for website designers is growing, this career field is open to almost anyone with the capability, aptitude, and inclination to succeed. Successful designers include people from all backgrounds and experience levels, and in some instances include junior high and high school students. As the Internet and the World Wide Web become more of a force in the marketplace, structured educational programs are sure to develop. In the meantime, artistic skill, creativity, technical knowledge of computers and software programs, computer programming, and computer science are invaluable aids in this career path. A bachelor's degree in computer science, art, graphics design, advertising, or marketing would undoubtedly be helpful in this freelance career as well. An associate's degree in art, multimedia design, or computer science is also desirable. There are also vocational programs available to the career-minded website designer. Your local vocational center can provide excellent direction for preparation and training in this dynamic new field.

For More Information

@ www.graphics.com: links and resources for graphic designers and website designers

@ www.gag.org: the website for the Graphic Artists Guild, with online resources and industry information for graphic artists and website designers

@ www.freelancers.com: the website of Creative Freelancers Online, which connects freelancers with companies in need of website designers, illustrators, writers, and editors

@ www.creativemoonlighter.com: a website to help you find part-time, temporary, and freelance jobs for website and graphic design, copy writing, advertising, and publishing

@ www.findcreative.com: a job-search and -posting site for the creative freelancer working in graphic and website design, illustration, photography, advertising, and copy writing

Full site reviews appear in Part Four of this book.

Chapter 6
Virtual Recruitment:
*Inter*netting a Job

If you're a professional freelancer, expect to be recruited online. In order to deal with the scarcity of skilled workers in today's markets, large corporations and small business alike have turned to online means for worker recruitment. Studies show, in fact, that more than 98 percent of all companies will post their available jobs online by 2002.

Why are so many companies turning to online means to find qualified people? For convenience and reduced costs, that's why. Even in economic downturns as experienced in 2000, the trend toward electronic recruitment increased as firms across the country and around the world sought reductions in recruitment costs by adopting e-recruitment policies and techniques. In a survey conducted by 6figurejobs.com, more than 97 percent of employer respondents indicated that e-mail was their preferred method of accepting résumés and proposals. Reduced cost was their biggest reason, followed by broad reach, twenty-four-hour access, and speed. So, even a bad economy encourages online recruitment.

Speed is a critical issue for online recruiters. On the Internet, would-be employers and contractors can post projects and jobs instantly where they can be viewed by millions of potential contract candidates throughout the world. One such example is the MRPAnet hosted by the Michigan Recreation and Park Association (MRPA). Through their MRPA membership, park and recreation facilities throughout the state of Michigan can access the association website at www.mrpaonline.org and freely post vacancies for parks and recreation positions or contracts. Postings include the title of the job or position available, its intended pay rate, the facility contact name, and a brief job description. The speed at which a job or project can be posted offers organizations such as this an excellent edge over the competition in finding work candidates, especially in the recruitment of high-demand job candidates and freelancers.

"We have found the Career Opportunities page to be the most popular and dynamic component of our website," says MRPA executive director Michael J. Maisner. "Providing the opportunity for real-time job postings is a great service for our parks and recreation departments throughout Michigan, as well as the individual members of the Association. Agencies can now post job vacancies as soon as they become available, and professionals seeking advancement in the field can access the site at any time to find the latest work opportunities the industry has to offer."

Of course, this is just one example of the seemingly infinite number of successful job sites. "Every city, every profession, it seems, has its own job search website," wrote Rebecca Vesely in her column, "Pounding the Virtual Pavement," for *Business 2.0* in June 1999. "Directmarketingcareers.com caters to direct marketing professionals seeking career advancement. College grads can click over to CampusCareerCenter Worldwide for first-time jobs and internships. Computer geeks can hit Computerjobs.com. The electronic recruiting market was estimated at $4.5 billion in September 1998 and is growing at an annual rate of 100 percent according to interbiz.com's 1999 Electronic Recruiting Index. And, today, as record numbers work in temporary and contract [freelance] positions, they have no choice but to perpetually be pounding the pavement. Just as consumers go online to browse for a new computer book, they can also surf for a job."

Personal Websites

Having your own website is a great idea, and you may be tempted to try to get your own website to show up in various search engines. You can do this by visiting individual search engine sites and cyberplow through their sloughs of online instruction on how to submit your site to them, but this process is extremely time-consuming. Your time would probably be better spent on more productive aspects of your job search. There are a number of online companies that will submit your website to dozens or even hundreds of search engines for a fee, or sell you software that automates the registration process for you. Some of these services assert that they will get a "high ranking" on these search engines for you and that your personal website will be listed toward the top of the results page if a would-be employer happens to search for a website like yours. Unless you have money to gamble on the underwhelming odds, don't waste your time with these services. No matter how high you rank in search engine results, if you get ranked on search engines at all, prospective employers are most unlikely to use search engines to shop for employees. In order to find freelance work online, you're better off taking a more direct approach by using job-search sites, viewing employer websites, and making direct e-mail inquiries.

E-Spiders: How Your Résumé Gets Noticed

To better facilitate the search for qualified contract workers, many companies have further automated the electronic recruitment process by employing résumé spiders for a fee on the World Wide Web. Résumé spiders are software programs that automate the résumé search by trolling the Internet for key words on select résumés. With the mass posting of more than 6 million résumés online, these sophisticated programs scan résumé websites for a match to contract employers' specifications. When a résumé for a potential candidate is indexed as a possibility, the software delivers an automated e-mail message from the recruiting firm to the résumé owner. The software searches and queries a multitude of search engines and reports a list of potential hits to the personnel seeker using the service. The process can be completed in less than sixty minutes, believe it or not, depending upon how many hits have been discovered in the search. A private database of potential candidates is created so that the spider's and the searcher's lists of candidates continue to grow with every search. Many spider services, such as the Résumé Robot, revisit their database once a month to maintain an accurate searching mechanism. Old résumé pages are removed when they become ninety days old or if links to the résumés posted to the Web have been broken. The sites scanned by such résumé spiders include some of the largest résumé sites on the Web, including AltaVista, Snap, Webcrawler, Yahoo!, and Northern Lights. The service offers the potential for finding megavolumes of potential employees and contract workers for needy employers.

● The sheer numbers in recruitment exposure are a major reason why employers are flocking to online venues to post their contract job availability. With a worldwide audience, the Internet simply reaches more people with less effort than any other available mass medium. By using the limitless space of the Internet's virtual capabilities, employers can post less-costly advertisements that are not charged by the word or line. As a job seeker, that gives you a considerable advantage in your search for skilled contract or freelance work. For the posting company, it provides a significant benefit over traditional advertising, offering adequate space to thoroughly outline the job being advertised and its complete details. That's a valuable information tool for companies seeking highly skilled workers for specific contract jobs.

Gaggles and Droves: The Downside of E-recruitment

Posting job notices online can actually be *too* successful—so much so that many firms have had to temporarily discontinue the practice. "We've had to stop posting our jobs online," says one middle manager. "We've gotten so many résumés online that we couldn't process them all. Most of them were junk," that is, résumés with little or no applicability to the advertised work. Because the Internet offers the ability to respond to posting firms with no out-of-pocket expense, work candidates are not dissuaded from posting weak or inappropriate résumés.

Nevertheless, the majority of U.S. employers continue to post opportunities online. By 1997, the number of job postings placed online by employers was 1.2 million. That number has risen sharply by more than 44,000 jobs and projects per week, increasing steadily by an average of 1.2 percent per week. In fact, it is projected that there will be more than 8 million job postings online by 2002. With numbers like these, there's no doubt that the Internet has quickly become a megamarketplace for job postings with no clear end in sight.

Online Recruiting					
Corporate recruitment	1998	1999	2000	2001	2002
Website recruitment	29%	60%	79%	88%	98%
No website	14%	9%	0%	0%	0%
Source: iLogos Research					

Freed to Lance

Jeff Westover, in his report for Myjobsearch.com in February 2000, wrote of a Myjobsearch.com survey that found "fifteen freelancers for every project advertised online." He wrote also of another Myjobsearch.com survey conducted from October 1999 through March 2000, which concluded, "The response rate from job seekers applying for projects posted at Internet freelance job boards resulted in twenty-one responses per posting." Yet if it is true that there were more than 6 million project jobs advertised online during the year 2000 and there were 8.2 million independent contractors (including seasonal workers and independent contract workers), prospects for finding freelance work over the Internet would seem more lucrative. Other statistics show that there are more than 2 million workers in the United States alone who are temporary employees working through temporary agencies. Some experts include them in statistics on freelance and independent workers. When these 2 million are added to the 8.2 million workers that are independent contractors and the 14 million other workers who are self-employed, the total figure is a staggering 24 million people who could be considered self-employed, contracted free-agent, or freelance workers. "There's a new movement in the land," wrote Daniel H. Pink in his article "Free Agent Nation" for FastCompany.com. "From coast to coast in communities large and small, citizens are declaring their independence and drafting a new bill of rights." He speaks in his article of the more than 25 million workers in America who comprise what he called the Free Agent Nation. With those colossal figures comprising the current market of competitive freelance workers, you might be tempted to toss in your mouse for a more traditional method of netting work. Yet within the same article, Pink speaks of free agent Deborah Risi, who "declared herself a free agent [and] landed her first client four days later." So, although free agents, independent contractors, and freelance workers comprise a significant part of the workforce, this should not dissuade you from the increasingly profitable potential of seeking independent work using online means.

"For a freelance writer, the Internet is an indispensable tool," says Katherine Woodford, a freelance writer from Moneta, Virginia. "An experienced writer can quickly find the websites with legitimate job listings, tossing the fly-by-nights into the recycle bin. I receive weekly newsletters with fresh listings from these trusted sites and the National Writers Union, which I highly recommend.

"The Internet is now the communication of choice between editor and writer. I very seldom have voice contact with my editors. Instead I receive all my assignments via e-mail and send the completed work to them in the form of an attached file. My telephone interviews are set up via e-mail and often I send sample questions so that they are more relaxed when we begin talking. Without the Internet, I would be out of business until I worked out a new system."

Career Profile: Freelance Writer

How would you like to spend your days finding ways to express your creative talents by teaching the world about new technologies, interesting people, unusual experiences, or important world events? Does the world of words excite or intrigue you? Are you poetic or do you dream about seeing your picture-words in print? If so, then perhaps a career as a freelance writer can help you make a difference in our changing digital world. With so many new technologies such as the Internet and the World Wide Web available for exchanging thoughts, ideas, and information, demand for talented and creative writers continues to rise dramatically.

"The best thing about being a freelance writer," says Gregory Diamond, a freelance author and writer for more than fifteen years, with a mischievous smile, "is the freedom to be my own person. To write for whomever I want and about whatever I want. To boldly say what no one has said before." Diamond has written for scores of well-known and not-so-well-known publications, including the poetry anthology *The Ebbing Tide, Life Insurance Selling,* National Public Radio, and more. After fifteen years of, as he says, "working in the trenches," Diamond has recently enjoyed the development of national and international exposure for many of his writings. "I'm very lucky," he says. "I've been able to successfully support my family with the income I've earned from my writing."

But it's not the big-name publications that support his career. Rather, Diamond has found a successful niche writing for smaller, narrowly targeted publications and clients that most people have never seen or read about. "That's the key," he says, "to find a market for your work. Finding a niche and developing it to the point that you can support yourself with the income you earn. Once you accomplish that, you can take the job just about anywhere you want to go with it."

In Diamond's case, that meant writing lots of brochures, letters, and résumés for people, sometimes writing as many as ten or twelve résumés per week in order to pay the bills. "When you're in freelance work," says Diamond, "you're pretty much self-employed. It's not enough to be a good writer; you have to sell yourself—your creative abilities and writing skills. Convince editors that you are better than the competition at sharing ideas and telling stories. It's not just about being an author; it's selling yourself—owning your own business and trying to run it successfully." Now in his sixteenth year as a freelance author, it's the freedom of being his own boss that Diamond says he likes most about the job. He sets his own hours and develops his own standards for the work that he does, most of it using a laptop computer.

"That's the worst part of it for me," he says, "dealing with the computer. I use it to make my job a lot easier, but I'm not very good at learning new software programs." With many new word processing, HTML, voice recognition, and language translation programs now being introduced to the market, technology is becoming an important part of the job. "Fifteen years ago, you used to be able to do this job with a pencil and paper. Not any more, though. You really have to know your stuff when it comes to computers. You never know when an editor is going to ask you to submit your story over the Internet or upload it onto their magazine's Web page on the World Wide Web." Electronic technology is an important element in a freelance writing career.

You must express yourself well in order to develop a professional writing career. Thus, good English and grammar skills are essential. It's a competitive industry. Editors demand expressive and well-perfected abilities with English and grammar, as well as strong abilities to develop thoughts and organize ideas. Those considering freelance writing as a career will find an interest in literature and journalism helpful in improving their writing skills. College-level journalism, literature, and/or English will be important for those wishing to obtain a degree in the writing field. A bachelor's degree in English, literature, or journalism is most desirable.

There are many occupations related to a freelance writing career. You may find it helpful to investigate the following career alternatives:

- Magazine writer
- Content writer and editor
- Technical writer
- Journalist
- Speech writer
- Public relations professional
- Copy writer
- Copy editor
- Editor

Employment Outlook: Next Ten Years

The Bureau of Labor Statistics reports that there will be a 24 percent increase in the need for writers in the next decade.

Number of Writers	
Total writers as of 2000	340,000
Total needed by 2008	423,872
Need for new writers each year	10,375

Annual Earnings	
Starting salary	$35,000
After 5 years	$47,000
After 10 to 15 years	$55,000

Median annual income earned for full-time freelance writing ranges from $35,000 to $60,000 per year, with an average annual income of $44,000, although beginners should expect no more than $25,000 to $30,000. Concentrating on a specialty genre or niche can be especially helpful in acquiring a full-time income from a writing career. Specialty areas include

- Personal-experience writing
- Technical writing (instruction manuals, software manuals, etc.)
- How-to articles
- Profile stories (stories about interesting people)
- Travel stories
- Business articles

"I've done a story on just about everything you can think of," says Diamond. Those stories include skydiving from 10,000 feet, cruising the Mississippi on a riverboat, having a baby, and even getting a tattoo, which he did just so that he could do a story on the subject. "That's the best part of this job," he says. "You get a chance to do it all."

For More Information

- www.writersdigest.com: megabytes of information on writer's markets, writing workshops, and writing groups
- www.freelance.com/: a website devoted to connecting freelance artists with those who are looking for freelance writers, designers, and artists

@ www.sunoasis.com: a website for writers, editors, and copy writers who are looking for freelance work, with project postings from potential contractors

@ www.freelancewriting.com: a job bank website, with project postings for freelance writers, editors, and copy writers

Full site reviews appear in Part Four of this book.

A Fine E-line: Defining Teleworking and Freelancing

A growing number of freelance workers are discovering that the Internet is unequaled in its ability to help them find quality work alternatives. When it comes to landing a good paying contract job, the high-speed connectivity of the World Wide Web is hard to match in its job-searching capabilities. Advertising your skills and services is mandatory if you are to find good project work, and when it comes to advertising, nothing exceeds the potential of the Internet in broadcasting your work availability.

Although there has been recent negative coverage on the effectiveness of job-search and employment websites, landing work online continues to evolve into an ever-effective method for finding qualified projects and freelance work. Most of the negative press seems to stem from the fact that there simply isn't enough credible data on the productiveness of using the Internet to find work, freelance work included. There is also the tendency to confuse those seeking and completing work online with traditional workers in the IT industry, which has experienced a significant number of job losses since the financial market corrections of 2000. When it comes to analyzing the true numbers of freelancers, free agents, and independent workers in America, there's a lot of misconception surfing around.

In the confusion, there is one mistake that you will not want to make in the definition of freelance work online, and that's the difference between online freelance work and telework, a concept discussed earlier in this book. It's a big difference. Although all freelancers working online are teleworkers, all teleworkers are not necessarily freelancers. That's a big distinction in many ways. Teleworkers are those who work for companies via electronic means, usually at a location other than their primary place of employment. Although teleworkers use online means to deliver work to their employers, they are usually employed on a permanent payroll. They are not independent workers; they are employees. Though it was the movement toward teleworking in the mid-1970s that fully feathered the coming renaissance toward a full-scale freelance workforce, the two movements are separate and distinct occurrences.

Teleworkers work at their primary place of employment most of the time, working away on an average of two days per week. The purpose of their teleworking arrangement is productive convenience. Teleworkers enjoy many benefits, including less commute time and more time with their families, and are generally more productive as their work time is expanded with the reduction of their travel needs. As reported by the International Telework Association and Council, "Telecommuting employs telecommunications to avoid the drudgery and risks of the traditional commute to the office." Teleworkers have taxes withheld from their paychecks by their employers. They take direct instruction from their employers, who control their day-to-day actions, including when and where they work. They are trained by a specific company or employer to complete a defined task for the firm.

Freelance workers, on the other hand, are independent and sovereign self-employed people. They are not employed on a payroll, and most would wretch severely at the mere suggestion. They assume their own expenses in performing the tasks that they are contracted to complete and wouldn't have it any other way. They bear 100 percent of the fruits of their labor and 100 percent of the risks involved in the conduct of their business affairs. Their work is performed as part of a contract or agreement to complete a specific service for a set fee, and they use their own methods and resources in the performance of those agreements. They all prefer to work for themselves (or they wouldn't be doing it), and most enjoy working from home.

If you have decided to go freelance or have been working freelance, you are part of a growing trend toward an independent workforce, a long-term shift in the work and employment paradigm. Of the 21 to 25 million self-employed workers in the United States (it depends on what report you read), about one in five today is an independent contractor that can be classified as a freelance, free-agent, or independent worker. These are people who are not paid a salary or wage. All in all, about 6 million people in the United States are now self-employed, according to a survey conducted by the Bureau of Labor Statistics. More than 4 million of these self-employed independent freelancers work in a home-based business. The majority of these home-based businesses—65 percent of them—perform service-related activities. That's more than 2.6 million people. What's more, an additional 1.8 million people in the United States are now doing independent contract work as a source of second income. That means that there's more than 4.4 million others who, like you, are doing free-agent work in America.

@ Independent contract workers own almost 50 percent of all small businesses in the United States.

@ Almost 50 percent of all home-based freelance workers have been freelancers for more than ten years.

@ More than 35 percent of all U.S. workers confirm that they telework from home.

@ There are more than 2 million home-based freelance businesses started in the United States each year.

@ About 25 percent of those who are self-employed use the wired way to deliver their work assignments.

Freelance workers using telecommunications as a mode of procurement and delivery for their work are doing so as a requirement for their project. They generally do so for one of three reasons.

1. They are located at a significant distance from their contracting employer.

2. It is a more efficient method to find and deliver their work.

3. It is the required method in which they must deliver work to their hiring parties.

The case of Fred Damsen is a typical example. Damsen, the owner and operator of the Japan Woodworker in Alameda, California, and the Japan Woodworking Fine Catalog of Tools, employs a freelance writer to develop his marketing and public relations materials and projects for the media. His freelance writer is located in the Midwest, almost 2,500 miles away. The work the writer does for Damsen is delivered online via e-mail and e-mail attachments.

"I use a freelancer online because it would be hard to find someone locally who is a marketing specialist and knows woodworking equipment," says Damsen. "Online I was able to find a marketing specialist to help me develop my marketing and public relations material for my specialty woodworking tools. The fact that he is halfway across the country makes no difference because he delivers his work to me online. He prepares press releases for me to send to woodworking editors throughout the country and writes marketing material for me. When we have to include photography in our releases, we simply send file attachments back and forth. So, online we are able to accomplish as much or more than we could otherwise."

Unlike teleworkers, freelancers work online in order to extend their work reach beyond their own locale and to expand their professional horizons. Working over the Internet, freelancers suffer no geographic limitations. Service work that is information-oriented, such as that completed by Damsen's freelance writer, is especially suitable for online completion. Those completing independent work online don't do it for convenience; they do so to operate their business relationships more efficiently. There are many hundreds of freelance occupations that you can operate successfully online. Stories like that of Steve Tiano, a freelancer in the cyberworld, are becoming common.

Says Tiano, "In 1978, to eat—I wasn't really fit for any other kind of work; summer work in construction was somehow gratifying, but only because I knew it would come to an end—I went to work in publishing as a proofreader/copy editor at a loose-leaf tax law periodical publisher. A husband-and-wife team ran this computer typesetter of science and math books and journals. I thought he was brilliant, a professor of computer science who'd written this earth-shattering program for typesetting math. They also managed the business, a mistake once they started to grow. She was production manager, even though they had other guys in that title with real experience, some of whom had come from England and Ireland.

"I decided there that if I ever could afford computer equipment myself I could probably do it myself and make a living. That is, if I remembered not to get too big and just kept it in my home, a cottage industry. After getting a full-time civil service job for security, I moonlighted nights and weekends as a page designer/layout artist on my own [computer] equipment at home. At first I trolled the newspaper classifieds, *Newsday* on Long Island and *The New York Times*. Publishing work seems a natural for off-site freelance, but it's not always easy to find work.

"I've gotten two long-running clients from Freelance Online. [The] first one is an odd story. Five years after a previous employer, a computer typesetter, folded— they'd been in bankruptcy for years—I answered a Freelance Online posting. I got an e-mail back: 'Steve, is that you?' An old friend from the computer typesetter who'd moved to Florida was the person hiring freelancers. So I got steady work laying out science/math journals. It paid poorly, but it was experience. I later left them after my friend moved on.

"I got another client from Freelance Online that pays considerably better. We'll see where that leads. I've also gotten one that may prove ongoing from DCPUBS."

Stories like Tiano's prove just how ubiquitous the Internet is becoming in the development of freelance work overall. With access to the Internet, you can selectively pinpoint or extract specific types of freelance potential in other countries, other states, or even your hometown. Using online capabilities, you can locate freelance work anywhere. And every day brings new technologies and tools that can improve your abilities to be successful in wired work as a freelancer.

Tools Drive the Trends

The development of application service providers (ASPs) is one example of how emerging technologies are being used to spur the growth of successfully wired freelance operations. A relatively new phenomenon, ASPs offer their customers, such as freelancers, the ability to operate specific application software, such as Web page creation or desktop design software, from a Web-based server. An ASP is technically defined as an organization that provides and supports computer application capacity to a network of users via a WAN. The ASP leases the use of specific application software over the Internet for a contracted fee. The concept is especially useful in business activities for independent freelance workers who otherwise could not afford the money or space for the necessary equipment required to operate the software applications. By using the Internet in such a manner, you can fundamentally operate a computer workstation with minimal equipment, office space, and financial investment. For a monthly fee, freelancers can access application software for their business needs and operate it from a robust application server. ASPs usually offer twenty-four-hour service, and most are available for a modest monthly premium. Such services can provide even those with meek resources with the availability of leading software titles for every use imaginable, including mass e-mailing for marketing purposes, database management, website design, desktop design, spreadsheet calculations, and online credit card acceptance. Used properly, ASPs can save you a substantial grip of hard-earned dollars if you're working from a home-based office.

The trend toward ASP-based business operations is proving a boon to independent business operators, and some experts predict that it will grow into a $20 billion–per-year industry by the end of 2003. Already, many key players in the software industry including Microsoft, Cisco, Oracle, and IBM are considering the development of ASP business services.

"The incremental cost differences could realistically allow the market penetration of application software suites to many of the small to medium-size enterprises that have been otherwise priced out of contention," writes Scott Jackson, vice president of Emerald Coast Jobs, Inc., in his article "Application Service Providers Introduce Yet Another Killer Application for the Internet" (published in *Climate Magazine*, July–August 2000). He adds, "ASP vendors will descend into the market en masse armed with industry bridesmaids to bring this concept into our business base." Once again, technology comes to your freelance rescue in the search for hot jobs online.

Another significant development in online tools is that of the personal communication device (PCD), also known as a personal digital assistant (PDA). Rarely can you attend a business meeting these days where professionals aren't whipping out their PCDs for all matters and purposes. PCDs are basically pocket-size PCs that make several forms of communication available to their users. The device is an electronic extension of your PC that links you directly to your primary communication channels, such as e-mail, as well as certain primary applications. Your PC wirelessly forwards incoming communications to your handheld PCD for instantaneous onsite communication. Commands can be sent from the PCD back to your PC for message forwarding, appointment scheduling, faxing, or other applications. The device can also retrieve key files stored on your PC for instant access. These flexible communication devices provide a completely independent, wireless link to your primary office location for a variety of needs and uses with a divergence of communication methods. Like R2D2 come alive, the device can be directly connected to the external port of other computers for remote operation or access to files and applications from another computer system.

Twenty-first-century work as a freelance agent is made easier for you with the many accoutrements and provisions that are now available online to help you with your job search. These tools have made home-based work for freelance professionals a practical reality. In finding freelance work online, as with all things digital, the tools drive the trends. But regardless of the service, whether it's an online database, an e-mail service, an ASP, a PCD, or another marketing utensil, making contact with potential contractors is what benefits you as a freelancer. Use good old-fashioned public relations—contact with those who are ready and willing to pay for your professional services. Even in an age of digital deals, human contact matters most, notwithstanding the fact that it is electronically delivered.

For more information on online tools, check out Part Three of this book.

Career Profile: Freelance Public Relations Expert

"You have to relate to others well, feel at ease with people, and communicate effectively," says Joseph Wallinski, who performs freelance public relations for the health-services industry and has been in public relations since graduating with a degree in political science in 1989. With his serious demeanor, the six-foot-tall, well-dressed executive is an imposing figure. His deep voice booms into the room, offering a sense of security and rock-solid stolidity. "My job is to develop the company's image—create a positive perception of the company and how it serves the interest of the public. The way people see my clients is essential to their building and maintaining a successful business. We want people to have a good attitude about what health services can do for them individually, and what it can do for the community as a whole. The only way this can be accomplished is with good communication between my clients and their publics. I am the go-between. A liaison, a bridge over which the company and the public can communicate with each other so that the needs of each are understood and nurtured."

The effectiveness of its public relations helps shape an organization—what it does and how it performs. To be successful, every company should have the support of the public it serves. Public relations experts like Wallinski, research, study, and evaluate the public's attitude toward the client's organization as a way to manage communication and understanding so that the public will support its efforts. A public relations expert is essentially an appearance builder whose job is to enhance the image of the company or organization as it is viewed by the public. A lot of what Wallinski does is produced electronically and delivered over the Internet, whether it's a press release written for a client or photos placed on a corporate client's website for journalists to download and print.

"I also do a lot of damage control," says Wallinski, straightening his shoulders as he speaks. "When something goes wrong it's my job to analyze the problem and fix it in a manner that is constructive and positive. Then I communicate that solution to the public through the press and other media so that our image is not tarnished and everyone is happy. The wrong message sent to the public could cost the company millions," he says. "I do my best to assure that doesn't happen."

In order to accomplish his mission, Wallinski relies on his contacts with local media and journalists, helping reporters make deadlines or providing them with source leads for developing stories. On any given day, he may also be required to write press releases, company literature such as an annual report to shareholders, or a speech for a company official. About half his work is completed online. Attending trade shows, conventions, and press conferences; speaking at special engagements; and overseeing advertising and promotions may also be important activities for a PR expert. It's a job that requires good written and verbal communication skills. "I wouldn't say that you *have* to like people to do the job, but it sure helps," says Wallinski. "Keeping the lines of communication open within the company is also a daily challenge. Management needs to understand the stockholders; stockholders need to understand management; management needs to understand employees; employees should understand stockholders. There's a lot of relation that needs to go on in a large organization. I work at making sure that these publics understand each other. That's why they call it public relations. It's challenging, rewarding, high-pressure, fast-paced, and never boring."

Can You Relate?

Public relations is a fast-paced career that demands the utmost in communication skills, online and offline, so good writing and speaking abilities are absolute requirements. Diplomacy and negotiation are the cornerstones of public relations. "A good PR person is creative and skillful," says Wallinski. "Someone who will keep his or her wits about, stay levelheaded while making quick decisions." Many of today's senior public relations professionals began their careers as journalists, reports the Public Relations Society of America (PRSA).

Does the Internet improve one's ability to work in the PR business?

"Sure," says Carrie Rathbun Hawks, president of the central Michigan chapter of the PRSA. "There are endless research opportunities, and a significant number of opportunities for grass-roots, word-of-mouth advocacy via chat rooms and bulletin boards. The Internet has also dramatically increased the speed with which information can be passed from one audience to another."

Does the Internet improve freelance abilities in the PR business?

"Absolutely," says Hawks. "There is much more opportunity to hook up with organizations you wouldn't otherwise be aware of to offer your writing, consulting, and media relations services."

There are many subcategories of public relations work that cover a broad range of income and opportunity. Some of these subcategories include

- @ Media relations
- @ Marketing and communications
- @ Community relations
- @ Fund-raising
- @ Employee relations
- @ Government relations
- @ Research and development

Employment Outlook: Next Ten Years

The Bureau of Labor Statistics reports that there will be a 25 percent increase in the need for public relations professionals in the next decade. The increased use of electronic communications and expansion in the communication industries will drive much of the growth in the public relations industry.

Number of Public Relations Professionals	
Total public relations professionals	122,329
Total needed by 2008	152,413
Need for new public relations professionals each year	3,083*

*due to the need for growth and total replacement

Annual Earnings	
Starting salary	$22,000
After 5 years	$35,000
After 10 to 15 years	$60,000

Executive public relations officers can earn even higher incomes, rising to an enviable $75,000 to $150,000 per year.

Education and Training

Public relations work is one of the fastest-growing career fields in America. It's not absolutely necessary to have a college degree to enter the public relations field, but it is strongly suggested. Most professionals agree that a liberal arts or business degree is most beneficial in this broad-ranging field. Jack Bergen, president of the Council of Public Relations Firms, says, "Business education is an excellent way to prepare for the business." Marketing, advertising, and journalism are also excellent academic preparation for a career in public relations. Journalism, speech, or mass communication schools administer most public relations curricula at accredited colleges or universities. The PRSA reports that there are more than 200 active PRSA chapters on college campuses nationwide. They are excellent sources of information on a freelance public relations career.

For More Information

@ www.prsa.org: the website for the Public Relations Society of America

@ www.prfirms.org: the website for the Council of Public Relations Firms, with resources for students seeking a career in public relations

@ www.elance.com: a job site with posts for public relations jobs, where freelancers can bid on contracts; independent contractors can post their profiles or view available projects

@ www.ActiMedia.com: a job site that offers a connection between media journalists and public relations jobs, where you can view journalism resources and search for media projects

Full site reviews appear in Part Four of this book.

Chapter 7

It Takes an E-village: Collaborating Online

For a freelancer, the ability to collaborate online with other professionals is one of the most powerful advantages of using the Internet. "Even a superb writer needs a good editor. A merely good writer needs a superb editor," says Dan Wilson, a freelance editor and owner of the Editor's DeskTop, an online editing service in Ontario, Canada. It is true: No one is good at everything, but everyone is good at something. One of the best avenues for finding freelance work online is being intelligent enough to ask for help when you need it. Multimedia capabilities such as the World Wide Web, e-mail, newsgroups, teleconferencing, bulletin boards, and Internet chat rooms enable you to collaborate with other professionals to view documents, modify files, and otherwise coordinate productive efforts. The ability to work with others in a virtual team environment can have a profound effect on finding and developing online contract work and can enable you to complete work that would otherwise be impossible.

Despite the rants from many of today's supposed freelance experts about the loneliness of working virtual, freelance over the wire does not by any stretch mean that you have to work alone. There are thousands of online communities available where free-agent workers can exchange ideas, share information, and collaborate on projects. Online collaboration can effectively bring people with important skills together and unite their talents into a dynamic and synergistic group. Wired collaboration between two or more freelancers enables them to develop and produce complex projects that could otherwise remain beyond their capabilities. Productive operations that would have taken days, weeks, or months in the twentieth century using traditional communication channels, such as the mail and the telephone, can occur instantaneously in the twenty-first century using high-speed electronic data transfers. Modern tools like Internet videoconferencing, file transferring, and file sharing can help you build a virtual dream team for completing your committed project work. These tools allow you to pull together people, skills, and facilities from anywhere on the planet at any time. This strategy can also be very effective in giving potential contractors the impression that your online freelance operations are larger than they actually are. Online collaboration can make a large office staff a virtual reality, a good way to bolster confidence in leery potential clients.

Online collaboration "has provided me with a rich and robust environment for completing top-notch work for my clients," says Dan Grove, an e-commerce consultant and Web application designer who provides his services online to customers all over the world. "If I'm developing a website for my customer who's an inventory service contractor, for example, I need to know specifics about inventory protocol and operating systems so I can properly integrate their website into their everyday business operations. In a case such as that I will bring in inventory specialists to either consult or help me complete the programming work that needs to be done. There's no way I could do it alone. Try finding an inventory control specialist locally. Right. That's not going to happen. The only way I can do this kind of work is by collaborating with other people who can help me when I need it."

Collaborating on projects for other freelance professionals or hiring out your services to others in a business-to-business environment is another online trend that is bringing success to a good number of freelance workers. The Editor's DeskTop (www.editorsdesktop.com), the Internet-based freelance editing service owned by Wilson, is a typical example. Says Wilson, "I run a very successful one-person, Internet-based editing service (it grew to five people years ago, but I killed that when I found myself managing for forty hours, and hardly editing at all). I have a stable of solid, reliable producers of projects, and I supplement that stable by taking occasional contract jobs from my website."

Wilson says that over the wire, word-of-mouth advertising produces more contracts for him than his website does. "But my website is very sober and fact-filled, and has few bells or whistles. It might be that if I souped up the site, I'd get more project requests from it, but there are two reasons for my not souping it up: I have more work than I can handle already, and of those who find me on the Web, only about one in twenty meets my standards for acceptable professional editing projects. Almost all of the contacts I get from the website (who haven't been referred to the website by other clients of mine) are "vanity" author-publishers who want to get something published that no reputable publisher will touch. I turn those down immediately.

"I think the best possibility for getting freelance work though a Web page lies in two things: getting links to that website set up on as many client-targeted websites as possible (I used to target sites that were frequented by publishers and writers), and getting listed carefully, individually, and repeatedly on the top handful of search engines."

Although online collaboration and networking will never fully replace the value of personal contact and face-to-face communication, it is an increasingly efficient method for attracting, obtaining, and maintaining profitable freelance work.

The Worst of It

You've got to take the good with the bad, and that also applies to online freelance work. Although there are some undeniable advantages to working wired in the twenty-first century, there are some disadvantages that you will want to consider. There is an unfortunate and common delusion that putting your résumé online will elicit an electronic avalanche of job offers and project contracts. This isn't true. In an age when thousands of websites are devoted to the distribution of résumés and career development, your online résumé, business card, or Web page is but one in millions. People are flocking to the Internet and the Web as the easy way of finding work. But you may be contributing only to the proliferation of online résumés that wait in vain for virtual work offers. Of the 6 million résumés online in 2000, part-time freelancers, dreamers, and hobbyists posted 2 million of them. Part-timers and hobbyists can often interfere with the project-seeking activities of legitimate free agents and freelancers by diluting the effectiveness of everyone's online postings.

"There have been complaints from employers who have legitimate telecommuting jobs listed on this and other sites about those applying for these positions," posted one freelance, work-at-home job listings site. "This is important: When applying for a job, PLEASE do not try to CONVINCE the employer through e-mail to hire you if you do not have the experience, qualifications, or employment stated in the listing. Doing this just makes employers reluctant to advertise legitimate 'work-at-home' opportunities in the future and that means we ALL lose in the end."

The growth of online résumé services has greatly simplified the task of job and project hunting for many a freelancer, but it has also made it easy for those who misrepresent their abilities and those who are not serious or legitimate freelancers to overwhelm the markets with weak-kneed potentials.

"From the 200 or so hits per month, ten to twenty e-mail messages result," says Wilson. "About half to two-thirds of those are editing wanna-bes or others who are not potential clients. If you had found me through my website, you would have been one of the latter group."

The current state of the find-it-online job markets has heavily swayed in favor of job seekers, with even easier ways to create, post, and e-mail résumés. But the slew of contractors and job providers flooding the recruitment gates are also increasingly putting the burden for finding work on the job seeker. So even in these days of digital job disbursement, it's up to you to go out and find the work. If you're a serious freelance worker or independent services contractor, be prepared to do your homework and seek out new project employers—to boldly inquire where no part-timer or hobbyist has gone before, so to speak. Don't get bogged down in the electronic nebula of online résumés out in cyberspace; set yourself apart from the others in a professional manner. Use the full capabilities of the Internet to your maximum advantage.

"The truth is," says Anton Malko, content manager at The Princeton Review, "there are so many people who are new at the Web publishing format, and there are so many pretenders out there, yet so many genuinely talented people too .... At the risk of sounding like a political candidate, I'd like to quote Hunter S. Thompson: 'When the going gets tough, the weird turn pro.' No offense—I'm among those pros.

"In one case in my work with an author, he came to our site and made an unsolicited offer to sell his work. We were reputable, in his eyes, because we have a brick-and-mortar history in our field. He was seemingly reputable because of a reassuring body of work online that I could browse and take into consideration, as well as a résumé that reflected the ability to do the task at hand and an open channel of communication via e-mail (we've never spoken directly) to coordinate an assignment customized to my needs. To top it off, he delivered publishable work on time and I paid him the amount we agreed on, a big key to building a strong relationship."

Although résumé banks can be an asset in your electronic arsenal to finding freelance work, they are apparently no substitute for old-fashioned proposals and queries, albeit in a digital format.

"I have only two 'résumés' out there now: one in Freelance Online's directory and another on a site I can't seem to find in my bookmarks or files just now," says Wilson. "I don't believe I've ever taken a contract from either listing, but I have had the occasional inquiry that cited one of them. I did post frequently to newsgroups and bulletin boards in the early years. Less so now, because I can't find the time." So, even in successful online freelance operations, résumé posting will most likely play a secondary role to more traditional methods for job inquiries.

Promises, Promises

When it comes to posting your résumé online, don't be fooled by the site's marketing pitch. "Do you want to earn serious money online?" asked FreelanceWorkExchange.com. "As a professional freelancer," boasted the Web page, "you can. Now you can learn to do the same—or perhaps even better. Whatever your specialization, you can be sure that right now there are companies looking for people with your skills and experience. If you're in a hurry to get started, you can sign up for your *free report* on the top-producing freelance markets, or check the key markets section for a list of the top freelance work exchanges. You can also get your free *Introduction to Million Dollar Freelancing* by sending us a blank e-mail here." When we followed the link for the free report, we were required to register an e-mail address. Continuing through the process toward the promise of freelance work landed us on a page forwarding interested freelancers to HotJobs.com, a third-party site, to create and register a résumé online. The offer for the free report never fully materialized online, nor was it ever sent later in an e-mail format as promised. The following screen said:"Thanks to the Internet, you now achieve twice as much in half the time. Make no mistake about it—the world is changing, and changing fast. For those who seize the opportunity now, the future is exciting indeed. But you must begin today. You need to act quickly to carve your niche in the global freelance market and exploit it to the fullest. Fortunately, getting started is easy. Just click below to sign up through our secure order form. Normal monthly membership is just $19.95." Further material suggested that obtaining freelance work using the Internet could enable you to "turn your hobby into a full-time career; give up your job and work from home; have a career that fits around your lifestyle; work anywhere in the world; earn more than you thought possible." Although the site may have provided some form of legitimate service in exchange for the suggested monthly fee, such offers seem dubious at best. As with anything else, on the Internet, if it sounds too good to be true, it usually is.

Career Profile: Freelance Proofreader

"It takes a keen eye and sharp English skills to work as a proofreader," says Dolores Fitzpatrick, a freelance proofreader. "You have to stay focused and riveted to your work for extended periods of time. If you lose a second's concentration, a mistake is likely to slip by in your copy. That's the worst thing that could happen."

Proofreaders review and correct copy (written documents and materials) to assure that it is grammatically proper and free of errors. When a mistake is detected, they suggest corrections by using standardized proofing symbols to indicate where the corrections should be made. Typographical errors, incorrect sentence structure, misspelled words, and poor text positions are just a few of the things proofreaders look to correct. They check the corrected version of text against the original copy to assure that it is accurate, or return it to the original author so that the suggested corrections can be made. "We often do fact-checking, too," says Fitzpatrick, "checking to see that the dates, statistics, and other numerical or historical data within the work is correct." Although she still proofs text on hard copy (text printed out on paper), word processing on a computer is her method of choice. "It's quicker and easier to simply make the corrections directly onto a word processor than it is to proof it, mark it, and then have it corrected," says Fitzpatrick. "So most of my work is done copy editing at the computer. I put the finished work on a disk for my editor or client."

Fitzpatrick says that proofreading can be exhausting work. "After you've been reading, editing, and proofing for eight to ten hours, everything can get jumbled together," she says. "You have to take frequent breaks to freshen yourself." She rates her work a 7 in job satisfaction on a scale of 1 to 10. "I get a chance to read interesting new things and learn every day."

There are many occupations related to a freelance proofreading career. You may find it helpful to investigate the following career alternatives:

@ Editor

@ Writer

@ Library technician

@ Court reporter

@ Data entry professional

Employment Outlook: Next Ten Years

Because of the increasing use of computers and sophisticated software programs for conducting proofreading work, the demand for proofreaders will dwindle in the years ahead. The U.S. Department of Labor, Bureau of Labor Statistics reports that there will be a 17 percent net reduction in the need for proofreaders in the next decade. A significant need for replacements, however, will continue.

Number of Proofreaders	
Total proofreaders as of 2000	41,000
Total needed by 2010	34,000
Need for new proofreaders each year	900*

*due to the need for growth and total replacement

Annual Earnings	
Starting salary	$22,000
After 5 years	$29,120
After 10 to 15 years	$41,600

Annual earnings ratios for this career category are moderate.

Necessary Skills

"Superior grammar and English skills" are what Fitzpatrick says are most important for a proofreading career. Those who pursue this work should be excellent spellers with a strong ability to use and craft words. They should enjoy conducting work of a repetitive, routine nature and have the ability to easily spot errors in typewritten materials. The ability to concentrate for extended periods of time, read and comprehend a wide variety of information, and quickly interpret written communications are beneficial qualities for proofreaders. Since most proofreading work is done with a word processor, the capability to operate computers and understand word processing software is essential.

Education and Training

Although there is no formal educational requirement for becoming a proofreader, most employers prefer to hire those with a two- or four-year college degree. Those with a degree in journalism, English, writing, or literature will greatly improve their abilities for finding work. Many employers provide training to their newly hired proofreaders. This will usually consist of three or four weeks of on-the-job training under the supervision of an experienced proofreader or editor. Many community colleges and vocational educational facilities also offer curricula to help students toward a successful proofreading career.

For More Information

@ www.freelanceonline.com: a website devoted to the interests of freelance writers, editors, and proofreaders, with information about developing a career as a proofreader

@ www.asme.magazine.org: the website for the American Society of Magazine Editors, with information, resources, and links for those pursuing editorial or proofreading careers

@ www.apme.com: the website for the Associated Press Managing Editors Association, with information, resources, and links on editorial careers

@ www.athomejobs.org: a Web digest that posts in-home jobs including writing, editing, data entry, and proofreading

@ www.homeworkers.org: the website for the Independent Home Workers Alliance, with project and job listings for freelance proofreaders, writers, and editors

@ www.freelancers.net: a Web service that matches freelance and contract Internet and multimedia professionals with freelance and contract vacancies/jobs

No Secrets on the Internet

Confidentiality is a concern you should have about freelancing openly on the Web or other Internet channels, like newsgroups or bulletin boards. Résumé spiders frequently grab posted résumés to build their databases, and it is easy for electronically posted material to get duplicated. Internet spider services scour for active résumés to create large databases that they can charge potential employers to search. You may never know where your résumé will end up. Jealous employers will also scrub the Internet for employee résumés in an attempt to find out which of their key workers may be freelancing on the side or planning to leave their employ. These scrupulous employers "salvage" or "scour" the Internet with thorough automated searches for résumés posted by their own employees. Is it an invasion of your privacy? Perhaps, but that's tough to assert when the résumé is openly posted over the World Wide Web and accessible to millions of potential viewers. If you're working for an employer that does not allow employees to work for others, you'll want to think twice before posting for freelance work online. You don't need the legal trouble, and employers in such cases may have a legitimate legal case or dispute.

If you are planning to post your freelance résumé online and don't want the world to view it, there are several precautions that you should heed. Posting only to sites with active firewalls is wise. Firewalls are built specifically to prevent outside sources from gaining access to the information held within the site. Most of the larger, well-known résumé sites are firewall-protected, but you should inquire to be sure. Sites that require a user password most likely are firewall-protected or use a secure user registration process; those that don't are risky at best. If at all possible, you should avoid posting personal information and identifiers such as your telephone number or street address. There are a lot of wackos out there whom you would not want to have such information.

Chapter 8
Online Theft: Identity Crises

Identity theft, a growing problem over the Internet, may be another concern and risk when posting work and personal information online. Using the Internet is an incredibly easy way to obtain information—intimate information—about people, including you. Your social security number, professional work history, personal address, and telephone numbers are most likely available and accessible online in seconds whether you know it or not. Various Web-based services and software packages such as Net Detective or Cyber Detective are created for the very purpose of finding out "everything you ever wanted to know about your friends, neighbors, employees, and even your boss." Software packages are openly available for download and purchase for as little as $29.95. Shareware can be downloaded from dozens of sites at no charge. There are even software packages—Trojan Horse programs—that under the guise of an e-mail message can gain access to another person's PC. When the e-mail is opened, someone else on the Internet can wander around unnoticed on your hard drive from another TCP/IP connection.

The nightmarish scenarios are endless. For instance, if someone else should obtain your social security number online, they could initiate an all-out rip-off of your personal identity. Using your name and vital information, they could place charges on your credit cards, gain access to your bank accounts, post messages throughout the Internet with your e-mail address, or use your online IP address as their own.

The Cookie Monsters

Albeit a slim one, there is a potential for personal disaster for those using online means to obtain freelance work or for anyone else using the Internet. While you haphazardly bounce from website to website as you search for project work or assignments, someone else could be learning more about you than you ever intended. Using cookie technology, many commercial and private websites and Internet users are able to place their own data on your computer's hard drive by embedding it into the HTML code shared between your and their machines. The original server can access this data whenever your machine is in contact with their Web server (but at no other time). Most times this contact between their server and the cookie on your machine goes completely unnoticed, as most Web browsers and operating systems will allow such contact to occur as a background activity on your computer. In most cases, cookies are silently transferred to your machine without your knowledge. Each time your machine is in contact with theirs, it can tell them detailed information about you, including where you've browsed the Internet or the World Wide Web. By employing such technology, third parties can amass a tremendous amount of information about you—enough to develop a profile of your personal behavior. Such technology has prompted public statements such as this proclamation by Scott McNealy of Sun Microsystems: "You have zero privacy on the Internet anyway." You may feel as though you are traveling cyberspace anonymously or in private contact with your potential customers and clients. In reality, however, you could be leaving a heavy trail of tell-tale personal information on the Internet, coaxing would-be thieves and spies home to your hard drive. At the very least, you could be providing commercial institutions with a lot of information about you that they could use or otherwise sell.

Protect Yourself

There are several simple things that you can do to minimize or alleviate the privacy risks involved in searching for work online.

@ Install virus protection software to guard against outside viral infection of your computer from websites and e-mail documents. Norton Antivirus and McAfee VirusScan are two such reputable programs that can protect your hard drive from computer viruses. These software programs can be purchased at retail locations such as CompUSA or Best Buy or downloaded online.

@ Install firewall protection on your PC. All computers that are connected online, especially those with broadband connections, should be firewall-protected from outside invasion. There are many reputable commercially developed software packages suitable for in-home use by freelancers who can afford such protection. There are also several well-respected shareware programs available for in-home use, such as ZoneAlarm or Sygate, that are available for a small fee.

@ Set your browser to disable cookies. Your Web browser can be set to disable the placement of cookies on your computer's hard drive. Go to Preferences in your Web browser and set its security levels to disable the use of cookies. To remove existing cookies and the list of sites you've frequented, delete the temporary files stored by your Web browser.

@ Never publish your personal address or phone numbers online or on your Web pages. Use a post office box or personal mailbox in all your online communications, and never reveal your intimate personal data. Use a third-party e-mail account, such as a Yahoo! account, when sending or receiving e-mail from unfamiliar parties.

@ Never download material from an unfamiliar website. Check the credentials and reputation of the site and its owner thoroughly before accepting downloads of software or other information, as dangerous viruses and Trojan Horse programs can lie dormant in such downloads.

@ Be careful when giving out intimate information about yourself in newsgroups, in Usenet, in e-mail, or on the Web. Keep your private information, such as credit card numbers, social security number, and family information offline.

@ Never release your name or personal identifier on an unsecured site or purchase products or services from an unsecured Web server. Your credit card or bank account information could be subject to open viewing along Internet lines if you do. Protected and secured websites will normally announce that they are secured before allowing access to their pages. Secured websites with authenticity certificates verifying that they are properly registered and identified will route your online purchase to an https Web address. Https addresses on the World Wide Web are secured on a private Web server under protected firewalls.

@ When making purchases or doing other business online, use an insured credit card with Internet insurance only. Many credit card companies will provide protection against the unauthorized use of a credit card for making online purchases.

The Vampires

There's a lot of "cheap e-lance" out there in the cyberworld. If you've committed yourself to freelancing and finding work on the Internet, watch out for e-world bloodsuckers who would have you provide your services cheaply or for free.

"Beware of the vampires who are out there waiting for new blood to emerge on the market," says Katherine Woodford, an online freelance writer from Moneta, Virginia. "They prey on hungry writers, knowing that the idea of seeing their name in print will excite them to the point that they are persuaded to sign away all rights and take little or no compensation for their work. Working for free doesn't pay the rent."

The relative anonymity inherent in online interaction between freelancers and their paying contractors can encourage otherwise reputable firms and organizations to take distinct advantage of freelance workers. This is especially true for those who are inexperienced or new to their field. It is so easy to communicate to a mass of potential freelancers online that the opportunities to lure innocent or otherwise ignorant freelancers into a virtual snare trap may be too much for some people.

"Some bonehead with a national flooring company tried to dupe me into some free work," says one freelance Web content developer who wants to remain anonymous. "I sent a query to his nationwide floor-covering association pitching some profiles I had written about floor-covering installers. His immediate response was: 'Send me the article and I'll let you know if I'm interested.' Give me a break. I sent him a reply explaining that I did not work on speculation, and that I could not allow him to see the finished product before he agreed to buy it. I was stupid enough to let a few other people pull that one on me before. Of course, these other people after seeing my stuff told me they weren't interested in my work even though some very similar content went up on their website shortly thereafter. I told this guy, who, by the way, was the president of this national floor-covering association, that it just wasn't good business for me to show him my work before he committed to paying me for it. He shot back a long-winded, snobby e-mail about how when he bought his Mercedes-Benz, the dealership let him look at it, test-drive it, and take it home for a few days before he committed to buying it. That I wasn't a professional because I would not let him 'review' my work like test-driving a car. He then explained that I had left him with a poor business impression and that he would not be interested in my services or my article. I sent him a response telling him that I was sorry that he wasn't interested in my working for him as a freelancer but that I was interested in obtaining some hardwood flooring for my home. Of course I explained to him that I couldn't purchase an expensive maple hardwood floor for my home without a chance to 'review' it or 'test-drive' it. That he would have to send one of his association members out to my residence to install the floor in my house— let me take it home for a few days and use it for a while before I made a decision on whether or not I would buy it. I never heard back from him. A good thing, I think. I just hope no one else gets ripped off by this cyberjerk."

There is an intrinsic downside to using the Internet as a mechanism for finding and delivering freelance work. Because of its ability to amass a volume of potential names for contracting employers and contractors, many organizations use it as a means for obtaining the lowest possible price for the work they contract. Oftentimes these savvy and shrewd businesses pit freelancer against freelancer in an all-out bidding war to assure that they receive the lowest rate for the work that they have to offer. Freelance work posted on some sites can consequently become fixated on price at the wholesale sacrifice of quality.

"I have found Internet job sites for freelancers to be terrible," says Jennifer Lawler, a freelance writer and editor. "The pay is low, the clients are looking for the cheapest supplier, and it's difficult to distinguish legitimate clients from the scammers."

Cathy Moore, an instructional writer who works freelance online, agrees. "The sites I've seen that are aimed at freelancers appear to attract the very hungry, both hungry clients looking for cheap work and hungry writers willing to work for nothing. Even the better sites like SmarterWork seem to attract too many unprofessional clients. I use the Internet to identify and qualify prospects. My field is narrow enough that I can identify good possibilities with a well-worded search. I put their contact information in a database and occasionally do an e-mail blitz. I've done this twice and have gotten strong nibbles so far from some good companies in other states and the U.K."

A look at a few project postings on SmarterWork.com may tell the story. Below is a table breaking down a list of research project postings placed by freelance-wanting contractors and the resulting number of bids that were received for those research projects by freelance researchers. The project postings appeared in the Research category of the View Projects forum on SmarterWork.com on July 2, 2001. Also shown is the highest freelancer bid that had been placed on that particular project at that time.

Name of Research Project Posted by Contractor	Number of bids	High Bid	Low Bid
Webmaster list	37	$175	$97
Home	23	$1,736	$228
Exhibition market	19	$1,700	$172
U.K. building site	32	$1,169	$70
For Mor	50	$1,058	$30
Airport maintenance	23	$1,500	$1,108
Envirograss	25	$1,108	$233
DVD players/SW/NO	13	$492	$201
Distributors	10	$1,492	$151
Ad research—Brazil	6	$2,703	$1,776
Tornado maths physic	7	$9,829	$299
Call center	4	$657	$566
Free websites	42	$341	$28
Alcohol/food	8	$1,039	$338
Can you help	23	$197	$55
Who's our competitor	20	$714	$146
Children's marketing	20	$6,904	$350

Such wide cost variances as these provide a clear picture as to how the Internet, with its hypercommunications ability, can foster an overaggressive and hostile marketplace where would-be contractors can nickel-and-dime you to death. A recent Myjob.com survey found that more than 70 percent of those bidding against one another for freelance work online were not qualified for the work that they were trying to acquire. Furthermore, more than 80 percent of those bidding had never been paid professionally for the work that they were attempting to gain. More than 97 percent of them had never been paid from a freelance job found using online means. These statistics give rise to a cheap and inexperienced pool of freelance work that is highly competitive—a poor arena in which to find quality freelance work. Contractors taking advantage of this marketplace will often demand that work be performed on speculation—a let-us-see-it-first-and-we'll-tell-you-if-we-want-it kind of arrangement. Spec work can be an effective door opener for getting better work later, but most firms using the technique simply move on when demands for higher pay are made, traveling down the information superhighway and picking up other inexperienced freelancers like hitchhikers along the road to cheap labor. Needless to say, whether you're posting your freelance availability online or just searching sites for potential projects, it is wise to "beware of the vampires."

Keep Your Fingers to the Mouse

Not everyone is suited to the independence of freelance life; it takes iron-willed resolve and discipline to manage the many distractions and challenges that you may face on a daily basis. The unstructured nature of independent free-agent work lends itself easily to diversion. There is no boss to whom you must answer, no time clock to punch, no staff to supervise, and no job description to which you must adhere. If you do not have the necessary motivation to complete the task at hand—finding quality paying projects and jobs—you may find this way of making a living unproductive. If you're planning to earn full-time pay, you should plan on spending full-time working hours earning it. Freelance work from home is not the easy way out of making a living. The temptation to turn Starbucks, the bookstore, the mall, or the local beach into your new office location may prove too tempting. There are also pitfalls to watch out for if you chose the opposite approach toward freelancing. Motivated and highly focused individuals may find it difficult to prevent work time from sneaking into their family time. The lack of a defined office environment with specified work hours can lend itself to a workaholic mentality and lifestyle.

Tipping Your Hats

The number of hats that you must wear as a freelance agent can also be distracting and confusing. To work independently you must be responsible for your own tax payments, clerical support, sales activity, telephone reception, public relations, customer satisfaction, and bookkeeping. Operating a Small Office/Home Office or so-called SOHO can be a time-consuming and intensive endeavor and is not for the lighthearted. The expense of wiring your home, equipping an officelike operation, and dedicating office space within your home are important and costly considerations. Even then, finding quality work online may not be any easier than using traditional methods for finding work. Those with a disposition to worry may find it overwhelming in times when paychecks appear few and far between. "In my early years, I went six months without a paycheck, getting things going," said one independent in an online forum discussion group.

Chapter 9

Down the Line:
What the Future Holds

Whether you know it or not, there is a human renaissance in the works—a digital new world that will fundamentally change the way you work and play and live. As it did so dramatically in the Renaissance, the first Industrial Revolution, and the second Industrial Revolution, life will change. This revolution, this rotation in the circle of our lives, however, promises to be more climactic and more exciting. It will affect not just the fundamental ways in which we work but the essential ways in and reasons for which we live. This course in human history is unfolding around us like a digital tsunami, carrying in its wake the discarded, old, outmoded, and obsolete ways and means of past eras. Set firmly in its direction by eons of economic development and human evolution, a new era in world advancement is taking rise, bringing with it, believe it or not, a return to some very ancient human desires. A cultural, social, and spiritual rebirth, fostered by a new generation dominated by a new digital morality, is on the rise, and you don't want to miss it.

Although life holds big changes for you environmentally in the years ahead, little has changed in basic human behavior over the past 1,000 years. Slavery is still the fundamental method by which we get our work completed. The only difference is that today we enslave technology. In the twenty-first century, trucks carry the loads that used to be carried by first-century slaves, and tractors plant the very same fields that knaves and peasants tended 1,000 years ago. Automation, fueled by ever-developing technology, continues to legitimately free the human species from the more burdensome of life's tasks. Fueling stations are automated with gasoline pumps that accept credit cards; social security checks are directly deposited by the government into waiting bank accounts; and voice-activated software programs record and process dictation. These functions used to be completed by human beings. The prospect of cybernetics (artificial intelligence and robotics), combined with high-speed communication, promises to further progress the automation of life. Life in manual terms will become radically less labor-intensive but nonetheless more profound.

Working Smarter, Not Harder

With automation alleviating many of the manual drudgeries of everyday life, world citizens will be freed to pursue higher education, more leisure time, and increased mobility. A smarter, more intelligent workforce equalizes power and encourages a more mobile workforce. Mobility, along with higher levels of education (made possible by the automation of manual responsibilities), will promote a more independent work world where individuals are liberated and appreciated independently, delivering the product of their work—information—from autonomous, self-owned, home-based offices. The workforce will become freelance- or free agent–based—not as author Daniel Pink proclaims, as a "Free Agent Nation," but more along the lines of a Free Agent World. The nation of Italy, for example, in a 1999 study conducted by the Censis Research Centre of Italy, found that many Italian workers were abandoning their attitudes toward traditional work alternatives in favor of "atypical" or freelance work. Between 1997 and 1999, the number of Italians working freelance rose from 1 million to more than 1.6 million, a figure that represents more than 8 percent of the nation's total workforce. The new freelance workers in Italy were found to have a higher education level and an average age of forty-four. More than 41 percent of the Italian freelancers, when polled, stated that they preferred freelance employment and considered it an "emerging model of employment." The growth of atypical or freelance work in Italy has been so prolific in recent years that the country's political parties have introduced a series of proposals that would regulate and integrate freelance workers into the nation's social programs.

As pointed out by Steve Klein in his article "Free at Last . . . Free at Last?" for *Content Exchange* in June 2001, a work world dominated by freelance workers and contractors will go "Internetrepreneurial."

"The Netpreneurial program, which encourages and advances Internet-related entrepreneurial innovation in the Metro D.C. area as part of the Morino Institute," wrote Klein, "is a wonderful resource, and it is interesting to see how the community has changed in these economically challenging times." Seeking to converge a centralized, economically bound, and associated group of Internet-related workers and businesses, the program fosters an environment of innovation and advancement for workers who deliver their work through digital networks and electronic means. The program is focused on workers and business people who produce products and services that they refer to as "Net-centric"—that is, services dependent upon the use of the Internet. One of the program's primary objectives is to bolster and nourish new ways to use Net innovation in business. Those considered Internetrepreneurial, or "Netpreneurial," are creators of products and services that are delivered digitally.

"About 33 million, or one out of every four American workers," will be free-agent workers by the end of the decade, wrote Klein. "It's a bigger workforce than the entire public sector, yet it is outside the traditional tax codes, health system, disability insurance, and retirement plans that most Americans encounter."

The continued evolution of these kinds of programs and the individual worker within the scope of such programs, as well as of society and everyday work life overall, equalizes the political, social, and economic powers that bind our culture. It places more freedom and power at the disposal of the average worker. Behind the keypad of a digital age, whether it's government, a large corporation, or a singular individual, all are equal. Delivering information to waiting contractors and employers from behind a PC on the Internet, a WAN, or a LAN connection is an indiscriminate process that obliterates preconceived notion and prejudice. The new millennium will bring the age of empowerment for the average worker, regardless of his or her personal disposition.

As a catalyst of human interaction and communication, the Internet further improves modern-day opportunities for higher education and increased mobility. Using advanced tools such as websites, wireless communications, e-commerce, and high-speed data communications, the individual, armed with higher education and increased mobility, is placed on a balanced footing with organizations large and small, whether for political, social, economic, or spiritual purposes. In such an environment, information will become the consumer good of highest value—

the very foundation upon which economic value, desirability, and importance rests. More than money and more than gold, the future will be purchased with information. The products—hard goods—are easy to produce in an age of mass production dominated by automation. The cereal produced by its manufacturer and packaged in the big, colorful, glitzy box will not be as valuable as the information we can obtain about it: who's buying the cereal, why they're buying it, how much they're willing to pay for it, where they're most likely to buy it, what color they're most likely to buy it in, and where they will buy it repeatedly. Information will transmit the future into the next millennium. This will change the very nature of our economy and escort the industrial age to its natural end. The information age will fully arrive, based on an economy of information and service. In the future you will pay more for the information and services that people can provide than you will pay for the products they can sell to you. But because that information is accessible to everyone at any time, in any place, and for any reason through the development of open and free mass communication, no one person, government, or corporation can claim or impose superiority.

"Knowledge is a unique economic throttle," wrote Blake Harris in his article "Training for Light-Speed" for *Government Technology* magazine (May 2001). "While the fruits of knowledge—such as a patent, a trademark, or the expression of an idea—can be owned, knowledge itself can never be exclusively possessed, at least not in the way capital or physical property can be. Nor can it be controlled in the way physical resources are controlled by national and other interests."

The Internet will become the world's great equalizer, the central communication hub of the human species, tying all facets of life together into a planetwide civilized integration. Information will be shared not for the power that can be attached to it, but in open distribution for the purpose of improving the condition of the whole, for improving the human condition. Because of our hypercommunications ability, and because "there is no privacy on the Internet anyway," these realities will actualize.

Generation One

The next generation to live and work and grow will not be Generation Y or Generation X; it will be Generation One. Through their interconnectedness—

largely through the Internet—people of this new generation will learn more and be more mobile than any generation that ever lived. Their knowledge and mobility will foster a new way of living—a new philosophy and morality—with fresh and innovative directions for our planet. Filtered by a myriad of worldwide races, religions, and social philosophies and bound together in an online, effervescent, single-bound existence, a more holistic approach to life will prevail. In the course of human history, what can be had has been had. There is nothing new but newness itself. Raised in a world that can provide them at least virtually with anything they want, people of Generation One will see materialistic ideologies resentfully sputter to their demise. But so, too, will the uncertainty of environmental, economic, and political chaos. Smarter and more resourceful than any other generation, Generation One will pursue the new horizon of a "we" culture, compelled to create a cleaner, safer, more modest, and indiscriminate world. And they are willing to work hard for it.

In 1993, for example, notice was placed over the Internet that PepsiCo had involvement and investment in a country held unwillingly by a brutal military government that had refused to relinquish power to a democratically elected official. Harvard students responding to the Internet notice objected and opposed their educational institution's involvement with PepsiCo. Student Internet communication with other universities instigated the call for a universal boycott of Pepsi products throughout the United States. PepsiCo, in a sensitive response to the situation, disentangled itself from involvement in the country. This is but one rich and fertile example of the new moralities of Generation One and the tremendous and positive absolution they will bring into a tiring world. The ability to communicate simultaneously with all members of our global society plugs them in to life as never before. Generation One will enjoy the physical ability to access a computer terminal from home, an office, or a mobile location that tangibly connects them to every corner of our shrinking planet at the touch of a button. Generation One will be truly connected in ways that could never have been imagined only a few years ago. An American in Michigan can learn of his Portuguese heritage from an Internet acquaintance in Portugal. Russian schoolchildren can videoconference over the World Wide Web with their counterparts in Dubuque, Iowa, to share their latest academic accomplishments.

For now, the Internet is making this new generation possible, and in one way or another, you are part of that generation.

An Intimate Affair

Despite its appearance, the Internet is an intensely intimate and personal medium. It is easy to misperceive the Net as a huge, oceanic cybervoid that connects people at a distance. The truth, however, is that it tangibly connects people in ways that are unimaginable or were just a few years ago. Through the connections of the Internet—both electronic and psychological—people are able to share their lives. People who might be otherwise removed from one another can connect, share information, share thoughts, share feelings. The recent phenomenon of Internet marriages is one small realized example of how the Internet is being used to increase intimacy among people. Every day seems to bring another fantastic story about how the Internet was used to find somebody. A long-lost cousin discovers his family in Lisbon. Twin sisters separated from each other at birth find each other and use the Internet to track down their birth parents. Regardless of the physical distance that lies between communicating parties, the Internet brings them closer together, at home, at work, and at play. A recent AOL/Roper study found that 75 percent of those online said that they used the Internet to stay in touch with family and friends, 41 percent said that they had used it to find someone with whom they had lost touch, and 75 percent said that more people know their e-mail address than their personal telephone number.

The Internet is also an awesome tool for facilitating personal contact in a freelance career. "The Internet has helped me get the contact information for agencies like AFP and Gamma-Laison, along with other organizations I had never heard of, who say that they want freelancers," says Alicia Wagner Calzada, a freelance photographer who runs her business from www.aliciawagner.com. Calzada uses the National Press Photographers Association site, where a job information bank called the JIB List posts available freelance contracts. "They also have staff jobs, and I have used that successfully in the past to find a staff job," she says. Calzada outlined the three ways in which she uses the Internet to further her freelance business.

@ I have a website so that when a new client expresses interest in seeing my work, I can refer them to it. This saves me from having to send them a portfolio and then trying to get it back. They can instantly look me up and see that I am skilled. I have also e-mailed my résumé on many occasions.

@ I often shoot things "on spec" with my digital camera. I can then transmit the image within a few minutes to all the clients I think might be interested in it. The risk for shooting without a prior commitment of payment is low since I have no additional expenses, and I can get the images to them in a timely manner.

@ Many agencies and groups have their contracts available online, or will e-mail them to me if I request them, which saves the trouble of using snail mail or the expense of calling Australia just to find out if the terms are to my liking.

"So, for me," Calzada says, "the Internet is not so much the answer to all my prayers in the hunt for work but an extremely useful tool, without which my life as a freelancer would be much more difficult. I'm fairly convinced that if we were not in this digital age, I would not have the ability to freelance and live where I live." Calzada lives on a remote island that has no mail delivery and is several hours' drive from the closest photo lab.

For freelancers and free-agent workers like Calzada, the Internet has advanced a freelance boon. It offers the intimacy, diversity, and attunement that will effectively bring rural economies into the world's economic infrastructure. As a result, small, individually operated home-based freelance businesses will expand rapidly in the coming years. The cumulative effects of these expanding rural freelance operations are bringing with them what some have referred to as the High-Tech Rural Renaissance, a more productive lifestyle characterized by the return of rural living and more relaxed attitudes.

Information technology will allow for close-up communication among an independent workforce largely driven by freelance employment. Corporations of the future, driven more by the need for information than the need for space, raw materials, and resources, will negate their requirements for high-cost employees, long commutes, and high rent costs with virtual business environments organized into online networks and workgroups. "In the last fifteen years," wrote Robert D. Atkinson and Paul Gottlieb in their article "The Metropolitan New Economy Index" for the Progressive Policy Institute, "a New Economy has emerged in the United States. Among its defining characteristics are a fundamentally altered industrial and occupational order, a dramatic trend toward globalization, and unprecedented levels of entrepreneurial dynamism and competition—all of which have been spurred to one degree or another by revolutionary advances in information technologies." The magnitude of cutbacks and downsizing experienced in recent history lie witness to this general movement in American and worldwide work life.

The advent of the Internet and its improving capabilities for high-speed data communication will to some degree undermine the very purpose for which cities were created during the industrial age: to condense resources and the workforce into convenient urban areas to facilitate the manufacture and distribution of mass-produced products. Consequently, we are witnessing the decline of industrialization. As a result, the ability to communicate quickly and easily over vast distances and operate efficiently in a virtual environment will stimulate to some degree, as George Gilder, a highly publicized and well-known futurist and a pioneer of supply-side economics, has prophesized, a movement away from city metropolises and a return to a more rural and intimate existence. "As the IT revolution gives companies and workers more location freedom," wrote Atkinson and Gottlieb, "a smaller share of employment is located in the largest metropolitan areas than was the case just ten years ago. The share of employment located in the largest sixty-one metropolitan areas actually declined by 1.5 percent between 1988 and 1997, from 55.1 percent to 53.6 percent. In contrast, the share of jobs in mid-size metros (between 250,000 and 1 million) increased by 4 percent, and the share in small metro areas (between 50,000 and 250,000) increased by 7 percent."

In the Driver's Seat

For most of our relationship with technology, it has driven us. Largely dominated by the need for increased industrialization, computers and automation have made it possible to speed up the living process—to do your job more quickly, get your car fixed more easily, make your dinner in less time, write your letters more swiftly, pay your taxes more rapidly, save (or spend) your money more rapidly, or teach your children more in less time. The technologies that we've created have been driving you, whether you know it or not. Thanks to technology, the average person in 2002 is expected to produce 50 percent more than that of the average worker in 1960. Life, thanks to human technology, has become harried and hectic, a frantic race.

The eventual fall of the industrial age, however, will bring a relative ambivalence toward materialist values. So why be employed? To what end will you be employed? Certainly not for material values—why would you want things that everyone else has or that have no intrinsic value? You wouldn't. The only logical conclusion is that you will be employed to earn the value of time—the one commodity that will be cherished by all but available only in a limited amount for a limited duration: precious time.

Rebelling against the madness, Generation One will use the superior abilities of technology to their advantage and seek more time. They will remove their families and themselves from the perils of urbanization and its exposure to unsuitable environments. They will cherish and exercise their abilities to live and work detached and independently, while simultaneously having the right to communicate openly and freely throughout the world. Their values for individual human rights and equality and their synchronistic power to enforce them with instant communication won't conflict with the advancement of technology and economic progress; it will inextricably fuse with it. They will use the resources of technology to promote their human interests in family, friends, and community.

This is not to say that cities will die. There will *always* be a need for industrialized products and processes. Neither will rural areas benefit overabundantly by such a shift in population demographics. There will be, however, a large shift in the methods by which you work and live. Recent reports have misinterpreted this movement toward rural areas, asserting that high-tech job growth has continued in urban areas at a faster rate than that of rural areas. This fosters, however, the mistaken assumption that growth in rural areas will be commercially based and associated with high-tech. This couldn't be further from the truth. The growth will be individually based. The "forty acres and a modem" that *The New York Times* has in recent years implied as the future of small business is a direct correlation to the movement of individuals—freelancers, free agents, and independent contractors—toward rural areas. It is an indication of the whims of individual people, the members of Generation One who are compelled to use technology for why it was developed: to improve the quality of our lives and increase the time in our lives, to finally drive technology rather than allowing it to drive us. For you, today, the Internet makes it possible.

Part Three
Online Tips, Tools, and Tricks

Chapter 10

Be Prepared: Computer Skills You Will Need

So, what do you need to get started with this job-surfing stuff? A pocket protector? A virtual surfboard? A $3,000 computer system? One thing *not* to get is overwhelmed. First of all, don't think of job surfing as a technical task. Think of it as a life improvement project. Like a home improvement project, you just need the right tools and a little know-how to be successful. Think of this section as your personal Bob Vila, a strong foundation for both your job search and your presentation to prospective employers.

Your Tool Kit

The two most important items to have in your tool kit are

@ A computer (and the know-how to use it)

@ Access to the Internet (and the know-how to use it)

Need Some Help?

If you're an accomplished Net surfer and e-mailer who already utilizes the power of the Internet, this book will help take you to the next level. But what if "the know-how to use it" parts of the tool kit seem daunting to you? Perhaps you're not particularly computer-savvy. Don't feel bad; even Bill Gates once knew nothing about computers. The fact that you're reading this now proves that you're motivated—maybe not quite as motivated as Mr. Gates, but you certainly have enough gumption to become a proficient job surfer. The world of online computing may seem intimidating, but actually, it's relatively easy—that's why it became so popular so quickly. With only a minimal amount of effort, you can make effective use of this book.

There are many options available to improve your knowledge of computers. Depending on your personal preference, you can choose from one of the six methods below.

Courses

A good place to receive computer instruction is at any local college or university. Call and ask about continuing education or adult education courses. Many colleges and community centers have programs under these (or similar) names offering night and weekend classes in a wide variety of subjects, including basic computer and Internet skills.

You don't need to be enrolled in a degree course in order to sign up for these classes, and they can be surprisingly inexpensive. You might be able to make them even more inexpensive by asking about available financial aid. (You may be eligible for such aid and not even know it.) Also, if you're already employed, some employers may pay (or, more likely, reimburse you) for all or part of the cost of such courses.

If you decide to enroll in a computer course, try to find one that has a good student/instructor ratio. Large classes will likely teach you more about why large classes are a bad idea than they will about computers. It also helps to find a class that offers a reasonable number of total course hours (ten to fifteen hours should be sufficient for an introductory course) and is taught by a trained, reputable instructor. Be careful because there are a number of substandard operations that could leave you highly dissatisfied. Stick with accredited institutions. If you don't know whether an institution is accredited, ask. Then, be constructively paranoid and double-check to make sure that the accrediting agency is legitimate; you can do so by consulting the Council for Higher Education Accreditation's website at www.chea.org.

Even classes at prestigious colleges can be disappointing if they're taught by inexperienced or undertrained instructors. Try to check out the instructor's credentials before signing up; many institutions publish their instructors' course-related experience.

Professional computer training companies, which can be found in the Yellow Pages, are another source for computer courses. These companies are usually geared toward training professionals on specific software, but they may be well suited to training you as well. Training companies can vary widely in the quality of their instruction; looking for ones that offer "Novell certified" or "Microsoft certified" training is a good call—this usually indicates a general level of competence in all of the company's instruction.

Video

You might find that you're most comfortable with your best friend, the television. In this case, watching a videotape on computer instruction might be right up your alley. There are some good computer video-instruction series available, but here you need to be particularly wary of shoddy products. Some good ones are produced by EduPro Systems (www.eduprosystems.com).

Tutoring

Many people find that they learn most quickly when they get intensive, one-on-one tutoring. Professional or semiprofessional computer tutors can easily be found by inquiring at local computer stores and computer repair shops. Tutors may also advertise in local newspapers and on community bulletin boards.

Private tutors can be pricey, but there are ways of economizing. Ask around among your family and friends; you may find that someone knows of a computer whiz who would be willing to teach you for a reasonable fee. What amateur tutors lack in teaching experience, they make up for in bargain pricing. You may need to swallow your pride, though: It's quite likely that an inexpensive and informal tutor of this sort will be younger than you are. On the plus side, the younger they are, the cheaper they are. Go young enough, and you'll be able to pay them off with pizza and GameBoy cartridges.

Help from Your Computer

Most new computers come with built-in help—tutorials and help files on the computer itself that will help you learn how to use it. A well-designed computer will say "Howdy" (in one way or another) and offer to help you learn how to use it the very first time you turn it on. When buying a new computer, ask about the availability of this kind of help on the models that you're considering.

Help on the Web

Once you're online and surfing proficiently, you will find that the Internet itself is probably the best single source of information about computers (or pretty much anything else, for that matter). A simple Web search is often the best way to begin to educate yourself about a particular topic.

Let's say, for example, that you type in a Web address only to be confronted with the mysterious words "404 not found." Is this some strange code phrase? There's a simple way to clear up the mystery: Go to a Web search site, such as www.google.com, and type in "404 not found." You will instantly be taken to a page of links to websites that discuss and explain the "404 not found" phenomenon.

This simple strategy of using Web search sites, or search engines, will work with almost any topic. And there are more of these search engines that you can shake a stick at: Go to www.searchenginewatch.com for a near-definitive list, complete with reviews and rankings.

Books

You've already equipped yourself with one important tool: this book. Nice going—you have excellent judgment. This particular tool will take you through all of the basic information that you need to get online and ferret out exciting job opportunities.

While you were shopping for this book, you probably noticed that there are a lot of other books for sale. Once you're finished reading this book, you might want to look at some of them. You may want to learn more about designing websites, for instance, so that you can create an online presence that will truly leave potential employers gasping with admiration. Or you might want to develop some computer skills that will be useful in your work. There are books out there that can teach you all this and more. Other than the Harry Potter series, we can't recommend any books in particular, but do keep in mind that the printed word can be an invaluable resource as you continue your journey through the online world.

Completing Your Tool Kit

If you have computer and Internet skills in your tool kit, then all you need to complete the kit is a computer and an Internet connection. (We'll address these items in the next two sections.) Once your tool kit is complete, you'll be able to use your tools to embark upon your job search. As you begin this journey, keep your goals in mind. As a job surfer, your primary goals should be

@ To learn how to use a computer to create and print a professional-looking résumé

@ To learn how the Internet can help you to find a job

@ To learn how to create Web pages so that you can put your résumé and portfolio online

These last two items will be covered in Chapters 13, 14, and 15.

While using your tools to pursue these goals, keep in mind that your tool kit is never really complete. You will most likely find, at some point, that you need an item or skill that you hadn't anticipated. For instance, a freelance photographer might discover that a piece of hardware called a slide scanner needs to be added to the tool kit. This sort of thing will come up all the time, but don't panic; armed with a computer, an Internet connection, and the knowledge of how to use them, you can harness the Internet as a research tool to find out exactly what you need and how it works.

Chapter 11

Past, Present, and Future: The History of the Internet

Even if you've been living in an underwater cave for the past ten years, you've probably noticed that the Internet has become quite a big deal in an extraordinarily short amount of time. Less than twenty years ago, personal computers were the latest technological novelty, and almost no one had heard of the Internet. Less than ten years ago, the Internet was still the near-exclusive playground of computer scientists and hard-core techno-geeks. It was completely lacking in graphics—a text-only world. And then, in the short span of six years, one area of the Internet, the World Wide Web—armed with dazzling multimedia capabilities—evolved from an interesting invention into a major sector of the economy and, in one overused phrase, "the repository of all human knowledge" (and, of course, of endless pictures of Anna Kournikova).

The Origins of the Internet

A long time ago—before MTV, even before the Beatles broke up—the U.S. government was fighting the Cold War, and among the tools in its mighty arsenal were gigantic, refrigerator-size computers—and the doughty, inventive scientists who ran them. As U.S. tax dollars poured out of Washington, D.C., to fund the high-tech number-crunching of these scientists, some of the money landed on college and university campuses, where it was used to develop these "supercomputers," which were about as powerful as a modern pocket calculator.

Many of these scientists were working with these supercomputers on large projects in collaboration with one another. To be more efficient, they needed to be able to share data with their coworkers—people who might be working on a campus on the other side of the continent. Sure, they could call one another and discuss the projects, and they could mail each other punch cards and printouts.

But there was a much faster way to share information—by networking these widely separated computers to communicate directly.

And so, in 1969, the Department of Defense's Advanced Research Projects Agency (ARPA) proposed a project called ARPANET, in which the government's far-flung research computers would be connected to one another via dedicated telephone lines (supplied by Ma Bell).

ARPANET had a unique decentralized design—it was specifically designed to survive a nuclear war. This requirement dictated that there be no single essential component of the network; if a nuclear strike took out, say, Stanford and the University of Utah, destroying their ARPANET-connected computers, the ARPANET computers at UCLA and the University of Michigan would still be able to communicate unimpeded.

One consequence of this decentralized design was that, once ARPANET was up and running, it was remarkably easy to hook a computer up to this expanding network. All you needed was a way for your computer to speak the computer-networking language, TCP/IP (Transmission Control Protocol/Internet Protocol), and a physical connection (usually a dedicated phone line) to the network. There was no way that a central authority could prevent someone from connecting to the network, and there was no way to control the content of the network. The seed of the Internet was planted.

The Infant Internet

Fast-forward to 1991. Thanks to the invention of the silicon chip, computers have become small enough to fit on your desk and no longer require air conditioners. They have keyboards and monitors instead of punch cards and Teletype-style printers. And ARPANET no longer officially exists. Its decentralized, easy-to-connect-to nature has caused it to evolve into something much larger: the Internet, to which more than 100,000 computers are connected (mostly on college and university campuses). The users of the infant Internet seemed to be coming up with new and creative operations for it every day.

In the next few years, the network spilled out of the academia and stormed the mainstream of American society. The darn thing was just so (relatively) easy to use, and it allowed all sorts of convenient communications between computers.

By the early 1990s, a large number of Americans were using personal computers, and most universities and large businesses were using mainframe (large, shared) computers with terminals. The Internet allowed the users of these computers to, among other things, swap computer programs using a system called FTP, or File Transfer Protocol; send messages using a system called electronic mail, or e-mail; and play text-only games using a system called Telnet.

One of the most popular areas of the Internet was a system called Usenet, which consisted (and still consists) of text-only bulletin boards on which Internet users could post messages on various topics, from microbiology to cartoons. To access Usenet, you would fire up a piece of software called a newsreader (the bulletin boards are called newsgroups). Nowadays, Usenet is more easily accessible via the website groups. One of the earliest topics pursued on Usenet was employment, both seeking and offering. Because Internet users were almost exclusively scientists or some other sorts of techies, the job postings were almost all for scientific and computer-related jobs.

The Dot-Com Gold Rush

A decade ago, the Internet had its great leap forward: Between 1989 and 1991, a interesting new use for the Internet called the World Wide Web was developed in Switzerland. It allowed Internet-based information to be displayed on Web pages, which could be accessed using programs called Web browsers.

In 1993, Mosaic, a graphics-capable browser for the Web, was written and released. The following year, the author of Mosaic, Marc Andreesen (at age twenty-two), founded Netscape Communications Corporation. Suddenly, the Internet was no longer a text-only environment; the addition of the World Wide Web's graphics capabilities made the Internet much richer, easier to understand, and more fun to look at. Most important, this rich graphical environment was interactive—it allowed Web surfers to send information, such as addresses and credit card numbers, to websites. It was clear that it was (at least theoretically) possible to make a lot of money in this new Web environment. The gold rush was on.

This sense of expansive opportunity led to a frenzy of Wall Street investing. A lot of Internet entrepreneurs and the investors who financed them made a lot of money during the next few years—and in those same few years, the Internet became a major financial and cultural phenomenon. Most Americans had never heard of the Internet before 1994; by 2001, most have done at least a little Web surfing, and millions have Internet access in their homes.

Most of these millions of Internet newcomers tend to think of the World Wide Web and the Internet as being the same thing. But old-timers who were on the Internet before 1994 know that text-only areas of the Internet such as e-mail and Usenet were around for many years before anyone ever clicked on a link to buy a book at Amazon or make a bid on eBay. The old-timers did not always welcome the massive tide of Internet newcomers, who were lured in by the millions by the World Wide Web's ease of use. These old-timers often complained that the "newbies" were technologically ignorant and lacking in "Netiquette," the honor code of manners that (in theory at least) guided online interactions. But no one could stop the stunningly swift expansion of the Internet because of its anarchic, easy-to-connect-to nature. Like most things on the anarchic Internet, job-board websites started out as small-scale, nonprofit ventures. But with the dot-com investing boom on Wall Street, job-board sites became slick, commercial, and very heavily trafficked as employers desperately sought qualified employees and workers sought to cash in on the boom.

The Dot-Com Bust

By the summer of 2000, the dot-com bubble began to burst. Greed—or, if you prefer, irrational exuberance—had driven the stock values for Internet-related firms far higher than could ever be justified. When a large number of heavily financed Internet startup companies continued to fail to show profits, investors began pulling back, triggering a chain reaction that brought the high-flying Internet financial juggernaut back to Earth. Employment-oriented Internet ventures were not spared; although no major jobs website has actually gone out of business, many had to resort to layoffs in 2001.

The crash of the Internet companies—massive layoffs, bankruptcies, etc.— has perhaps led to an excessive backlash against the Internet in the public mind. Unfortunately, such is the nature of our hype-driven culture; depending on whose hype you encounter, the Internet is either a dangerous digital swamp full of pedophiles and scam artists or the greatest American invention since television, guaranteed to lead us into a future of unlimited economic growth. The truth, of course, does not lie at either extreme. The Internet is anarchy, and humanity's worst and greediest impulses find easy expression there. But the expansive possibilities of the Internet as a commercial tool are still just as present as they ever were; it's simply become apparent that it may not be quite so easy to make fast, easy cash from these extraordinary possibilities. Fortunately for you, it appears that there will always be a market for jobs-related websites, no matter how many millions are lost or won on Wall Street.

The Future

What's next for the Internet? If present trends continue, bandwidth (the speed at which information can travel over the Internet) will continue to increase. What does this mean for job surfers like you? Well, in just a few years, it may be quite common to conduct job interviews via the Internet as it becomes more feasible to transmit high-quality video and audio. It will become much more common for people to have their own Web servers in their homes instead of paying for space on commercial servers. This will allow job seekers to store a lot of personal information, including extensive interactive portfolios, on their home computers and will allow people to access this information via the Internet.

Clever people will continue to find new ways to apply the Internet's ever-increasing bandwidth to the tasks of sharing information, collaborating, playing, working, and communicating. And the Internet-using public, the final judge of such matters, will decide for itself which of these new applications it wants to use. There's one thing you can count on, though: The Internet will continue to become a more powerful tool for many aspects of our lives. As a job seeker, you will need to understand this tool and know how to use it effectively. This won't necessarily make you a geek—it'll be much more likely to help put you on the path to a satisfying and well-paid career.

Chapter 12

Getting Wired: Obtaining Internet Access

If you, like millions of Americans, already have access to the Internet, then you may be tempted to skip this section. Not so fast, hotshot: There are a number of issues we'll cover here that you've probably never considered. For instance, do you know what ADSL is? GHz? No? Then consider this: At some point in your job-surfing endeavors, you may need help resolving a problem with your computer or your Internet connection. If only to prepare yourself for intellectual combat with the arrogant techies who often staff the computer help desks (they will sadistically try to humble you by slinging acronyms), you should read this section.

Although there are many factors to consider when trying to get connected to the Internet, it's quite simple. All you need are

1. A computer

2. A connection from the computer to the Internet

3. TCP/IP software (software that allows the computer to communicate on the Internet)

4. Internet software

Note that the most important piece of Internet software you'll need is a Web browser, which will allow you to access World Wide Web pages. You'll also need other Internet software (e-mail software, for example), which we'll discuss in more detail in the next section.

For the sake of argument, let's assume that you have none of these things at the moment, and let's look at each of them in turn.

A Computer

If you want to take full advantage of the Internet, then you should have a fairly modern computer. You wouldn't try to drive on an interstate with a Model T, right? Well, given the progress of the computer industry, a computer bought five years ago is basically a Model T by today's standards. As of 2002, there are certain specs that your computer should possess at the minimum. The recommended computer features listed below are comparable to the sensible family car. See pages 136–141 for a more detailed explanation.

- @ 10 GB hard drive

- @ 128 MB RAM

- @ Built-in Ethernet and modem

- @ Pentium II processor or higher, 500 MHz (PC)
  G3 processor or higher, 400 MHz (Macintosh)

- @ CD-ROM drive

There are dozens of features and specifications with which you'll be confronted while you're shopping for a computer—different kinds of graphics cards, sound cards, RAM, and more. You don't have to worry too much about these things (or even what they mean). As long as your computer meets the requirements we outline for you, your Internet-navigating experience will be a smooth one.

Buying or Upgrading a Computer

Have you decided that you need a new computer to help you land that perfect job? Who knows, maybe you'll even use it for work-related tasks once you're hired. Well, you have two basic options if you really need your own modern system: upgrading your old computer (if you've got one) or buying a new one.

Upgrading an Older Computer

On the following pages, you'll find a list of specifications—all the stuff that your computer should have if want to have a good job-surfing experience. If you currently own a computer but it doesn't measure up to these specifications, you could try to have it upgraded. There are many ways to upgrade an older computer, such as to add RAM, a bigger hard drive, or even a better processor. This process can be expensive, though, not to mention tricky. Some computers are not upgradable, some can be only slightly upgraded, and some can have only some basic features upgraded.

To find out whether your computer is upgradable, you can do any of the following three things:

1. Get the computer's model number. Sometimes this is clearly printed on the front of the computer, but it's usually on the back or the bottom. The model number should be near the computer's serial number. The model number, like the serial number, is usually some arcane series of numbers and letters. On most computers, this information should be fairly easy to find. If it's not, you can call up the manufacturer's help desk and yell at them.

2. Contact the computer's manufacturer. If you're armed with the model number, tech support should be able to tell you what's upgradable on your machine.

3. If you have no luck with method 1 or 2, take your computer to a local computer repair shop. They can help you figure out if you're able to upgrade.

Before taking the final step of paying for upgrades, it's important to evaluate cost versus benefit: unless the total cost of the upgrade is significantly lower than the cost of a new computer, you should buy a new computer. Putting money into an old computer is like putting money into an old car: You may keep it on the road for a bit longer, but who knows what will break or become outdated?

Buying a New Computer

Hopefully you have good self-esteem, because shopping for a computer can be a humbling experience. First you wade through oceans of maddening acronyms to try to figure out what you need, then you buy an expensive machine that you hope you'll understand how to use, and then, a few weeks later, you see an ad for a computer that's much cheaper and that seems much better than the one you've got. You've got one advantage on your side, though: this section. Read it thoroughly and you'll be able to avoid the most annoying aspects of this process.

Choosing an Operating System (OS)

One thing to consider when buying a computer is which operating system (OS) you would like to use. An OS—also referred to as the computer's system software—is the software that gives a computer its particular personality. Different operating systems give you different ways to access your documents and folders, run programs, and change the computer's settings. The OS basically controls the computer, so it's pretty important to choose the right one.

There are many different personal-computer operating systems available today for you to choose from (see sidebar). Keep in mind that choosing an OS for your computer will forever dictate what software and hardware you buy for your computer, because they have to be compatible with your computer's OS.

You may already be familiar with a particular OS listed in our sidebar, so you may already know which you would want on a new computer. If you are undecided, however, be wary of the commonly heard advice that one OS is "the only one to use" or "much better than all the rest." Each OS has its strengths and weaknesses, and you should choose the one that you like best. You might want to go to computer stores and try out the different ones that are available. Don't obsess over it *too* much, though—pretty much any OS that you can buy today will meet your needs as a job surfer.

The Lowdown on Operating Systems

Windows

There are many flavors of Windows available—so many that it's downright confusing. The best way to cut through this confusion is to choose one of the most recent versions of Windows; you'll avoid many potential problems (software incompatibilities chief among them) by doing so. As of this writing, the most recent versions of Windows are

@ Windows ME: A reasonable choice, especially for older machines or for machines that just barely meet the specs listed above in the "A Computer" section.

@ Windows 2000: This is the best choice in the Windows family, especially if you share your computer with others. It's more stable (meaning it crashes and freezes less) than other versions of Windows.

@ Windows XP: Looks promising from a user-friendliness standpoint, but it's a bit risky to commit to an OS that's so new—there may still be bugs that will be worked out in updates. Check on its progress in the next couple of years.

Macintosh

Apple aficionados have an easier time figuring out which OS to choose because they're consecutively numbered. As of this writing, your two Mac OS choices are

@ Mac OS 9: Remarkably easy to use. However, many PC games and some Windows-compatible software do not have Mac OS versions or equivalents.

@ Mac OS X: Combines Mac OS 9–style user-friendliness with Windows 2000–style stability. Very promising, but it's also very new—make sure that there is enough software available for it.

Linux

Linux is the most stable and most flexible of all the major operating systems, and it will run on almost any kind of computer. However, it's really only for hard-core technophiles. Mostly used for running Web servers and similar tasks, Linux requires an in-depth knowledge of computers, and it takes a long time to set up.

Tips on Purchasing a Computer

Sure, you can just go out to the nearest computer shop and buy yourself a new machine, using the specs listed later in this chapter under "Computer Specs." However, given the rapid advancement of the computer industry, this will probably work only within a year or so of the publication of this book. Beyond that point, the computer industry will surely have come out with computers that are twice as fast, are probably a bit cheaper, and incorporate features that don't even exist at this writing. So how do you figure out which computer to buy if things keep changing? If you crack open a computer catalog, the choices may seem overwhelming. You don't want to buy an enticingly inexpensive machine that turns out to be a lemon; nor do you want to saddle yourself with a mega-expensive, top-of-the-line computer that has many accessories you'll never use.

There is a rule of thumb that can help you through this thorny problem: In general, look at computers that are not quite top-of-the-line (i.e., not quite the most expensive). Computers that fall at this price point tend not to be packed with unnecessary features yet powerful enough to last you for a few years.

But don't just use this rule of thumb to quickly choose a computer! Instead, get detailed specifications for models at that price point, and then

@ Comparison shop. Try to find models by other reputable manufacturers that have the same (or very similar) specs, and see if the price is better.

@ Look for special deals. You may find a similar model offered bundled with additional RAM, a color printer, a scanner, or even a digital camera.

Dirt-Cheap Computers

In the past few years, many extremely low-cost Windows-based computer systems have become available on the market, often costing less than $500. Why are they so cheap? Because they are built around certain kinds of non-Pentium processors, which are significantly less expensive than Pentiums—and significantly slower. If this is all that you can afford, then you might be able to get by with one of these super-cheap computers. Just don't expect such a machine to be fast or to last you a long time.

Warranties and Tech Support

Before purchasing a computer, find out what sort of warranty and technical support are included in the price. A computer with a very limited warranty and pay-per-use tech support may not be as good a value if you intend on using the tech support frequently. Novice computer users should probably pay for a computer with slightly lower specs but with a better warranty and free tech support.

How Long Will It Last?

One of the most frustrating things about buying computers is how quickly they become obsolete. It would be ridiculous if a five-year-old car were not drivable, yet that's essentially the situation with computers.

You can expect a top-notch new computer to be useful for about three years. This limit can be stretched another year or two if you make sure you buy a computer that's easily upgradable; ask the retailer if the processor and other components of the system can be upgraded in the future.

Save a Few Bucks

If you can't afford a new computer, look for a secondhand machine. It shouldn't be too difficult to find one that meets the minimum specifications outlined below. You can look in the for-sale ads in your local newspaper, in computer stores, and in computer repair shops. It also doesn't hurt to ask around among your family, friends, and colleagues.

You can, of course, also find used computers online, assuming that you can get online to do so! Auction sites such as eBay are good places to find used computer equipment.

The main advantage of getting a new computer rather than a used one is that new computers come with warranties and (usually) free telephone technical support. Also, a new computer's hardware and software should be in pristine condition—something that you cannot count on with used computers.

Another cost-saving option available to you is a refurbished computer. These are computers that were returned to the manufacturer for one reason or another.

Usually returned because they were broken, they have been fixed and are now being resold at a lower cost. Refurbished computers are often sold without a warranty, but refurbished computers with warranties can be found.

Shared and Public-Access Computers

If these cost-saving tips are still beyond your means, then you should take advantage of public-access computers. If you're a student, then your school might have Internet-connected computers that you can use outside class time.

If you're not a student, then your workplace (if you're employed) might have Internet-connected computers that you can use. Unfortunately, most companies have policies against using company computers for personal Internet browsing. It can't hurt to check with your employer, though. Your company might allow its employees to surf the Web during specific nonbusiness times. Just be careful not to job-surf at work. Whatever your workplace's policy, you don't want to lose your present job because you were surfing for a new one!

Another option for cheap access to the Internet is a public library. Most public libraries offer the use of Internet-connected computers. Unfortunately, old and malfunctioning machines are, sadly, quite common in public libraries. If you're fortunate enough to have access to a public library with good Internet services, be sure that you understand their policies. You may need to reserve time on a computer and agree to time limits and other restrictions.

Finally, you could contact your state or local employment office—look under Employment in the government listings section of your phone book. Some of these offices have Internet-connected computers that they will make available to job searchers under certain conditions. They may also be able to direct you to other publicly accessible Internet-connected computers.

Computer Specs

The most important things to focus on when shopping for a computer are its specifications, or specs. (The color of a computer shouldn't really be a factor, so we won't cover that. Personally, though, we like translucent yellow.) The most important specs are outlined here.

Hard Drive Size

A hard drive is a disk inside the computer. All of the computer's programs and files, as well as its operating system, are stored on the hard drive. Hard drives from the 1980s and 1990s were measured in megabytes (MB), which are millions of bytes. Now that technology has increased the efficiency of hard drives, drives today are measured in gigabytes, or GB (there are a thousand megabytes in a gigabyte). A 10 GB drive is our recommended minimum. Watch out, though: as program sizes get bigger, this requirement is climbing fast. Soon we'll be measuring hard drives in TB—terabytes, or 1,000 gigabytes!

RAM

Do these computer acronyms make you nauseous? Don't worry. You don't really need to know what it stands for. (But if you're curious, RAM stands for random access memory.) What you *do* need to know is that RAM is the memory of your computer. The RAM is what helps you run several programs at once without slowing down your whole computer. RAM consists of little chips inside your computer, and the memory on those chips is used to run programs and store temporary information.

Don't confuse RAM with hard disk space. If your computer ever tells you that it's "out of memory," that means it needs more RAM, not a larger hard drive. RAM is measured in megabytes, or MB. *We recommend at least 128 MB of RAM for your computer.* If you plan on working with graphics and layout, you probably want to upgrade to at least 256 MB. Of course, it wasn't too long ago that even a few megabytes of memory was a lot, but today's programs are bigger and more complicated, and they demand more RAM. Therefore, it probably won't be too long until we measure memory in gigabytes; try to stay on top of what's required of your system and purchase a bit more memory than you'll need. That should keep your computer from becoming obsolete for at least a little while.

And the Keyboards Were Made of Stone

"640K [of memory] ought to be enough for anybody."

—Bill Gates, 1981

"64 megabytes (MB) of RAM recommended minimum; more memory generally improves responsiveness."

—Windows 2000 system requirements, as listed on Microsoft.com

Note: There are 1,000 kilobytes (KB) in a megabyte (MB). Therefore, we can see that Windows recommends at least 100 times the amount of RAM that Gates had deemed sufficient only nineteen years earlier!

Networking and Modem

A modem connects your computer using a phone line; networking hardware connects you directly to a network. (High-speed Internet connections such as DSL and cable, discussed later in this chapter, fall into the network category.) You'll need to use one or the other of these to connect to the Internet.

There are a number of different ways to connect to a network. By far the most common is with a system called Ethernet, in which the computer is connected directly to a network using Ethernet cables. Ethernet cables, also referred to as 10BaseT, 100BaseT, or Cat 5 cables, look like thick phone cords and use an RJ-45 connector (which looks like a phone jack connector, only slightly larger).

Wireless Ethernet networking—which uses radio waves, rather than cables, to connect your computer to a network—is just beginning to become competitive with cable networking. Wireless Ethernet uses a communications standard called 802.11 (Apple Computer calls it "Airport"), and it allows users to create a cable-free Ethernet network within a limited area, usually a single building. At the moment, very few computers come with wireless Ethernet built in, but this will probably become more widely available in the near future.

Networked computers connect to one another via a hub and to the Internet via a router. Make sure your computer includes a modem and Ethernet capability.

Processor Type and Speed

The processor is the heart of a computer, and it's the chip that operates all of the commands that pass through the computer. Computers can have a wide variety of processor types.

Processor speed is a very important spec, but it must be looked at in comparison to the computer system at hand. Processor speed is directly comparable only within a single processor type. For example, a 900-MHz Pentium II is faster than a 700-MHz Pentium II. However, a 700-MHz Pentium III is significantly faster than a 766-MHz Celeron.

In 2001, computer-chip makers created the first 2-GHz computer (2,000 MHz). This means that computer processor speed will soon be measured in GHz rather than MHz.

Removable-Media Drive

Computers can be outfitted with a number of different kinds of media drives. Drives can help you store and transport information easily using portable disks.

The most important kind of media drive is a CD-ROM, which stands for Compact Disc-Read Only Memory. A CD-ROM contains about 650 MB of data, which can easily be used to store just about any type of computer software you could use. In fact, most software today needs to be installed from CD-ROMs.

Ready to 'Ware

Hardware is your computer and any other physical stuff (printers, etc.) that's connected to it. Software refers to the programs that you run on your computer. Software is "soft" because it's ephemeral—it can crash, but it won't leave any broken glass on your floor.

There are many different kinds of drives that can read CD-ROMs; the most common kind right now is the DVD-ROM drive. This is a drive that can play DVDs (CD-size disks that contain movies) as well as CD-ROMs. Other kinds of removable-media drives include floppy disk drives and Zip drives.

Other Specs

There are a number of other, less important specs for computers that you should probably know about. A semicomprehensive list follows.

Expansion Cards

Expansion cards (often referred to as PCI cards) can greatly expand a computer's capabilities. These cards generally serve to allow you to attach external devices, such as scanners and external disk drives.

This spec is becoming less important with the growing popularity of USB and FireWire ports (see next section), which can perform the same functions.

Ports

Computers are connected to other devices using ports. A computer might have several kinds of ports, such as parallel, serial, networking, USB, and/or FireWire (a.k.a. IEEE 1394). Just like expansion cards, these ports are used to connect devices such as printers and scanners.

USB and FireWire are the most advanced and convenient types of ports available. It's a good idea to find a computer that has them or (if you already have a computer and it doesn't have these kinds of ports) to look into buying USB and FireWire PCI cards.

Graphics Cards

Graphic design professionals and computer-gaming enthusiasts are particularly interested in the specifications for a computer's graphics card, which connects the computer to a monitor. The better the graphics card, the better the image on the monitor—especially animated images.

There are a wide variety of graphics cards that could come with any given computer, but don't sweat this particular spec too much—the card that comes with your computer is probably just fine for your job-surfing needs. If you are involved in a graphics-intensive career such as digital video or online animation, then you might want to invest in a higher-powered graphics card. If you're a computer-gaming aficionado, then you might also want a top-of-the-line graphics card so that you can slaughter aliens and mutants in rich, vibrant color. Note, however, that this is unlikely to contribute in any meaningful way to your job search.

Sound Cards

Sound cards can provide different levels of amplification and richness of sound, as well as different kinds of sound input. Just as with graphics cards, you'll find that the sound card that comes with your computer should be sufficient for your needs. If you're involved with digital music editing (or, again, if you want to blast aliens with extraordinary realism), then you'll need a high-quality sound card.

Other specifications are limited only by the ingenuity of the computer industry. There will no doubt soon be features available that we can't even imagine now.

The important thing to remember when buying a computer is that the specs should fit your needs. Don't be bowled over by sales pitches for computers with features that you don't need or don't understand.

An Internet Connection

This is the trickiest item on our list of Internet access requirements. That's because the Internet service provider (ISP) industry is in a constant and often very confusing state of flux. In most parts of the United States, there are several options for connecting to the Internet. Usually, you will find that there are several ISPs to choose from—perhaps one or two local ISPs, and then as many as a half-dozen regional or national ISPs. Once you've picked an ISP, there are still different physical methods of connection to choose from. This section aims to help you find your way through this plethora of choices.

Until about 1999, if you were considering your Internet connection choices, you would have been thinking about modem speeds and a second phone line. In the past couple of years, however, there has been a high-speed Internet access revolution, and there are now several ways of getting "high-speed, always-on" Internet connections that do not require a traditional modem. These services allow you to use your telephone while you're online and (in most cases) to remain connected to the Internet whenever your computer is turned on. If you plan to be spending a lot of time online (and in order to effectively use the Internet to find employment, you will need to do so), then a high-speed (also called broadband) Internet connection is for you. While such connections are not cheap, their prices are competitive with traditional modem connections, and they are likely to become more affordable in the near future.

Internet Connection Options

Before you choose an ISP, you may wish to consider what kind of Internet connection you need. Here are the different kinds of connections that are currently available.

Modem

A modem connection allows your computer to connect to the Internet via a regular telephone line (using an infernal cacophony of clicks, beeps, and whines). This option is not going to give you the speed and convenience that you should have in order to effectively job-surf (or download porn, if that's your bag). However, in many parts of the country and in most of the world, a modem is the only option.

Despite the galloping speed of the high-speed Internet revolution, which is rapidly making modems obsolete, most computers still come with built-in modems. These modems are the fastest available: 56kbps (kilobits per second), also known as 56k or v.90. If a modem connection is your only Internet connection option, make sure you are using a 56k modem. Modems slower than 56k are responsible for those super-slow load times; unless you really enjoy watching Web pages take thirty to sixty seconds to load, we recommend never, ever using a modem slower than 56k.

Cable

Also known as a cable modem connection, this type of connection comes into your home via a television cable line. The cable line then gets split in two; one segment goes into your television (for regular cable-TV service) and the other goes into a cable modem box, which connects to your computer.

If a cable modem connection is an option for you, this is probably the best kind of connection that you can (relatively cheaply) get. If cable Internet connections are available in your area, you can usually buy the connection from your local cable company. Recently, however, the federal government has been putting pressure on cable companies to allow other ISPs to use their cable lines to provide Internet access. As a result, there may be some added competition in the cable modem sector soon, and you'll be able to choose between your cable company and other ISPs for a cable modem connection.

DSL

A digital subscriber line (DSL) Internet connection comes into your home via a regular phone line; the line then gets split between your telephone and a DSL modem box, which in turn is connected to your computer. Despite the fact that DSL uses your phone line, you will still be able to use your telephone while online.

DSL is the most complex Internet connection option. For technical reasons, you need to be within a few miles of a central office (a telephone switching station) in order for it to work, so DSL is rarely offered in rural areas. And although many DSL installations work smoothly, there is a much higher probability of running into problems when trying to get it installed than with other types of Internet connections.

There are two main factors that make DSL installation so complicated.

@ Most phone companies are now also ISPs, and most offer DSL access. However, the equipment that these companies are using is complex and often alarmingly antiquated by technological standards (it may be older than you are), and well-trained technicians who understand the equipment are in short supply. As a result, it can take a long time to set up a DSL line, and there are serious problems with reliability.

@ Other ISPs are allowed to use the phone company's lines to provide you with DSL service—but in order to do so, they need the phone company's help. The service problems noted above make coordination difficult. And, it must be said, the phone companies often seem reluctant to provide fast, quality service to other ISPs—who are, after all, competing with them to offer you ISP service.

When shopping for DSL service, you may hear the term *ADSL*. This stands for asynchronous DSL—the kind of DSL service that's generally offered to residential customers. Other flavors of DSL tend to be significantly more expensive (though also faster) and are intended for business customers.

Satellite

Internet access via satellite dish is, in many rural areas, the only option for high-speed Internet access. While not quite as fast as DSL or a cable modem, it's significantly faster than a traditional modem.

Until recently, satellite Internet access had one major Achilles' heel: It only allowed you to download (receive information) from the Internet at high speed. In order to upload (send information, such as e-mail), you had to be simultaneously connected via a traditional modem. For most users, who do a lot more Web surfing (which generally involves only downloading) than uploading, this still provides acceptable speeds. However, you're still saddled with the inconvenience of a modem connection.

Recent satellite ISPs don't require a phone line to upload files. While the upload speed is still slow, at least you don't have to have a second phone line installed in order to use your telephone while online.

There are still several serious drawbacks to satellite Internet: The speeds are slower than other cable modems or DSL; the initial installation cost is high; and there is a longer "lag time" while your data bounces back and forth from Earth into orbit, making applications such as online gaming or instant messaging annoyingly slow.

Wireless

Wireless Internet access is just normal Internet access via a specially designed dedicated cell phone. While this provides an incomparable measure of freedom—especially if you're a laptop user—it does have some drawbacks: It's slower than other high-speed options (only four times faster than a modem); availability is limited to major cities (and is spotty even there); and it's pricey.

T1 and Ethernet

This is the sort of Internet connection that many schools and larger businesses have. A T1 is a high-capacity dedicated phone line that allows many computers to access the Internet at the same time. Ethernet is the networking system that distributes this connection to individual computers. A few places in the world (such as the Blacksburg Electronic Village in Virginia: www.bev.net/project/brochures/about.html) offer this sort of high-speed connection in apartment buildings. This arrangement is likely to become more common in the future.

Choosing an ISP

Once you've figured out which kind of connection best fits your situation, you can go shopping for an Internet service provider.

A-O-(HEL)L?

"So easy to use, no wonder it's number one!" America Online's ubiquitous ads, and junk-mailed installation CDs, have helped to make it by far the largest ISP. AOL is a good choice for newcomers to the Internet because it's designed entirely for beginners. The worldwide availability of the service and twenty-four-hour technical support are also powerful advantages.

AOL does have disadvantages, though: More than any other ISP, it's saturated with advertising, which you must wade through or past to get to your online tasks. AOL also requires that you use its unique Internet-navigation system, which is a far inferior product to either Microsoft Explorer or Netscape Navigator. While this is fine for many people, AOL users miss out on the richness and flexibility of the Internet experience.

Also, AOL mostly offers traditional modem connections, though it has begun to branch out into broadband connections.

Local and Regional ISPs

Not too long ago, local and small regional ISPs dominated the market that was left over from AOL. In recent years, however, larger ISPs have bought out these smaller players at an alarming rate, reducing competition.

Fortunately, many of these smaller ISPs are still surviving. Look in your Yellow Pages under "Internet." Or, if you can get online, do a search on www.yahoo.com for "ISP directories" for a list of several websites that can help you search for an ISP.

Although local ISPs are more likely than national ISPs to be bought out or go out of business, they tend to offer friendlier, more accessible customer service and can generally be more flexible.

Larger ISPs

While large regional or national ISPs may keep you on hold longer than local ISPs, they often have longer tech support hours, and you can move to another part of the country without switching ISPs.

Specialty ISPs

You might find that there is an ISP that offers exactly what you want from the Internet. Some ISPs specialize in providing Internet access to corporations only; some specialize in a particular kind of connection, such as satellite; and at least one (www.speakeasy.net) specializes in providing Internet access to online gaming enthusiasts.

Free ISPs

Beware of free or extremely cheap Internet access. A number of companies offering this sort of access appeared in the late 1990s, but many of them have gone under in the dot-com bust, and there is no guarantee that the remaining ones will not do likewise. As is the case in so many other places in life, you get what you pay for; these bargain ISPs generally require that part of your computer screen be taken up by advertisements, and the services are not noted for their high speeds or reliability.

AOL

Web address: aolplus.aol.com/highspeed/
Modem? Yes
Cable? No
DSL? Yes
Satellite? No
Wireless? No
Monthly cost: $43.85
Installation/equipment charges: $0

Earthlink

Web address: www.earthlink.net/home/broadband/
Modem? Yes
Cable? Yes
DSL? Yes
Satellite? Yes
Wireless? No
Monthly cost: $49.95
Installation/equipment charges: $100

MSN

Web address: essentials.msn.com/access/broadband.asp
Modem? Yes
Cable? No
DSL? Yes
Satellite? No
Wireless? No
Monthly cost: $39.95
Installation/equipment charges: $99

Verizon

Web address: www.verizon.net
Modem? Yes
Cable? No
DSL? Yes
Satellite? No
Wireless? No
Monthly cost: $49.95
Installation/equipment charges: $50

DirecPC

Web address: www.direcpc.com
Modem? No
Cable? No
DSL? No
Satellite? Yes
Wireless? No
Monthly cost: $49.99
Installation/equipment charges: $690

Time Warner Cable

Web address: www.roadrunner.net
Modem? Yes
Cable? No
DSL? Yes
Satellite? No
Wireless? No
Monthly cost: $39.95
Installation/equipment charges: $100

Wireless Web Connect!

Web address: www.wwc.com/products/anywhere/
Modem? No
Cable? Yes
DSL? No
Satellite? No
Wireless? No
Monthly cost: $59.95 (additional telephone charges may be applied; see website for details)
Installation/equipment charges: $300

All prices are for basic residential DSL service, with the exception of DirecPC, Time Warner Cable, and Wireless Web Connect.

Keep in mind that this information is changing all the time—even month to month and week to week! You might consider updating this chart yourself by visiting the websites of the ISPs listed and seeing what their current offerings are.

A Checklist for ISPs

When choosing an ISP, there are a number of factors to keep in mind.

Connection Type

You should first determine what kind of connection you want, based on the choices available in your area. Ideally, you want the fastest and most reliable connection available, but cost must naturally be taken into account. Of the most common types of affordable residential Internet connections, these are kinds to look for, in order of desirability: cable, DSL, and satellite. Modem connections should be used only as a last resort.

Customer Service

The best Internet connection in the world is useless if no one can help you to set it up and use it. Before signing up with an ISP, check out their telephone support hours. Call their customer service line and ask about their services. Are the customer service people polite, and do they appear to be well trained? Find out if you might ever have to pay extra for telephone tech support; ideally, it should always be free!

E-mail

When you buy Internet access, your ISP will provide you with an e-mail account. Since e-mail may now become your most important communication tool with potential and future employers, you should review the details of an ISP's e-mail offerings before signing on. Here are some things to look for.

@ IMAP Compatibility

With most e-mail systems, you need to always check your e-mail from a single computer. If you move around from computer to computer, you'll be able to access only messages that you haven't read yet; none of your older messages—ones that you've already read—will be accessible. IMAP-compatible e-mail systems allow you to move around from computer to computer while retaining access to your entire e-mail collection. If you plan to commonly use multiple computers, this could be an important consideration.

In order to use IMAP, you will need to use an IMAP-compatible e-mail client, such as Eudora or Netscape (Netscape includes an e-mail program in its Web browser package).

@ **Attachment Size Limits**

Most ISPs have restrictions on the maximum size of a file that can be sent or received as an e-mail attachment. If this size limit is too low—1 MB, for example—this could be a problem if your work requires you to send and receive large files, such as image files. Word processing files will usually fall far below any attachment size limit. However, if you have attachments (such as pictures) on your word processing résumé, you might not be able to send them.

@ **Webmail**

Many ISPs will offer Web-based access to your incoming mail—a very convenient feature if you are often away from your own computer. Note, however, that this feature does not give you access to e-mail that you've already read.

@ **Extra E-mail Accounts**

Many ISPs offer extra e-mail addresses for free or for a small fee. Don't confuse this with having multiple Internet access accounts (which you don't need)—think of it this way: one Internet access account, multiple e-mail addresses.

For job surfers, having multiple e-mail accounts allows you to separate your business-related e-mail from your personal e-mail. This will help you avoid overlooking business-related correspondence, which can easily happen if you receive a lot of personal e-mail.

Free Webmail

If your ISP does not provide you with extra e-mail accounts, you may want to use a Web-based e-mail service, such as Yahoo! or Hotmail. These services are free, and they do not require that you use special e-mail software; the mail system is accessed using a Web browser. An enormous advantage of these services, as with IMAP, is that you don't have to be at your computer to see your e-mail; you can get into your e-mail from any Internet-connected computer.

Web Space

Does the ISP offer free Web space, and if so, how much? Can you pay extra to get more space? Will they help you to register a domain name (personal Web address) for your Web space? These will be important considerations when it comes time to publish your online résumé and/or portfolio.

Contracts

Are you required to sign a time-specific (e.g., one-year) contract with the ISP? Is there a penalty for canceling the contract?

There are a couple of online resources that help evaluate an ISP, so find some time on an Internet-connected computer and check out www.dslreports.com. Although this site is geared toward DSL consumers, it also provides information on other kinds of connections and on ISPs in general. The Community Forums section features lively discussion of the merits and sins of many ISPs. Another terrific resource is www.cnet.com/internet/0-3761.html. This page, on the technology-industry site cnet.com, offers a number of interesting links related to the ISP industry.

Now Go Get It!

Okay—you've chosen your ISP and connection type, and you're ready to get connected to the Internet at (hopefully) a blazing-fast speed. The next step is to contact that ISP and tell them what you want. The ISP's customer service department should take it from there, sending you all of the information, hardware, and software you will need in order to get connected.

TCP/IP Software

TCP/IP is the language that computers on the Internet use to communicate. (TCP/IP stands for Transmission Control Protocol/Internet Protocol. Use this little-known fact to amaze and delight people at parties.) Fortunately, all personal computers made since 1995 that came with Microsoft Windows (including Windows 95, Windows 98, Windows NT, Windows 2000, and Windows ME) or the Macintosh OS (any version) have TCP/IP software built in.

You *will* need to configure the TCP/IP settings on your computer, however. When you sign up with an ISP, you will receive instructions on how to do this. Sometimes you will receive a CD-ROM that contains a software installer that will do the TCP/IP configuring for you.

A typical TCP/IP configuration dialog box for Windows looks like this:

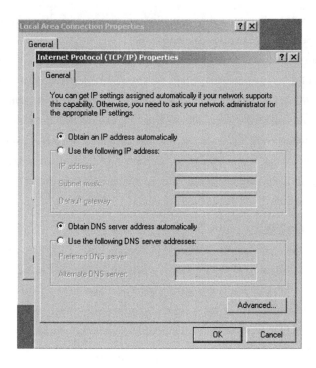

A typical TCP/IP configuration dialog box on a Macintosh looks like this:

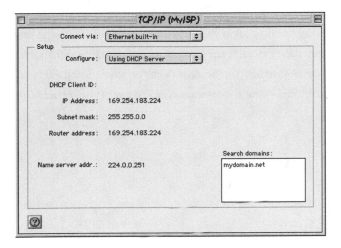

The actual numbers that appear in these boxes may be quite different on your computer.

This process can seem very technical, but it's usually quite easy. Every computer that's connected to the Internet needs to have a unique IP address; configuring the TCP/IP settings on your computer will give it such an address. Think of an IP address as being like your street address: In order for information to reach your computer from the Internet, your computer needs to have an address.

Internet Software

Any new computer should come preloaded with some Internet software. In fact, Windows comes preloaded with Microsoft Internet Explorer, which is a very competent Web browser. Netscape Communicator, the second most popular Web browser, can be downloaded for free from www.netscape.com.

As a job surfer, you'll need some software in addition to the Internet software to help you find your dream job. This software includes a word processor, an e-mail program, an FTP program, and a Web page editor. We'll discuss how to acquire and use this software in the next chapter.

Keeping Up with New Internet Resources

Once you've taken your first steps toward being a successful online job searcher, remember that the Internet is constantly shifting. By the time you read this, there may be some great sites and useful resources that aren't in this book because they didn't exist at the time of its printing. In order to keep up with these new developments, you should do some creative surfing. Periodically search for job-related sites using www.yahoo.com and any of your other favorite search engines.

Chapter 13
Sharpening Your Tools: Basic Internet Software and Skills

Okay, here are just a few more little things before we go on to the really fun stuff like creating online résumés. Once you've got Internet access, it's time to get familiar with some of the basic software tools that you'll need to master the online environment. This includes not only the obvious and all-important Web browser but also a plethora of other programs that will help you to take full advantage of your Internet connection.

Web Browsers

The most essential tool for a job surfer is the surfboard: a Web browser. There are a number of Web browsers available today, and most of them are free. Netscape Navigator was the first mass-market Web browser, but in the late 1990s, Microsoft aggressively marketed its Web browser, Internet Explorer, which now dominates the market.

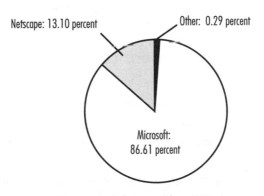

Netscape: 13.10 percent

Other: 0.29 percent

Microsoft: 86.61 percent

(Source: www.websidestory.com, February 2001)

Some folks prefer Netscape, others Internet Explorer. As you can see from the percentages in the pie chart, most prefer Explorer. In fact, Explorer is essentially the better of the two at this point—it's more stable and user-friendly than Netscape. On the other hand, Netscape has built-in e-mail, Usenet, and Web design software. The choice is yours. (Netscape wishes that you and other Web surfers had been given more of a choice in the past—the central issue in the antitrust lawsuits against Microsoft is the aggressive marketing techniques used to propel Internet Explorer's market share past Netscape's.)

Why would anyone use one of the browsers found in the .29 percent group? Because Netscape and Microsoft, in their brutal war for market share, have packed their browsers with numerous features and released new versions as quickly as possible. As a result, both browsers are somewhat buggy, take up a lot of disk space and RAM, and have features that you'll probably never use. The alternative Web browsers that make up much of the .29 percent, such as Opera and iCab, have tried to exploit these weaknesses by being smaller and more stable.

If you want to explore other Web browsers (not all of which are free), you can find a list at dir.yahoo.com/Computers_and_Internet/Software/Internet/World_Wide_Web/Browsers/.

Keep in mind that your ISP may provide support for only Netscape and Explorer, or possibly only Explorer. Check with your ISP to see which Web browsers they support. If you use any others, you'll be on your own if you run into trouble.

Using Your Browser to Stay Organized

As you find effective job sites that help you meet your job-searching goals, you'll want to bookmark them for future reference. Bookmarking is a feature available in all Web browsers that allows you to save sites (usually in a pull-down menu). It may have different names in different browsers; Internet Explorer calls it Favorites.

You should also familiarize yourself with the history feature of your Web browser. This feature gives you a complete list of all the websites that have been visited by the browser—up to a limit that's predefined in the browser's preferences. This feature is particularly useful when you want to return to a job site that you've forgotten to bookmark, but remember: Any *other* site that you may have visited within that specified time is also public domain.

Web Add-Ons

Internet Explorer and Netscape Navigator can deal with most Web content (text and pictures), but they need a little help with the fancier online sounds and animations. For example, to hear high-quality music or see video clips, you'll likely need an add-on to your Web browser. In fact, your Web-surfing experience will be much smoother if you outfit yourself ahead of time with the most commonly needed plug-ins. Our brief list below shows a few of the essential plug-ins. As you surf the Web you may discover that you need another plug-in. You'll be told what you need and where to get it on the website, so installation should be a snap.

WinZip (for Windows Users Only)

Many files that you get from the Web will be zipped, which is just a fancy way to say compressed. (The file's size gets shrunk so that it can be downloaded more quickly.) WinZip allows you to decompress these files so that you can use them. This program, unfortunately, is not free, even though it isn't expensive by computer software standards.

This nifty piece of software is available at www.winzip.com. You should also download and install the WinZip Internet Browser Support Add-On, available at www.winzip.com/ibrowser.htm.

A note for Mac users: You don't need software of this type because all Macs come with a program called Stuffit Expander, which performs the same function.

Shockwave

This oft-used bit of Internet software allows you to view complex, beautiful, sometimes interactive Shockwave animations. As more sites use its animations, the plug-in becomes even more essential to have. It is available for free at www.macromedia.com/shockwave/download.

Adobe Acrobat Reader

Acrobat Reader allows you view and print PDF (portable document format) documents. This format is often used for downloadable forms, and you're likely to need it at least once or twice in your job hunt. This free software is available at www.adobe.com/products/acrobat/readstep.html.

Windows Media Player, QuickTime, and RealPlayer

These three fiercely competing packages allow you to view a wide range of video and audio content on the Web. As a job surfer, you should equip yourself with all three to ensure that your computer can handle almost all audio/video stuff that you'll encounter.

QuickTime and RealPlayer are available in both free and commercial versions; the commercial versions have more features, but the free versions will provide you with the basic playback that you need.

Media Player is available at www.microsoft.com/windows/windowsmedia/en/download/default.asp; QuickTime is available at www.apple.com/quicktime/download; and RealPlayer is available at www.real.com/player.

E-mail

Once you're fully online, you may find that e-mail will begin to replace the telephone as your most important communication tool. You'll need an e-mail program first, though. Fortunately, most new computers come with a copy of Microsoft Outlook Express preinstalled.

If you don't have Outlook Express on your computer, you can download this freeware program from www.microsoft.com/windows/oe.

Another popular e-mail program is Eudora, available in both freeware and shareware versions from www.eudora.com.

Using E-mail Effectively

There's more to using e-mail than catching up with your crazy uncle Morty, who just got connected. Using e-mail is not necessarily as simple as it appears, and there are a number of ways to use it more effectively. Here are some pitfalls to watch out for so that you don't make some embarrassing mistakes.

@ Avoid being overly informal. Just because e-mail allows you to communicate with the world while wearing pajamas doesn't mean that you should use the same tone with your business correspondents as you would with your family and friends. It's generally acceptable to be slightly less informal than you would be in a business letter. Pretend that you're writing an interoffice memo. Use salutations and closings, and check your messages for spelling and grammar mistakes before sending them.

@ Do not argue or attempt to settle disputes via e-mail. It's easy to convince yourself that you're having a real conversation via e-mail, but e-mail lacks the often subtle visual and audible cues that are present in a real conversation—cues that communicate whether a person is angry or sarcastic, for instance. It's very easy to misread the other party's tone and to misinterpret his or her intentions; also, people tend to be less restrained via e-mail, because unlike a face-to-face or telephone communication, e-mail conversations lack the potential for immediate negative consequences. As a result of these factors, e-mail arguments can quickly escalate. As soon as a tone becomes strained, initiate personal contact to resolve the issue.

@ One of the most serious breaches of Netiquette (online etiquette) is spamming—sending out bulk e-mail to a number of people whom you don't necessarily know. Should you somehow get hold of e-mail addresses for a number of potential employers, you may be tempted to send job queries or résumés to them. Don't do this. Most people do not like to receive impersonal, unsolicited e-mail, and any potential benefit of this strategy will likely be more than offset by the annoyance you will cause.

@ If you want to contact potential employers, try using the telephone first; a personal contact will make a much better impression. If you must e-mail someone you don't know, keep the message brief, polite, and professional, and do not attach a résumé; because many viruses these days come in the form of attachments, an unsolicited e-mail with an attachment is likely to be immediately deleted.

@ Keep your e-mail organized. As we mentioned, one way that you
can stay organized is to keep separate e-mail accounts for personal
and business e-mail. Within an e-mail account, you should also
organize your e-mail carefully: Create folders (or mailboxes) for
different topics and/or correspondents, and keep your inbox empty.

@ Erasing a message will usually erase any attachments that came
with it, so copy any important attachments to a secondary
location.

Transferring Files on the Internet

The Internet is, above all, a communications device. Part of the communicating
that you'll engage in as a job surfer will probably include sending and receiving
files. In general, when you send a file over the Internet, it's called uploading;
when you receive a file, it's called downloading.

Receiving Files

Web browsers make it easy to download files. If you want to download a file from the Web it will usually be fairly clear how to do so. For example, at www.snood.com, you can download the shareware game Snood by clicking on one of the links in the section labeled Download Snood. (For maximum job-searching productivity, however, you might want to wait until *after* you've found some work before downloading this insanely addictive game.)

After clicking on the right place, your Web browser will either simply download the program to your desktop or ask you where on your hard drive you'd like to have the file saved.

When you download a program, you will often be downloading not the program itself but only an installer of the program. Once the download is complete, you need to locate the installer (wherever it is on your hard drive) and double-click on it. The program will then be installed.

If an individual wants to send you a file, the easiest way to do this is via e-mail. Most e-mail programs have an attachment feature that allows you to do this.

Sending Files

Sending a file to an individual is also fairly straightforward; you simply e-mail the file as an attachment.

However, if you're going to be creating Web pages for an online résumé and/or portfolio, as described in the next chapter, you'll need to be able to transfer the Web pages that you create to a Web server (a computer that allows worldwide access to Web pages). To do this, you'll need FTP software. Yes, it's yet another scary-looking computer acronym, but it's actually quite easy to learn.

FTP stands for File Transfer Protocol, and FTP software allows you to move files between your computer and other Internet-connected computers, such as Web servers. You'll need FTP software if you want to publish Web pages, such as an online résumé.

Share and Share Alike

Most of the software that's available for downloading from the Internet falls into one of two categories: freeware and shareware. Freeware is software that you may download and use for no charge; shareware can be downloaded for free, but you are expected to pay a (usually quite modest) fee to the author if you use it. Although shareware licensing fees are essentially unenforceable, we urge you to be a good Netizen (citizen of the Internet) and pay your shareware fees—you will encourage the continuation of the generosity of the amateur programmers who write most shareware programs.

How can you tell if a particular program is freeware or shareware? There will rarely be any mystery to it; most shareware programs will frequently and prominently present you with reminders to pay the shareware fee.

There are many different FTP software packages to choose from. One of the most popular FTP programs for Windows computers is WS_FTP, which can be downloaded from www.ipswitch.com. It comes in both Pro and Limited Edition versions. The latter has fewer functions but is free under certain conditions. If you're a Macintosh user, download Fetch from www.fetchsoftworks.com. It's not free, but it does come with a cute little animated doggie.

Word Processors

We know, word processors are not actually Internet programs. Still, the word processor will become a major component of your online tool kit. Although you may deliver résumés, cover letters, and other business correspondence via the Internet, you will often create these documents using a word processor.

Microsoft Word is by far the most popular word processing program. Although you can choose to use any of a number of other word processors, you will guarantee maximum compatibility with the rest of the world if you get a copy of Word. (It often comes preinstalled on new PCs, which is a very easy way to acquire it!)

Like many other word processors, Word also has a convenient feature that allows you save any document as a Web page, ready to be published on the Web.

Web Editors

With its Save as Web Page feature, Microsoft Word can be considered a very basic Web editor. However, there are other, much better programs specifically designed to create Web pages. You'll find this sort of program helpful when you start building Web pages of your own, such as an online résumé and portfolio.

There are two types of Web editors: HTML assistants and WYSIWYG ("what you see is what you get") editors. HTML assistants are programs that help you with HyperText Markup Language, the programming language in which Web pages are written; toolbars and pull-down menus give you access to HTML tags so that you don't have to remember them. WYSIWYG editors allow you to design Web pages graphically, bypassing HTML entirely. The Web-editing software acts as the interface between the computer language and you. (You don't ever have to see it.)

Many HTML assistants are freeware or shareware programs; you can find a list by going to www.versiontracker.com and searching for "HTML assistant." The industry-leading WYSIWYG Web editors are the commercial products Macromedia Dreamweaver and Adobe GoLive.

In addition, many text- and graphics-oriented programs (such as Microsoft Word, as we mentioned) have basic Web page editing or exporting features built into them.

Chapter 14

Online Résumés

If you want to be a truly efficient job surfer, you're going to need a well-made online résumé, which allows you to deliver your résumé to potential employers instantaneously. Instead of mailing a paper résumé, you can simply e-mail the address of your Web résumé. An online résumé also demonstrates your familiarity with the Internet. A proper online résumé shows a flair for design and a comfort level with the Internet. No matter what your career is, an eye for production and Web savvy are very desirable traits.

Before we show you how to create an online résumé, let's show you what else you must have before you can create this supplemental (and serviceable) second résumé.

One Résumé, Many Formats

You should create and maintain your résumé in the following formats:

@ **Microsoft Word**

Having a résumé in Microsoft Word allows for easy e-mailing. Most employers who accept résumés via e-mail require that the résumé be in this format.

@ **Plain Text (ASCII)**

Most word processing programs allow you to save your résumé in plain text, or ASCII, format. This is useful in several circumstances. Some employment websites ask you to type in an entire résumé; pasting your plain-text résumé will allow you to do this quickly. (Pasting text from standard Microsoft Word documents usually does not work correctly.)

Some people who receive résumés in e-mail attachments may have trouble reading a Microsoft Word attachment. (Maybe your prospective employer isn't very computer-literate.) In these cases, you can copy and paste your plain-text résumé into a regular e-mail message.

@ PDF (Portable Document Format)

This format allows you to create documents that incorporate both text and high-quality graphics, yet are small enough to be easily delivered via the Internet. To read PDFs, you need the free product Adobe Acrobat Reader; unfortunately, to create PDFs, you need the rather expensive software package Adobe Acrobat.

This format is used extensively in computer graphics–oriented industries, such as advertising and design, and may make a good impression when seeking work in those fields. Keep in mind, though, that the person who receives your résumé may be a not-particularly-computer-savvy human resources staffer, and therefore may not be familiar with the PDF format.

Before using any of these formats to deliver your résumé to a prospective employer, make sure that the person receiving your résumé can read that particular format. In many ways, an online résumé is the safest of the formats, because most employers will have no problem accessing a Web page.

@ Online (HTML)

Making yourself visible as a prospective employee on the Web can be challenging. There are literally millions of other job seekers who already have online résumés, with thousands more coming online every week. Keeping that in mind, an online résumé is still a must-have. Although it may be challenging to make yourself stand out from the masses, a well-designed online résumé can be an effective and convenient way to communicate your abilities to prospective employers.

The Plain Text (ASCII) Résumé

If you insist on using plain text, your options are limited. That doesn't mean your plain text résumé has to be, well, plain. Here are five handy tips when creating a regular résumé, whether it's for e-mail or an online database.

@ Delete any special formatting. ASCII does not understand underlining, italics, bold, bullets, links, or colors. Make sure to eliminate any of these fancy formatting features before uploading your plain text résumé. You can use asterisks or tildes (~) in lieu of the standard bullets that you see in HTML (or a Word document).

@ Maintain a page width of sixty characters. Different e-mail readers will view your résumé differently. Therefore, you have to play it safe and assume that their screen can only view sixty characters per line. If you go over this limit, you run the risk of having your text spill over to the next line.

@ Eliminate abbreviations and symbols. Don't expect everyone to understand your career-specific abbreviations. Consider that many of the viewers of your online résumé will be human relations personnel or headhunters, and they won't understand your job lingo. On the same note, never use &, %, or + in your online résumé. Spell those characters out.

@ Remove all tabs. Any tabs that you have used to help format your résumé in regular text may show up as garbled gobbledygook. Replace your tabs with spaces, and your résumé will look the same regardless of who is looking at it.

@ Review your résumé first. If you're going to e-mail a résumé to a potential employer, send a copy to a friend or to yourself first. That way you can review it first for typos, grammatical errors, and layout before anybody important sets their eyes on it. This point can't be stressed enough.

The Online Résumé

The first instinctive act of most online job seekers is to post a résumé on one of the popular Web-based job boards, such as Monster.com or HotJobs.com. These sites offer the tantalizing promise of near-effortless job searching: Post your résumé, and thousands of employers can view it. These sites are great—and we heartily recommend them—but you can take their usefulness to another level with your own HTML.

Some job sites allow you to post your résumé in HTML format, but very few require it. When given the choice, most people choose to send their résumé in plain text. However, we recommend taking advantage of any HTML option; that's your chance to stand out.

If you create a personal account at Monster.com (which you can do by going to my.monster.com) and choose to create a résumé, you will be led through a series of screens that allow you to create a very detailed résumé. It has some limitations, however; you are limited to the categories that Monster.com gives you; you can't make the résumé look particularly snazzy (from a graphic design standpoint, all Monster.com résumés look exactly alike); and you can't attach samples of your work. In other words, Monster.com makes it rather difficult for you to communicate a sense of your uniqueness through the use of graphic design and multimedia elements.

HotJobs.com's résumé feature is even more basic and less flexible than Monster.com's. Making yourself stand out from the many thousands of résumé-posters on the site is very challenging indeed.

If you do decide to post your resume on a job-board site, keep an eye out for an "add a URL" feature. URL stands for universal resource locator. All it means is "Web address." Like many other job-board sites, Monster.com gives you a chance to put a personal Web address on your résumé. If you have a résumé and/or portfolio somewhere else on the World Wide Web, you can use these little boxes to post a link to a much more personalized, comprehensive, and (potentially) effective advertisement for yourself. Think of this as a side door out of their cramped résumé environments into the limitless possibilities of the Internet.

Creating an Online (HTML) Résumé

Before you can enter anything into one of those "your URL" boxes, though, you need to have an résumé somewhere on the Web! If you already know something about Web design, then you're way ahead of the game. For the rest of us, though, let's learn how to create a basic (yet professional-looking) résumé Web page using HTML.

Web pages are written in a simple programming language called HyperText Markup Language, better know by its acronym, HTML. Web designers create HTML documents, which Web browsers interpret and display as Web pages.

There are ways to create Web pages without learning any HTML whatsoever. There are a number of specialized programs, such as Netscape Composer (which is free) or Dreamweaver, that are designed specifically to help you avoid using HTML at all. However, it's a good idea to know at least a little bit about HTML. It helps you to understand the Web's limitations and possibilities, and makes it easier for you to solve problems with Web pages that you may create. In many cases, it's easier to fix a minor problem with a Web page by quickly editing the HTML code rather than using a Web editor program (like Dreamweaver or Composer) to try to fix the problem.

HTML Basics

HTML is a simple computer language used almost exclusively for the Internet. The language uses "tags" to assign colors, pictures, text, and formatting for your browser. In fact, if you click View on the top navigation bar of your browser and choose Source (in Netscape, choose Page Source) from the drop-down menu, a Notepad file will open up containing all the HTML code for whatever page you might happen to be viewing. You will see that each page is formatted in HTML using a < at the start and a > at the end for each tag. A slash is used to end a format. Take a look at the following examples of basic HTML tags:

If you type this in HTML:	It will look like this:
Joe Bloggs	Joe Bloggs
Joe Bloggs	**Joe Bloggs**
<u>Joe Bloggs</u>	<u>Joe Bloggs</u>
<i>Joe Bloggs</i>	*Joe Bloggs*

That's not too difficult, right? (We told you so.) Here are a few more important HTML tags to know to make the most of your HTML résumé:

<center>Joe Bloggs**</center>**
Will center the text.

<div align=right>Joe Bloggs**</div>**
Will right-justify the text in the tag.

**
**
Will add a line break. You need this to separate the text in your résumé.

<hr>
Will add a horizontal line across the screen. This is a nice feature if you want to divide the sections on your résumé.

<font size=+1>Joe Bloggs**</font>**
Will increase the size of the text in the tag. You can also make the font size larger (+2, +3, etc.) or smaller (−1, −2, etc.).

<ul>
Creates a bulleted list (useful for listing job duties).

<li>
Creates a single bulleted item in a list.

Two additional tags are important to know for creating a successful HTML résumé.

Type **<html>** at the start of the file, and put **</html>** at the very end. This tells the Web browser that it's looking at an HTML file.

When you're ready for the text of the résumé, type **<body>**, and type **</body>** when you're done.

Okay, so now you know the basics. Already you know more than 99 percent of the Web-surfing public. Before you get too cocky, there are a few more HTML tags that can really enhance your online presence. And before you get too attached to the way anything looks on your screen, consider which browser you are using to view the page.

HTML Headings

There is a neat feature with HTML programming called meta tags, which can help your résumé get noticed. These specialized tags allow you to put text in the file that won't actually be visible in the real résumé. Why would you want this? A brief description in your résumé will allow you to pop up on more employer searches. For example, look at the following two lines of HTML code:

```
<META NAME=DescriptionCONTENT =Description
I am a terrific worker.>

<META NAME=Key WordsCONTENT=
HTML, Quark, Adobe, workaholic>
```

Putting the above two lines at the top of your HTML file will automatically direct employers to you if they search for the words listed under CONTENT. You can put as many words in that description as you want. The more, the merrier.

Giving your HTML résumé a title will also help to get it noticed. The title is what you see in the top left corner of your browser's screen:

```
<title>Joseph Bloggs Résumé</title>
Will add a title to your page.
```

Since the title of your HTML résumé and meta tags aren't part of the body of the résumé, they go before the **<body>** tag. Instead, these heading codes have their own tag, which is **<head>** and **</head>**. A typical introduction to an HTML résumé looks like this:

```
<html>

<head>

<METANAME=DescriptionCONTENT= Description
I am a terrific worker.>

<META NAME=Key WordsCONTENT=
HTML, Quark, Adobe, workaholic>

<title>This is my awesome résumé!
</title>
```

```
</head>

<body>
```

Links

Links are one of the most convenient features of the Internet. They allow users to hop around the Web with a simple click of the mouse, yet they're incredibly simple to create. For your résumé, linking prior jobs to their respective websites is a professional and handy way to say, "Look where I've worked." A prospective employer should appreciate your effort to make his or her research as simple as possible. Check out the following two lines of HTML code.

```
<a href= "http://www.review.com">
Review.com</a>

<ahref= "mailto:joe_bloggs@review.com">Joe Bloggs</a>
```

The first line above links Review.com to its URL. The second line links to Joe Bloggs's e-mail. Just use **<a href=** "http://www.x.com"**>** before the text you want to link, and a **</a>** to complete the tag. Link as many companies and references as possible. The easier you make it for employers to learn about you, the better chance you have of getting hired. Always remember to add the http:// at the start of a linked URL.

Tables

Tables are the jewels of simple HTML coding. They are a bit more complicated than the other coding tags, but learning them opens you up to whole new range of options. If you look at the most professionally designed Web pages (see www.review.com/career/car_wh_HTMLresume_bloggs.html), you'll notice that résumé information is justified on both the left and the right of the same line, creating an orderly layout that covers the screen—regardless of its size. This is done with a table.

<table COLS=2 WIDTH=100%>

The above tag sets up a table that looks like this:

Column 1	Column 2

The table, like the code says, has two columns and is the width of 100 percent of the screen. You can always add more columns or make the width smaller. It's up to you. You won't actually see the border of the table unless you type the word "border" (with no quotes) after the word "table." Play around and experiment with different border sizes.

You can enter information in either cell of the table separately, and then you can alter the text inside it without affecting the other information in the table. For instance, let's say you wanted to put your last job in the left box and the dates you worked there in the right. You start entering data in a table with a **<tr>** and end the data with a **</tr>**. Then the information in the individual boxes is marked with **<td>** and **</td>** tags. Check out the code below and the table that it produces:

```
<table COLS=2 WIDTH=100%>
<tr>
<td>Tenfold</td>
<td>August 1999–present</td>
</tr>
```

Tenfold	August 1999–present

Now, if you wanted to right-justify the dates of your last job, just type in the code for it before the text. To link to Tenfold, simply add the tags with the URL. Look at the HTML below:

```
<table COLS=2 WIDTH=100%>
<tr>
<td>
<a href= "http://www.tenfold.com">Tenfold</a>
</td>
<td><div align=right>August 1999–present</div>
</td>
</tr>
</table>
```

That's it. You've added justification and linked to your job. If you want to change the dimension of the cells, that's easy to do. If you want a cell to be 20 percent of the screen, just add **WIDTH=20%** as part of the **<td>** tag. Or if you want the cell to be 100 pixels wide, **WIDTH=100** will do it. Look at the code below:

```
<td WIDTH=30%><a href= "http://
www.tenfold.com">Tenfold<BF></a></td>
<td><div align=right>August 1999–present</div></td>
```

Your First Web Page

Believe it or not, you already know most of what you need to know to create your first Web page. Let's try it: First, locate a text editor on your computer. A text editor is a program that creates simple text documents. On a Windows PC, you can find a text editor named Notepad under Start Menu/Programs/ Accessories; on a Macintosh, you can usually find a similar program named SimpleText in the Applications folder on your hard drive.

Open your text editor and type in the following text. (We explained what each of these lines of codes mean earlier in this chapter.)

```
<html>
<head>
<title>
</title>
</head>
<body>
</body>
</html>
```

Between the **<title>** and **</title>** tags, enter a title for your résumé. Your full name followed by an apostrophe and then "Résumé" is usually a good bet. It'll look something like this when you're done:

> # Susan A. Jobseeker's Résumé

Between the **<body>** and **</body>** tags, type out your résumé using the format listed earlier (bullets, bold, tables, italics, different font sizes, and more!).

Line Breaks on Web Pages

 As you begin to experiment with HTML, you'll notice something strange about blank lines. Viewed in a Web browser, a document that contains this code:

```
<body>
Hello there!
Hello again!
</body>
```

will look exactly the same as a document that contains this code:

```
<body>
Hello there!


Hello again!
</body>
```

Because HTML is such a simple-minded language, it doesn't recognize the line breaks that you enter into your text editor. When you want to create a line break, you need to use the HTML tag <br>. You use it like this:

```
<body>
Hello there!
<br>
<br>
Hello again!
</body>
```

Don't forget to save your document. Be sure to note where you're saving it. It's probably easiest to save it on your computer's desktop.

You can give your HTML document a wide variety of names, but there are a few hard-and-fast rules.

@ The name must end in ".htm" or ".html" (the latter is preferred).

@ The name cannot contain spaces or certain nonalphanumeric characters (such as slash symbols). If you want the name to have a space in it, use an underscore (_).

@ Generally, the file name should be kept as short as possible.

You can now view your Web page using a Web browser.

First, locate a Web browser on your computer. Most computers come pre-equipped with a copy of Microsoft Internet Explorer and/or Netscape Navigator.

Use the Web browser's Open a Local File feature to open your HTML document. This feature has different names in different browsers, but it's usually called something like Open File.

Before you create your first Web page, you may want to use our sample résumés as guidelines. This will give you a head start on creating your own online résumé!

Sample Online Résumés

Take a look at the way a regular résumé can look in plain text—just the regular, standard résumé on the Web. Look below or at www.review.com/career/car_wh_htmlresume_bloggs_bad.html.

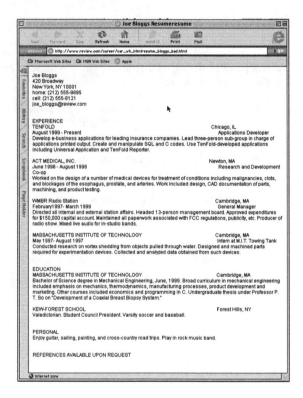

Now compare that plain (old) résumé with a polished online résumé. See below or at www.review.com/career/car_wh_htmlresume_Schmo.html. Notice how much more striking it is and how it fits the screen no matter what size you set it to. Check out the hyperlinks, which allow potential employers to learn about the companies you've worked for with one simple click. They'll appreciate the better presentation, and they'll value the ease with which they can research your background.

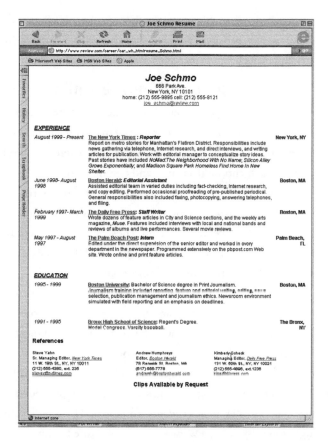

As you can see, the ability to apply advanced graphic design concepts can greatly enhance the inherent attractiveness of an online résumé. With a well-designed online résumé, it's possible to get the flavor of your personality across—and to provide a much more palpable sense of what you can offer potential employers.

Feel free to steal the HTML from the sample online résumé above. Put in your own information and pretend you did it from scratch; we won't tell. Be careful to copy this text very precisely; the smallest typo could drastically change how the page looks when you view it in a Web browser.

Take a look at how we've used the tags described earlier in this chapter. As you can see, these tags surround the text that you want to format. You'll soon see the dazzling results in your browser.

Getting Your Résumé Online

In order for you to share your résumé with the world, it needs to be copied onto a Web server—a computer that's connected to the Internet all the time and that's dedicated to hosting, or publishing, Web pages. There are two flavors of Web servers for you to choose from: free and commercial.

There are a number of popular free Web-hosting sites, including geocities.yahoo.com and www.tripod.com. An extensive list with reviews can be found at www.collfreewebhosting.com. These sites have the advantage of being easy to use, often requiring no knowledge of HTML or of FTP software. On the downside, most free Web-hosting sites offer only a very small amount of disk space—not enough to host a respectable portfolio. Also, advertisements will appear on every page that you create, and these sites can be excruciatingly slow to access. All in all, a free Web-hosting site may not communicate the most professional image, even if the price can't be beat.

Commercial Web servers allow you to buy Web space for a monthly or annual fee. Most ISPs offer Web-hosting packages. Some companies specialize in Web hosting and don't even offer Internet access. You can find hundreds of commercial Web-hosting options by doing a Web search for "website hosting."

Commercial Web-hosting sites are usually much faster than free sites and give you total control over the appearance and organization of your pages. You can also usually buy a cool personalized Web address (such as www.susansresume.com). To take advantage of these sites, though, you will need to learn some basic Web design and HTML skills, and you'll need to use FTP software. (If you remember from our Sending Files section on page 161, file transfer protocol software is free software that you can download from the Web and then use to send files to various places on the Internet—such as Web-hosting sites!)

Commercial Web space can be pricey, but you can economize by looking for hosting packages that offer only the features that you need: sufficient disk space

(20 to 30 MB should be enough to begin with), the ability to affordably add additional space, and domain-name registration services. In regard to the last item, don't be fooled by sites that merely offer you a "personalized Web address"; you may wind up with an address such as myportfolio.bobswebhosting.com. You need real domain registration, which allows you to choose any available Web address you want.

Do You Already Have Web Space?

You may already have Web space and not know it. Many Internet access accounts include a small amount of Web space; the space can be increased by paying a bit more per month. Contact your Internet service provider to find out if your account includes Web space.

Beyond the Basics: Learning Intermediate and Advanced Web Design

Once you have your online résumé up and running, you will no doubt be tempted to tweak it, update it, and give it a more attractive look. This is a good thing, as long as you don't neglect other aspects of your job search! There are many things that you can add to your online résumé, such as striking graphics, which we'll discuss in the next chapter.

In order to spiff up your online résumé, you're going to need to build up your Web design skills beyond what we've taught you here. The best place to learn about Web design is—you guessed it—on the Web. Do a Web search for "Web design tutorial" or "HTML tutorial," and you'll find many sites that can help you in this area. One of the best (and most amusing) intermediate Web design tutorial sites is www.webpagesthatsuck.com.

Many commercial Web editors also have design tutorials and Web page templates built into them; Web design how-to books are another option for improving your Web design skills.

Finally, Remember What You're Selling

It pays to put some time and thought into the graphic design/presentation aspect of your online résumé. Clumsy or ugly Web design may make a worse impression than not having a personal Web page at all. Put yourself in the position of a potential employer. What would a poorly designed online résumé communicate to you? It's a bit like showing up for an interview in a stained suit that's two sizes too small.

Chapter 15
Creating an Online Portfolio

Once you've started your online résumé, you may want to add samples of your work for prospective employers to peruse. Adding a few samples can change your online résumé into an interactive online portfolio.

The purpose of an online portfolio is the same as that of a physical portfolio: to showcase samples of your work for potential employers. If you've ever worked in a creative or media-related field, then you may already have a handsome bound folder full of writing samples or a cumbersome, coffee table–size imitation-leather bag full of drawings and/or printouts. An online portfolio fulfills the similar function of a traditional portfolio but with several interesting and advantageous differences.

- @ You can include a variety of nonpaper-based media such as animation, music, and programming samples.

- @ You can easily present your work in different ways for different audiences.

- @ An online portfolio is much easier to carry—just put the Web address of your online portfolio onto your résumé and/or business card.

Don't assume that you can't compile a portfolio just because your work is not creative. If you've produced work that can be in any way printed, transferred onto videotape or CD, photographed, or put onto a computer, then you have material to include in a portfolio. It's almost always possible to include some graphically attractive representation of the work you've done, no matter what your work may be.

In perhaps the most exciting development of all, it is now possible to include a wide array of multimedia (animation, sound, video, etc.) elements in an online résumé. With a little bit of imagination and the right tools, you can include such elements in your online portfolio. If they're done well, these multimedia elements rarely fail to impress.

An online portfolio is particularly important for freelancers. Employers on the lookout for contract employees will almost always be interested in seeing samples of your work, and the Internet can serve as an incredibly fast and convenient method of delivering such samples.

Gathering Your Materials

When deciding what to include in your online portfolio, you should keep in mind many of the same considerations that apply to physical portfolios.

@ Decide on a specific focus for your first portfolio (you can compile additional portfolios later). Ask yourself what kind of work you would like to do and in what environment you'd like to do it. The resulting focus can be as broad as "writing travel articles for websites" or as specific as a particular position at a particular company.

@ If you don't have enough existing material from school or previous jobs—and some of you might not have *any* such material—then create some. Be sure to dig through your archives, filing cabinets, and hard drives, and even contact previous employers if possible. You may have at some point in your career produced material that fits your focus.

@ Cut your compiled material down to a manageable size. The goal is to keep your portfolio as concise as possible; include only your best work, and make sure it is small enough to be quickly evaluated but still effectively showcases your skills.

This may mean different things in different contexts. You should include the pieces that you think will be most impressive to the particular companies or market to which you're targeting your portfolio. But the main point here is: Don't just put *all* of your work into your online portfolio—don't force potential employers to wade through material that may be of little interest to them. People who are responsible for hiring are almost always very busy. Don't make them spend half an hour sifting through your portfolio, fascinating though it may be.

@ Tailor your portfolio to the particular market in which you're seeking work.

The Internet provides remarkable flexibility and convenience in building a portfolio. Consider a person seeking work in both writing and photography. This person could put up a single portfolio page such as this:

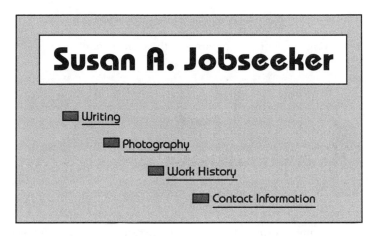

This method forces potential employers who are looking only for a writer to wade through the photography section of the portfolio—and for employers who are hiring only photographers to wade through the writing section. Not only does this waste employers' time—and the more time you make them waste, the more you risk losing their interest—but it also may give the impression that you are not wholly focused or specialized in one area. While some employers might consider multiple areas of expertise to be a selling point, others—perhaps most— might pass you over for someone equally qualified who specializes in the skill they're interested in.

The Internet gives you the flexibility to present multiple versions of your portfolio, each tailored to a specific market. Ms. Jobseeker, for example, could create two versions of her portfolio, one for writing and one for photography. She could then direct potential employers to one or the other.

You will probably be tempted to include material that you are particularly proud of. But just because it's good work doesn't necessarily mean that it's the sort of work that your potential employer is looking for. When compiling your portfolio, try to put yourself in the position of a prospective employer, and ask yourself, "Would this particular piece convince me that this person is right for the job?"

Design and Organization

When laying out your online portfolio, there are a couple of tips to keep in mind.

- @ Make the portfolio easy to understand. Include an introduction, an index with the title of each piece, and comments for each piece (attach these comments to the appropriate pieces).

- @ If possible, include testimonials and recommendations related to the work that you're showcasing.

You may be tempted to include quotes of recommendation as part of your online résumé, testifying to the quality of your work and to your reliability and worth as an employee. Including such generic recommendations is a bad idea. Potential employers are generally going to want to call your references anyway— and it's much better that they should hear words of praise directly from the source. By including these kinds of comments about yourself, you could make yourself seem immodest (and perhaps a bit desperate).

It can be very effective, however, to include specific comments about the work that's in your portfolio. If the people for whom you did the work can express their satisfaction with it—and, even better, be specific about how that particular work helped them to achieve their business goals—this can be a powerful selling point to others who may be in the market for your services.

Preparing Your Materials

Once you've decided what materials to include in your online portfolio, you need to prepare the materials for your website. If the material is already on your computer in one form or another, then you're halfway there. If not—if the material exists only in printed format or on videocassette, for instance—then you will need to digitize the material. That means you need to find a way to transfer it onto your computer.

Digitizing Text

If the material exists only on paper and you don't want to type the text in manually, then you'll need to scan the material into your computer. For text documents, you will need the following equipment:

@ A good scanner (600 dpi or better)

@ OCR (optical character recognition) software

Without OCR software, your scans will arrive on your computer as images, not as word processing documents. An image format does not allow for easy editing or for copying and pasting of the document's contents, and it's usually quite hard to read. This should definitely be avoided.

Once you've used the scanner and OCR software to get your documents onto your computer, you'll need to edit the documents, because OCR software is not 100 percent accurate. Depending on the quality of your scanner and which OCR software you're using, it'll be more like 98 percent—meaning that two words out of every 100 will be wrong. You'll need to track those words down in the document on your computer and correct them.

Also, OCR software usually does not deal very well with nontext elements on a printed page such as tables and graphics. This, too, will require editing in your word processor to correct.

Most OCR software has built-in features designed to help you get the best possible accuracy from your scans and to correct problems in the resulting word processing document. Read the software's manual carefully to learn about these features.

Digitizing Graphics

In order to transfer your noncomputer-based graphics work onto your computer, you will need

@ A scanner

@ Image-editing software

Since you are scanning only for the Web, a top-of-the line scanner is not required. Most scanners can handle only $8\frac{1}{2}$-by-11-inch or $8\frac{1}{2}$-by-14-inch documents. If you want to scan a larger piece, you have five options.

@ Locate a larger scanner.

@ Take a photograph of the work and scan the photo.

@ Take a digital photograph of the work and transfer the photo onto your computer.

@ Reduce the image on a photocopier and scan it (which will result in a loss of image quality, however, especially for photographic images).

@ Scan the piece in sections and reassemble the sections in Adobe Photoshop.

You will need Adobe Photoshop to edit your scanned document, because scans rarely, if ever, come out perfect. Photoshop is the industry standard for image-editing software, but you can use any such software as long as it allows you to save your images in GIF or JPEG format, which are the only two formats that are viewable with all Web browsers.

Digitizing Video

In order to transfer your work from videocassette to a computer, you'll need

@ An analog video capture card

@ Video-editing software

When selecting a capture card, keep in mind that you may want to output your computer-edited work back to videocassette; in that case, make sure that you get a capture card that has that capability.

If your work is in digital video format, then you'll need a FireWire (also called IEEE 1394) card instead of an analog video capture card. As with any other digitizing task, you'll want to edit your work once it's been transferred onto your computer.

Digitizing Audio

If your audio work is not already on your computer, you will need

@ A way to connect your audio device (minidisc player, DAT player, etc.) to your computer

@ Audio-editing software

Most computers have either an "audio in" or "microphone" ministereo jack, so all you will probably need to connect your audio device to your computer is a cable to connect to that jack.

If your audio work is on a CD, then (assuming that your computer has a CD drive) all you will need is CD-ripping software.

Optimizing Your Computer-Based Material

Once all of your portfolio pieces are on your computer, you will need to edit the material to make it presentable. When editing your material for uploading to your online portfolio, there are two major points to keep in mind.

@ You should make the material as attractive, impressive, and comprehensible as possible.

@ You should make the individual file sizes of your documents as small as possible. The less disk space your portfolio pieces take up, the less time it will take a prospective employer to download them. Try to keep your file size below 1 MB.

All of this digitizing and editing requires specialized hardware and software. If you can't find the appropriate tools, a sales associate at a good computer store should be able to help. Just don't let yourself get talked into shelling out big bucks. Educate yourself, evaluate your options, and decide what you really need. And keep in mind that copy shops and graphic service bureaus might be able to meet your needs more economically, especially if you need to use the services only once or twice.

Optimizing Text

If written material is going to be part of your portfolio, you have a number of different options for preparing it.

@ **Microsoft Word**

More likely than not, your material is in Microsoft Word format. If not, it's relatively easy to copy and paste the text into Word and save it as a Word document.

You can upload copies of your Word documents directly to your website, but this has several drawbacks. Not all prospective employers have a copy of Word or a compatible word processor. Even if they do, their version may be different than yours, which can cause strange things to happen when they try to open your Word documents. Also, Word documents are often replete with hidden codes and information. This may allow others to view, for instance, all of the deleted text and past revisions from your documents. Unless there is a compelling reason to use Microsoft Word format for your online text documents, you should choose one of the other options.

@ **HTML**

Word and some other word processors have an option to save any document as a Web page (or HTML document), which can then be uploaded to your portfolio site. Use what you've learned in chapter 14 to tweak your HTML document.

@ PDF

The PDF (portable document format) gives you total control over the fonts and general look of your documents; it's essentially like taking a snapshot of your document, except that those viewing the resulting PDF file can search, copy, and paste the text. If maintaining the exact look that your documents have on your computer's screen is important to you, then PDF is the best choice.

Virtually anyone on any kind of computer can read PDF documents. If you don't already have the necessary software, you can go to www.adobe.com and download it—it's called Adobe Acrobat Reader, and it's free. PDFs can be created from almost any kind of document, as long as the document contains only text and graphics. However, you'll need a copy of Adobe Acrobat (which costs several hundred bucks) to create PDFs.

Optimizing Graphics

If you have any work in Adobe Photoshop or Adobe Illustrator format, you could simply upload these files to your portfolio site, but there are two major drawbacks to using Photoshop or Illustrator files in your portfolio. First, the file sizes are huge compared to your other options. Second, anyone who wants to view them must have Photoshop or Illustrator. Instead, choose one of the compressed formats below. Photoshop, Illustrator, and most other computer graphics programs will allow you to save in these formats (or at least in the first two).

@ GIF

This format is the best choice for line drawings, cartoons, or any graphic that does not contain a huge number of gradients of colors. (Photographs almost always contain color gradients.)

@ JPEG

This format is the best choice for photos and anything with gradients of colors. When saving a document as a JPEG, you'll be given the option to set the "quality level"—usually from 1 to 10 or 1 to 100. The higher the quality level, the larger the file; the lower the quality level, the smaller the file, but the cruder it will look. This loss of quality will usually manifest itself in the form of fuzzy "halos" around the edges of objects; text usually becomes unreadable. We recommend choosing a quality level in the intermediate range.

@ **PDF**

Once again, this is a great choice for complex compositions including both text and graphics. (This is especially useful in advertising and graphic design work.)

Most Adobe products will allow you to save in PDF format directly from the product. When this is not possible, you will need to use the Adobe Acrobat software package.

Optimizing Video

If any of your work is already in the form of digitized (computer-based) video, then it's probably in one of the following formats:

@ QuickTime (.mov)

@ Video for Windows (.avi)

@ MPEG (.mpg)

Any one of these formats will be fine for inclusion in an online portfolio, but in general, QuickTime is your best bet. It is easily readable on both Windows and Macintosh computers (which are very common in creative industries) by downloading the free QuickTime Player from www.apple.com/quicktime. It also provides good image quality with relatively small file sizes.

If you're working on a Macintosh, Cleaner from Terran Interactive Software (www.terran.com/cleaner) is a great software tool for minimizing video file sizes while maintaining high image quality.

Optimizing Audio

If you have digitized audio files that you'd like to include in your online portfolio, the MP3 format is your best bet. It can provide CD-quality sound while keeping file sizes small. (The only exception to this might be in the case of electronically composed music, where the MIDI format is the industry standard.)

Optimizing Web Work

If you want to include Web design work that you've done, the simplest thing to do is to include a link on your portfolio website. Beware, though: Unless you have full control over it, work that you've done in the past may be taken offline or updated. To protect yourself, always keep a copy of Web design work that you've done.

If you haven't kept a copy on your computer, or if the online version looks better than your copy as a result of design work done by others, you can download your Web pages (including graphics and other content) using a program such as PageSucker.

If you choose to include Web pages that include work by others, you should first get permission from them. Then you should credit the collaborators in your portfolio.

Online Hosting Options

Once you have your material compiled, optimized, and ready to upload, you need to find a place to upload it. Choose one of three basic options: the free or commercial Web space discussed in the previous chapter or specialized portfolio-hosting sites.

You can upload your material to a site that hosts portfolios, such as www.elance.com or www.portfolios.com. These sites will charge you a monthly fee for this service. The advantage is that you usually don't need to know anything about Web design or HTML. The disadvantage is that you don't have total control over how your portfolio pages will look; usually, you will have to put your material onto pages that are predesigned by the website.

De-digitizing

As useful as online portfolios can be, there are still many circumstances in which you need a traditional physical portfolio. Perhaps the employer does not have Internet access, has a slow connection, or is simply not computer-savvy. Plus, physical portfolios are a requirement in some interviews.

When you're working on a physical portfolio, you may want to include computer-based material. Depending on the format of your work, you may have to create printouts, burn a CD, or output your work to videotape.

When "de-digitizing" your work, you'll want to achieve the highest-quality output possible. You will need specialized hardware and software to get the best results. Your local print shop or service bureau can help with some of this, and manuals included with the hardware can also provide guidance.

If you have computer-based work that you'd like to include in a physical portfolio, you should create a hard copy of your work. In the case of images, you will want to create high-quality printouts. If you don't have a high-quality printer, spend the extra money in a local print shop or service bureau; it's worth it. If you have access to a CD burner, you can also burn a CD of your work. (This presupposes that your interviewer is computer-literate.) When burning CDs, keep the same design rules in mind that you would use with an online portfolio. The CD needs to be easy to navigate, and the material needs to be well presented. You may want to include a Readme file explaining how to use the CD.

Unlike an online portfolio, a physical portfolio involves performing: Usually, you will need to present your physical portfolio in an interview. Be sure to practice presenting your portfolio first so that your presentation will seem natural, relaxed, and professional. And keep it short, or you risk losing the interviewer's interest!

Copyright Issues

The growing popularity of online portfolios raises a host of thorny copyright issues. Following the simple rules below will help keep you out of trouble.

Don't Rip Off Others

Make sure that you own everything you're including in your portfolio. In many cases, the employer for whom you produced a particular piece of work owns it. You'll need to get explicit written permission from the owner(s) of your work before uploading it to the Internet.

Don't Get Ripped Off by Others

If you are the owner of a piece that you're putting on your portfolio site, you'll want to protect yourself from potential thievery. Here are some tips.

- @ Incorporate copyright information into each of your pieces. It's easy to add copyright information to each of your Web pages. If you want to protect yourself, do it.

- @ Use the lowest quality digitizing that you can accept. For images, keep the image dimensions small and the quality less than top-notch; this will discourage theft.

- @ Consider using small sample portions of your material instead of entire works. For example, if your portfolio includes video or animation work, you might include just a few seconds of the work—enough to show your talents—rather than an entire piece, which could be stolen

- @ Add watermarks to images. Watermarks are available in Adobe Photoshop and other image-editing programs; they superimpose a semitransparent, embossed-looking image of your design over an image. Your watermark image can be simply a text-only copyright notice or your name, or it can include graphic elements.

Compiling Multiple Portfolios

If you have chosen more than one focus for your job search, you will want to compile more than one portfolio. This concept seems simple enough when applied to physical portfolios, but how should you go about creating multiple online portfolios? The answer depends on which Web-hosting option you've chosen.

@ If you've chosen free Web hosting, the easiest thing to do is simply to sign up for multiple free accounts with different user names.

@ If you've chosen a portfolio-hosting site, you should be able to create multiple portfolios showcasing different areas of talent. Consult the technical support for the particular site.

@ If you've chosen commercial Web space, put each of your portfolios into a different directory. You could create separate directories for a writing portfolio and a photography portfolio, which would allow you to use two different Web addresses. For example, www.susanjobseeker.com/writer and www.susanjobseeker.com/photographer would separate the portfolios.

Get Help and Get Inspired

Remember that the best place to learn about computers and the Internet is on the Internet. Having trouble with scanning? Go to your favorite search engine and do a search for "how to scan." Want to learn how to transfer your work from videocassette to the Web? Search for "how to digitize video." And because one of the most powerful learning tools for any task is to check out how others have done it before you, try searching for "online portfolio." You will find thousands of existing online portfolios to inspire you.

Finally, keep in mind that, just like an online résumé, an online portfolio is not a magic key to a job—it's a tool to add to your tool kit of online job-search strategies.

Chapter 16
Attracting Employers' Attention

Once you have an online résumé and/or portfolio, the next issue is what, exactly, to do with it. You should not expect potential employers to find your online presence on their own. Instead, think of your online presence as an enhancement to your traditional résumé and portfolio. You wouldn't leave your résumé and samples of your work posted on bus stops and bulletin boards around your town, would you? No, you would probably try to get your résumé and portfolio into the hands of people who are interested in hiring someone like you. The strategy should be the same with your website. You should try to get its address into the hands of people who might hire you.

Getting Your URL into the Hands of Employers

When trying to get your Web address into the hands of potential employers, keep in mind that a personal contact, rather than an e-mail, is best. Don't believe that you can run your entire life (or even the job-searching part of your life) via the Internet. E-mail from a stranger can be lost, overlooked, or easily deleted; a personal conversation will be remembered. You're better off sharing your Web addresses verbally once you've established a communication with the other person.

It can be awkward to give someone your Web address verbally, however, unless it's a remarkably simple one (such as www.myportfolio.com); this is one reason why it's great to have a very simple Web address. Unfortunately, for most Web addresses, you may well find yourself reduced to spelling out the address character by character. This is usually an annoying experience for both parties ("Right after the L, you should put a forward slash—no, a forward slash, not a backward slash—it's on the same key as the question mark . . . "). Rather than putting yourself through this painful process, you should use a different method of conveying your Web address.

@ If you're in a face-to-face meeting, write your Web address down. Better yet (to avoid misinterpretation of handwriting), present a business card or a résumé with the Web address highlighted.

@ If you're communicating via phone, ask for an e-mail address to which you can send your Web address or a fax number to which you can send a résumé that includes your Web address.

Put It on the Network

Another way to disseminate your Web address is to show your site to friends, colleagues, and acquaintances. You never know who might be in a position to further your job search. This kind of networking can be one of the most effective methods of job searching. If your website is impressive enough, they may pass it on to a potential employer via word of mouth.

Are *They* Searching for *You*?

You may want to get your website to show up in various search engines. You can do this by visiting search engine sites and reading their instructions on how to submit your site. When you're creating your pages, be sure to use meta tags, as described on page 171. Search engines use meta tags to help people find your site. For example, if you have a Key Words meta tag of "photographer," a Web search for "photographer" should list your page.

There are a few rules of thumb to follow when adding meta tags.

@ In the Description meta tag, make your description as, well, descriptive as possible. The entire contents of this tag may be displayed on a search results page, so try to make your description as intriguing as possible to potential employers.

@ In the Key Words meta tag, make your key words as specific as possible. For example, if you're a freelance writer for children's books, don't just put "freelance"; put "freelance, writer, write, writing, books, children, young, stories, creative, fun." The more key words you use, the more visitors you'll wind up attracting.

@ Make sure that you put meta tags on *all* of your pages, not just your main page. Some search engines will index every page of your site, which could either bring you higher up on the search results pages or give you more listings on those pages. Either way, the tags increase your chances of being found by a potential employer.

Adding meta tags alone isn't going to do the trick, though—it's like hoping that your business will flourish just because your phone number is in the Yellow Pages. So don't just sit there; go register your site with those Web search engines. By registering with a particular search engine, you guarantee that your site will show up (somewhere) on the results pages if someone does the right kind of search.

A good way to get started is to go to www.searchenginewatch.com. This useful site not only lists all of the major search engines but also gives you tips on how to register your site with each one. The process varies from search engine to search engine—it can be as simple as submitting your Web address, though most will ask for more extensive information. Just make sure that you read the site-submission instructions carefully (look for a link named something like Submit Your Site or Add a Site). Among other useful information, these instructions will also often tell you how long it will take for your site to be added to the search engine's database—a process that can sometimes take several weeks.

It's possible to purchase software that will do the grunt work of site submission for you, submitting your site to hundreds or even thousands of search engines. You should probably save your money for other endeavors; once your site has been submitted to the major search engines, other search engines will pick it up anyway.

Here's a trick that may help you show up more prominently on search engine results pages: Pretend you're an employer, go to a search engine site, and do a search for someone like you. Take a look at the top results. If you can mimic (without plagiarizing or misrepresenting yourself, of course) the content of these pages, then your site may also rise to the top of the results pages. Try looking at the HTML code for these top-ranked pages (most Web browsers allow you to do this) and see what meta tags they use.

Keep in mind that different search engines have different methods of generating search "hits" on your site. Some will simply use the information that you give when you submit your site; others will use your meta tags; some will index all of the words on your pages; some will use a combination of all of these methods. You can learn more about the nitty-gritty of how search engines do what they do at www.searchenginewatch.com/webmasters/work.html.

Another way to attract attention to your site is to submit your address to sites dedicated to your particular profession. (For example, Playbill.com offers a site-linking service for actors.) Rather than fishing for attention from the entire online world, you're advertising your site directly to your peers. Check with your favorite profession-related site to see if they have a service like this.

Don't forget to put your Web address on every piece of printed material that's related to your career: flyers, résumés, business cards, whatever. You'll probably be pleasantly surprised by the results—often, people who wouldn't go out of their way to learn more about you in the real world will take the time to check out a website.

Use Your Time Wisely

 The process of submitting your website to search engines is time-consuming, and your time might be better spent on other aspects of your job search. There are companies that will offer to submit your website to dozens of search engines for a fee or sell you software that purports to do the same thing. Some services will even assert that they can help you get a "high ranking" on these search engines—that is, that your website will show up near the top of results pages. Unless you have money to spare, don't waste your time with these services. No matter how high you rank in search engines, prospective employers rarely use search engines to shop for employees. See chapter 17 for more efficient job-hunting resources.

Chapter 17
Internet Job-Hunting Resources

The Internet is chock-full of resources for job seekers. There are sites that list open positions, sites that allow you to contact employers, sites that will give you general job-hunting tips, and even sites that provide real-time interviews. So where do you start?

Job Boards

Most people think of job hunting on the Web and immediately think of job-board sites, where employers post online Help Wanted ads. Think of these sites as more convenient versions of your local newspaper's help-wanted section. Job-board sites have some significant advantages over newspapers. First, the job postings online are searchable, which saves a lot of time and effort. Second, online job ads are usually quite detailed because the Web does not impose the same kind of space constraints that newspapers do.

Job-board sites can give you a good sense of what the job market is like; you can easily see what sort of skills are being sought by employers, which industries are hiring in your area, and so on. Among the most popular general-interest job-board sites are

@ www.monster.com

@ www.hotjobs.com

@ www.jobsonline.com

@ www.vault.com

@ www.careerbuilder.com

@ careers.yahoo.com

@ www.americasjobbank.com

@ www.flipdog.com

@ www.jobbankusa.com

@ www.headhunter.net

Freelancers' Sites

There are a few sites that cater specifically to the needs of people who prefer contract work rather than full-time employment.

Freelancers' sites simplify the contractor-search aspect of a freelancer's life by offering online contract job postings. Two of the most popular freelancer's sites are www.elance.com and www.guru.com. But www.elance.com has one major drawback: Only subscribers get access to the higher-paying contract jobs; www.guru.com has no such restrictions.

Industry-Specific Sites

You can significantly narrow your job search by visiting sites that have job postings for the particular industry in which you're interested. The Sites section of this book, beginning on page 207, will cover this area in great detail.

Individual Employers' Sites

One efficient online job-search strategy is to target specific employers and visit their specific websites to get employment information. Not all employers have actual job postings on their sites, but it's definitely worth looking. If you don't know an employer's Web address, you can, of course, search for the organization's site using your favorite search engine. If you still can't find it, you can always use that reliable nineteenth-century technology—the telephone. Call the employer's main number and ask if it has a website.

For sites that don't have job postings, you can at least educate yourself about the companies that you're targeting.

Usenet

Before the World Wide Web exploded in popularity in the mid-1990s, Usenet was one of the hottest spots in cyberspace. It has now been pushed aside because the Web is easier to use and because Usenet is text-only—no graphics or multimedia elements.

There are a number of different ways to access Usenet, but the simplest way is via the Web at groups.google.com. Many of the hierarchies (the links beginning with "alt," "biz," etc.) have job groups in them. Try this:

@ From groups.google.com, click on the alt link.

@ From the alt page, pull down the menu in the upper left-hand corner, and select the alphabetical range within which the word "jobs" falls.

@ On the resulting page, click on the "alt.jobs" link. You'll be taken to a page that has job listings and (at the top of the page) further subgroups with even more job listings

Due to the somewhat esoteric nature of Usenet, its job postings are heavily slanted toward highly technical, and especially computer-related, jobs. Other jobs may be found here as well, however, so it's worth a look.

Support, Advice, and Job Training

Finally, there are sites that, while they may not offer actual job listings, will help you become a better job surfer. These sites offer job-searching advice and information, sort of like an online employment center.

Many job sites have features like this built into them; Monster.com's subsite content.monster.com is one example. Two good sites that specialize in support and advice are www.jobsmart.com and www.jobhuntersbible.com.

Chapter 18
Moving Forward

The rest of this book will help you use the Internet to advance your job search. However, you should continue to research non-Internet-based strategies. You're already pursuing one of them by reading this book. In this book, you'll find sites that will in turn suggest more real-world job-search strategies. By exploring this complex interrelationship between the real world and the virtual world, you'll be empowered to search for jobs in ways that you never imagined—and that will give you an edge over the conventional job searcher.

Keeping Up with New Internet Resources

Once you've taken your first steps toward being a successful online job searcher, remember that the Internet is constantly shifting. By the time you read this, there may be some great sites and useful resources that aren't in this book because they didn't exist at the time of its printing. In order to keep up with these new developments, you should do some creative surfing. Periodically search for job-related sites on www.yahoo.com and your other favorite search engines.

Part Four

The Sites

The following list of freelance job-seeking websites has been rated on a five-star rating system, with one star indicating a general waste of precious online electrons and five stars indicating a virtual job-finding megastar. What's important to a writer, however, may not be to a graphic artist or Web page designer. Therefore, each site has been thoroughly surfed by qualified, watchful freelance eyes so that an accurate assessment can be made in several discriminate categories about its helpfulness to you as a freelance professional, a free agent, or an independent contract worker. Critical consideration has been given to a wide range of anticipated career concerns so that freelancers in all areas can determine the site's usefulness in finding jobs. Specific areas of interest are categorized. Categories critiqued include general information about the site, such as the primary market to which it is directed (employers, freelancers, or independent contractors); the specific features that can be used at the site, such as whether your résumé can be posted, how long it will stay posted, or if you will receive e-mail notifications from interested contractors after it is posted; and the notable services that are available at the site, such as links to worthwhile sites, interesting and valuable career articles, or helpful job-seeking tips.

When you are a freelancer, time is the most valuable asset you own. In order to maximize the savings of your assets, each review also provides a brief synopsis of the site's major weaknesses, its usability, and its general helpfulness to you as a freelancer or free-agent worker. Finally, we'll help you decide if the site is worth the investment of your inestimable freelance time.

Ajr.newslink

www.ajr.newslink.org

Markets Served

Employers:
> Yes.

Job seekers:
> Somewhat. For a potential employee (job seeker), this site is a good use of time and a good place to put your résumé online. While you wait for the employer to contact you, go to other websites and practice your key-word searching skills.

Fee for job seekers:
> No.

Type of professionals:
> As the JobLink page says, "JobLink, the fastest way to hire a journalist."

Information

Job listings:
> Yes, but the strength of this site is in the résumé-posting service. Without specifying jobs (no key words), we asked the JobLink for a list of jobs and received seventy-six openings.

Articles:
> Typing in "freelance writing" and clicking on the Search button brought back links to 1,746 articles in alphabetical order. That'll keep you busy.

Facts and figures:
> This site has excellent resources for working and job-seeking journalists. There are links to news, business, journalism organizations, e-mail forums, publishers and academic resources, newsletters, marketing research, lists of news sites, and good job-search starting points for journalists.

Contacts:
> Because this site is less commercialized than many others, you'll find plenty of contacts in the archives and news articles.

Training:
> No.

Recruitment:
> No.

Placement:
No.

Tools
Résumé posting:
There is a résumé-posting place called a JobLink ad. We put ours up for free. It looked cool!

E-mail from the website came immediately. It said: "This advertisement was posted free as a service to you as a job seeker. If you need to make changes, you must make them online. We regret that we are unable to accept changes to free ads by telephone or e-mail."

Portfolio:
If you have a website with some of your projects shown (photos of your trophies, your blue ribbon from the fair, your National Book Award), this site will allow a link from your want ad to your site.

Skills test:
No.

Edit résumé:
You can edit your résumé (they call it your work wanted ad) only until you click the button to send it to their database, so read it carefully. The e-mail said that you can make changes online, but it wasn't specific, nor did it explain how.

How long you will stay posted:
Your résumé will stay online for five weeks.

Automatic notice to employer if user inquires?
No.

Automatically sends your résumé?
Yes. Our first e-mail back explained that in addition to posting our JobLink advertisement on the website, they had "just completed e-mailing copies of it to four readers who previously registered to receive copies of all new ads in the combination of categories in which your ad is included."

Notification when a matching job is available?
No.

Perks
The search feature also works throughout their archives of news stories. Try "toothache" and you'll have no luck, but "salmon" will give you five articles.

Listing and Compensation Data
Number of employers offering jobs:
No data.

Good salary ranges?
> No data.

Overall Navigability
Strengths:
> You can decide to submit your own ad or look at newspaper jobs. You can also find good articles and features. This is a clean site with little advertising, which makes it an easy place to browse through.

Weaknesses:
> Job seekers may be worried about the cost of placing their résumé, because the site says the ads are "risk free." This is not a big weakness but one for the site owners to consider. The direct-marketing verbiage is suspect, so you'll think you're going to be charged or asked for a credit card number. The site owners should remove the word "risk" and replace it with the word "free."

Usability:
> Relatively easy.

General Review
Synopsis:
> This is a website for journalists, and although sales and marketing and Web programming and design jobs are included, the jobs are all within the journalism industry. It is primarily a place to sell your services, not a place to search for jobs.

Helpfulness and value to freelancers:
> Good.

Waste of time online?
> Not at all.

Aquent

Markets Served

Employers:
> Yes.

Job seekers:
> Yes.

Fee for job seekers:
> No.

Type of professionals:
> This organization places writers, editors, proofreaders, graphic designers, Web designers, production people, presentation graphics designers, illustrators, project managers, and desktop support staff in freelance, permanent, and "try-before-you-hire" jobs.

Information

Job listings:
> Before you apply to work for Aquent, you can peek at some available jobs. You don't learn much when you click on Express Interest in This Job, as they require you to have an Aquent application code number. The first job found was for a permanent position with an unnamed employer in our chosen city in our skills field, so you don't get only contract freelance work in your searches. Permanent work is not standard through a temp agency, so we clicked on the Chat Line, asked how that happened, and received the answer immediately: Many permanent workers wind up becoming an employee of the client.

Facts and figures:
> Aquent says that last year they "brought together" more than 30,000 professionals and client companies.

Contacts:
> You can chat in real time with someone from Aquent from 8 A.M. to 9 P.M. ET, or you can send Aquent e-mail. You can't contact any of their clients.

Training:
> Aquent has a partnership with two training companies that will give registered Aquent members "special rates" on training fees.

Recruitment:
   No.
Placement:
   Yes.

Tools
Résumé posting:
   Yes.
Portfolio:
   You can attach samples to your posted résumé.
Skills test:
   Yes.
Edit résumé:
   This site does not allow applicants to edit their résumés
   online. If you've applied to Aquent and would like to make
   changes to your résumé, send an e-mail to
   questions@Aquent.com. If you're a registered Aquent talent
   and have been given MyAquent access, you may attach an
   updated version of your résumé online using the Update
   Profile function. If you're registered to work through Aquent
   and don't have MyAquent access, contact your local office if
   you have one in your city.
How long you will stay posted:
   As long as you want.
Automatic notice to employer if user inquires?
   Yes.
Automatically sends your résumé?
   Yes.
Notification when a matching job is available?
   Yes.

Perks
   You can download and read (using Adobe Acrobat) several
   great free guides that are written for the employer client. They
   are chock-full of helpful data for the employee, too. The
   Proposal Skill & Price Guide tells what roles certain
   professionals can fill for the employer, defines what they do
   throughout the production process (of creating a printed
   piece, for example), and outlines what pay ranges the employer
   should be expected to offer.
       It's a little confusing, but the site offers two ways to get paid:
   directly from the client or directly from Aquent. The company
   website has a billing service for independent professionals. It says:
   "For a fee, which can go as low as 3 percent, a member enjoys all

the advantages of their own credit department: 1) payment for invoices within two days instead of thirty to ninety days; 2) a professional staff to make all follow-up collection calls; and 3) for established members, a credit-checking service for new clients." The company also provides an insurance brokerage service designed "exclusively for independent professionals who don't necessarily work through an agency."

Listing and Compensation Data

Number of employers offering jobs:
> No data.

Good salary ranges?
> According to Aquent's salary guide for employer clients, the salary ranges are very good.

Overall Navigability

Strengths:
> It is super easy for both talent and client to get what they need from this Internet agency.

Weaknesses:
> The company is not open enough. They are too reticent with pertinent details. Unless you are very talented in your specialty, you're probably not going to get in.

Usability:
> Good.

General Review

Synopsis:
> This is not really an online job search website. It is an employment agency that puts you and one of their clients together to get the client's job done. You are working for the agency, not the client, and either the client or the agency pays you. Time cards and benefits are included in the package. Because this is really a staffing agency that has recently jumped online, their seriousness with their task is obvious. You'll have to pass some qualifying tests and interviews to get on their lists, but that's to your advantage from the looks of Aquent's history.

Helpfulness and value to freelancers:
> You're not really working for yourself, and it may be hard to find home-based work, but it wouldn't hurt to get on board.

Waste of time online?
> No.

ArtHire

www.arthire.com

Markets Served

Employers:
> Yes.

Job seekers:
> Yes.

Fee for job seekers:
> No.

Type of professionals:
> Visual, sound, and writing are the main categories of skills. These have thirty-three, six, and ten subcategories, respectively, so there's lots of places for you to look for jobs.

Information

Job listings:
> To see the job openings, choose "Any" job, location, and type of contract, and you'll get twenty-eight jobs, from Web designer to exhibit fabricator artist to prepress production manager. We chose Creative Writing as a type of job, no specific location, no specific contract (i.e., full time, part time, temp, etc.). The two jobs found were one and two months old. To apply, you must join the website.

Articles:
> No.

Facts and figures:
> No.

Contacts:
> Employers cannot directly contact the artists.

Training:
> No.

Recruitment:
> No.

Placement:
> No.

Tools

Résumé posting:

You can create an extensive résumé and include photos or samples of your work.

Portfolio:

You'll want to be Web-savvy before you put your portfolio together for this website. They have specific requirements for visual artists, music/sound/voice artists, and writers. You may submit as many as ten samples in each category, a nice bonus. They give you a nice listing of the supported files, maximum pixel height and width, and byte maximums for posting. For writers, for example, the maximum number of characters allowed in each sample is 20,000, a good-size document.

Skills test:

No.

Edit résumé:

Yes.

How long you will stay posted:

No indication was given.

Automatic notice to employer if user inquires?

No

Automatically sends your résumé?

No information.

Notification when a matching job is available?

At their Auto Notify button it says: "Use Auto Notify to receive an e-mail whenever a new job (or new art list) meeting your search criteria is posted on ArtHire."

Perks

Employers looking for artists do not heavily use this site, so the best tool is the portfolio section. Find out what your fellow artists are doing. You'll find out about their rates, the quality of their work, and other important information.

The site has concise directions on how you can send in your work for display or for sale. A Store button allows people to view and purchase some of the art submitted to the site.

Listing and Compensation Data

Number of employers offering jobs:

Twenty-eight.

Good salary ranges?

Very little salary information is given.

Overall Navigability

Strengths:

There is a site map right behind the homepage, so you'll be happy.

Weaknesses:

We wonder if their Webmaster is on vacation. Either the submissions of several writers are definitely in the wrong category, or speech writing has changed since the days of Toastmasters. The speech-writing category contains e-mail marketing, a fiction story, and a newspaper article on gang violence.

Usability:

This is an extremely useful website for both employee and employer. It's a good site where the employers can silently "interview" talent and study résumés in the privacy of their laptop.

General Review

Synopsis:

As a freelancer, you need exposure to find jobs. This site's employment service allows you to list your own portfolio. You can also search for jobs by choosing Employment and then Job Search, where you enter the category of your skill. Give the site time, and perhaps it will catch the attention of employers. If you have a great-looking portfolio, this place is almost as good as having your own website.

Helpfulness and value to freelancers:

Very helpful.

Waste of time online?

Absolutely not.

BestJobsUSA +

www.bestjobsusa.com

Markets Served

Employers:
   Yes.

Job seekers:
   Yes.

Fee for job seekers:
   No.

Type of professionals:
   All types are invited here, but primarily those seeking full-time work.

Information

Job listings:
   Yes.

Articles:
   Go to Guidance in the Workplace from the Site Jump Menu at the bottom of each page. Christian pastors write the articles, which is bound to be a different experience for you than the standard freelance job-search site.

Facts and figures:
   There's good information here on many of the nation's larger cities, the location of career fairs and trade shows throughout the country, and ratings on the best places to live and work. Although there are some interesting statistics, most of it reads like the Encyclopedia Britannica.

Contacts:
   You'll find contacts only for employment agencies.

Training:
   No.

Recruitment:
   Check out Best Places to Live and Work. You may not agree with the choices, and your hometown may not be listed, but the links are very useful for someone serious about relocating. Each of the top twenty best places has a Web page created by BestJobsUSA to tell you about the community. It also lists thirty to forty of the largest employers in that area, a routine

that may be helpful in figuring out which could be approached for freelance work.

Placement:
Yes.

Tools

Résumé posting:
When you create a profile, you can post your résumé on it.

Portfolio:
No, but you can give your URL in your résumé.

Skills test:
No.

Edit résumé:
Yes.

How long you will stay posted:
You can remove your résumé whenever you want; otherwise it may stay for an undetermined time.

Automatic notice to employer if user inquires?
No.

Automatically sends your résumé?
No.

Notification when a matching job is available?
Yes. You can enter job categories, locations in which you are willing to take freelance work, and key words that will help potential employers locate you when they're searching for workers or freelancers with your skills. You can enter only three key words. If you are skilled in more than three classifications, you may want to post more than one résumé with this website.

Perks

Look for the Site Jump Menu at the bottom of the About Us page. It's not as visually helpful as a full-page site map, but it will let you see the many offerings.

The Career Fairs link is one of the best on the Internet. You'll be directed to career fairs throughout the country to find forty-seven in Oregon, thirty-seven in Missouri, and three in Maine. You can also find some good-quality lists of trade shows around the country.

The site is obvious in its displays to the Best Places to Live and Work pages. If you pick, say, Omaha and San Diego—two of their top twenty places—you'll get straightforward information, no tricky links to major national employers or employment services as you might expect. There are loads of cool data about the cities listed with opinions as to why they are best.

A helpful area is the list of major associations and federal government agencies in the United States. These organizations are designed to help you, the professional, research and keep updated on issues affecting your industry and career. You can connect to nearly 100 legitimate professional and trade associations in industries such as business, computers/IT, engineering, environmental, federal government, health care, human resources, and others.

Listing and Compensation Data
Number of employers offering jobs:
No data.
Good salary ranges?
Average.

Overall Navigability
Strengths:
This site is one of the easiest to navigate on the Internet, probably because of its clean design. There are no distracting banner ads, crazy animations, or flashy marquees scrolling across the page.
Weaknesses:
There were none noticeable enough to mention.
Usability:
Easy.

General Review
Synopsis:
This is the website of Resource Communications, a staffing firm. They claim that "each day company account executives speak to more than 1,500 hiring managers and human resource professionals. The company monitors national recruitment activity by subscribing and archiving in excess of 300 major newspapers' employment sections, and has a constantly updated database of over 300,000 professional candidates." That's disappointing if you don't want to wait in line behind 300,000 people. On the other hand, the Internet lets you look for freelance work while you're standing in the cyberline somewhere. So, posting your freelance résumé or portfolio here may put you in the right line at the right place. Good luck!
Helpfulness and value to freelancers:
The Job-Search database doesn't have a choice to categorize contract jobs. The key word "freelance" got twenty-six jobs, all in the graphic arts industry. Using "independent agent" got two job postings and "temporary" got seventy-nine. Hint: Even

though there isn't a category for contract workers, you can offer that kind of arrangement with a company that is looking for your specific skills or talents. On the Internet, as anywhere else, nothing ventured is nothing gained.

Waste of time online?

No.

Black-Collegian

www.black-collegian.com

Markets Served

Employers:

> Yes. The employer member profiles list a wide variety of fields, including state departments of education, the Social Security Administration, the military, school districts, accounting firms, banks, retail store chains, universities, and even the IRS.

Job seekers:

> Yes.

Fee for job seekers:

> No.

Type of professionals:

> According to the site, "Black collegians and all people of color seeking career and self-development information."

Information

Job listings:

> 1,000.

Articles:

> You bet! The site offers excellent and informative articles from *The Black Collegian* magazine on career advice specifically geared to the unique employment situations faced by people of color in the United States.

Facts and figures:

> You can find many statistics and helpful facts in the articles reprinted here.

Contacts:

> In addition to the many links to employers, there are links to other sources of information specific to minority issues, including those of Asian Americans, Hispanic Americans, Native Americans, and other world cultures.

Training:

> No.

Recruitment:

> It seems obvious that the employers that sponsor the site and buy the ads are seriously recruiting from among minority college-educated people. Many of the job postings are at the

senior level. When you open up one of the ads (i.e., senior nurse practitioner), you get extensive information about the pharmaceutical company that placed the ad, along with the job description. So even if you're not ready for senior level just yet, this is a good place to learn about the companies that appear committed to providing equal opportunities and diversity in the workplace.

Placement:

As far as placing you in a freelance position with a company, there doesn't seem to be many offerings. However, we emphasize that this is a good place to hang out and study the terrain.

Tools

Résumé posting:

You must create an account (no fee) to post your résumé. There's the typical form to fill out, and you'll choose a password.

Portfolio:

No.

Skills test:

No.

Edit résumé:

You can edit your résumé and profile.

How long you will stay posted:

No data.

Automatic notice to employer if user inquires?

We think so.

Automatically sends your résumé?

You choose to apply for a job that interests you.

Notification when a matching job is available?

You can create a search agent that will e-mail you when a job listing matches your criteria.

Perks

Click on Employer Profiles. You'll find links to more than fifty companies offering jobs through Black-Collegian.

Click on Graduate/Professional School in the index to move to a plethora of articles and links to "organizations assisting people of color in graduate and professional studies." Good substantive material has been placed on this great, serious website.

You may also ask that your identity be kept private. If you check "confidential," your information and current position will be hidden from potential employers. They can then contact you only via e-mail.

Listing and Compensation Data

Number of employers offering jobs:

Fifty-six.

Good salary ranges?

Example: The entry-level salary suggested for a retail sales worker in a major city is nothing to brag about and not much to live on in most big cities (high of $30,000).

Overall Navigability

Strengths:

The index on the homepage is great.

Weaknesses:

None, unless you were hoping for a bigger database of jobs.

Usability:

Good.

General Review

Synopsis:

It may say it's for college students and graduates, but this website is excellent for anyone curious about employment opportunities for people of color in this country. You're still in high school? Log on to learn about hundreds of roads ahead.

Helpfulness and value to freelancers:

Somewhat helpful, depending on the company.

Waste of time online?

No.

CareerBuilder

www.careerbuilder.com

Markets Served

Employers:
Yes.
Job seekers:
Yes.
Fee for job seekers:
No.
Type of professionals:
All.

Information

Job listings:
Using the site's Megajobsearch button, you can click on a map of the United States to find out what companies are hiring in each state. This is a cooperative venture with other job-search services. You can also choose a company (from an alphabetical list, if it's listed) to see if that company is hiring. We found that many of the jobs listed under a particular city are with national firms that put their data into many cities. (Tip: Kinko's is hiring everywhere!) Your chosen company may have an opening in your chosen city but also may list twenty other openings in other cities on the same page.

Articles:
This site has articles galore. There are seventy excellent articles on the subject "getting ahead at work" alone. There is also an article on the results of a survey conducted by this website. Specifically, the survey aimed to discern how the Internet has influenced our lives at work and at home, including the use of e-mail at work and home and whether we spend more or less time at work because of these new tools. There is a recommended reading list, and you can order the books by following the supplied link to Amazon.

Facts and figures:
The site's Megajobsearch will search seventy-five-plus sites for jobs from around the country.

Contacts:

The Contact Us page is disappointing, with a statement that says, "If you're a job seeker, our FAQs will answer the questions you have." However, on the same page are driving directions to their Reston, Virginia, headquarters and a phone number "if you get lost." The FAQs are well done and covered most of our questions.

Training:

No.

Recruitment:

You create a Personal Search Agent (PSA), which will track jobs within your parameters and e-mail you the results. In a day or so, we received the first e-mail, which contained two jobs. They were both freelance jobs! The e-mail has a link directly back to CareerBuilder, where you find a detailed job description waiting for you. Very efficient.

Placement:

Yes.

Tools

Résumé posting:

Your PSA will do this for you. You can define up to five PSAs and request e-mails daily or weekly.

Portfolio:

No.

Skills test:

No.

Edit résumé:

Yes.

How long you will stay posted:

No data.

Automatic notice to employer if user inquires?

No.

Automatically sends your résumé?

No data.

Notification when a matching job is available?

Yes, by e-mail.

Perks

The PSA stores specific job-search criteria. You can set it to periodically e-mail you new jobs, or you can run it anytime from the Job Search tab.

This site gives you the opportunity to search for specific jobs on other websites "outside the CareerBuilder network." You'll find this behind the Advanced Search button. Here is where you can specify "contract" work and the key word "freelance" or the key phrase "free agent." This can be a bit intimidating with all the databases you're searching. It will take time to find a real contract or freelance vacancy.

Listing and Compensation Data
Number of employers offering jobs:
No data.
Good salary ranges?
No data.

Overall Navigability
Strengths:
The networking aspect of this website—searching other sites at the same time—is great. You can even get a description of the other sites, what specialties they focus on, and for what type of individuals they are searching.
Weaknesses:
Because this site is so big, it takes hours to get used to.
Usability:
Fairly good for a massive site.

General Review
Synopsis:
This is a website dedicated to being one of the biggest in number of jobs posted. It is a good resource for the job searcher, although many of the jobs posted are through employment agencies.
Helpfulness and value to freelancers:
If you use key-word searches, you can land some possibilities.
Waste of time online?
No.

CareerCity

www.careercity.com

Markets Served
Employers:
>Yes.

Job seekers:
>Yes.

Fee for job seekers:
>No.

Type of professionals:
>All.

Information
Job listings:
>There are 12,024 jobs in the system.

Articles:
>There are a few articles and links to articles through the Career Services page.

Facts and figures:
>Not much data in this category.

Contacts:
>No.

Training:
>No.

Recruitment:
>No.

Placement:
>No.

Tools
Résumé posting:
>The short and simple form used to get your résumé into cyberspace is nice. Your own résumé can be posted in text and with the formatting you've chosen. You can also place it in a searchable database. The Posting page helps you through the process.

Portfolio:
>If you attach your Web page to your résumé, your portfolio is available to the viewer.

Skills test:
>No.

Edit résumé:
>Yes.

How long you will stay posted:
>No data.

Automatic notice to employer if user inquires?
>No.

Automatically sends your résumé?
>No.

Notification when a matching job is available?
>Yes.

Perks

This is a useful website for research information and career services such as résumé and interview techniques. The homepage gives you links to information about jobs in government, education, and health, as well as informative salary data. When you go to Links to Salary Surveys, you have to wade through fifty or so links before you actually find out how much you should charge for freelance labor. It's disappointing, but the data is somewhere on the site.

In the FAQ section (off the homepage), you'll find résumé help, job-posting help, and links to many other sites for job searches.

Listing and Compensation Data

Number of employers offering jobs:
>There is no employer data, but the postings were directly through employers and staffing agencies, like many of the Internet job sites.

Good salary ranges?
>Decent.

Overall Navigability

Strengths:
>You'll have no trouble navigating this site. It doesn't try to be all things to all people as some sites do. It has a clear and concise format.

Weaknesses:
>The job-search program isn't what it should be. For lack of a better term, it's wimpy.

>You will be disappointed if you go to the Diversity page. It appears as nothing more than window dressing, making a trite statement about the importance of diversity in the workplace. We asked for any jobs in all locations and found sixteen jobs.

At the top of the list was a posting for a maintenance person for an apartment complex in Oakland, California. Definitely not the freelance job you'll expect. The other fifteen jobs were standard, run-of-the-mill openings.

You might get a little perturbed when you try to find "teaching jobs in five states": Zero jobs were listed. A search for jobs in all locations under the category of "education" yielded one job at Harvard for a conservation librarian. All locations under several categories chosen at random received 500 matches. All locations in advertising found 322 matches. One location, Oregon, in the broadcast category resulted in seven listings for "various cities," including the navy, but none in Oregon itself.

Usability:

Except for some frustration when trying to find the job postings and where to post a résumé, this is user-friendly.

General Review

Synopsis:

In general, this site is not bad for a company that publishes books for job seekers. Their data is clean, but it's hard to figure out how and where to find the information.

Helpfulness and value to freelancers:

This is an okay site. There is some good data on how to handle yourself in an interview.

Waste of time online?

No.

CareerJournal

www.careerjournal.com

Markets Served

Employers:
> Yes.

Job seekers:
> Yes.

Fee for job seekers:
> No.

Type of professionals:
> On the About Us page, the site states that this is the "premier free site for executives." Don't be fooled. That doesn't mean that only executive jobs are offered; it could also mean the site is for executives who are looking for employees. Positions featured include senior and general management, sales, marketing, finance, technology, and a range of related fields. All things considered, though, we believe that the site is aimed primarily at executive recruitment.

Information

Job listings:
> The trick—with this and all other sites—is to figure out the search database. Searching for "hotel reservations" in any city in any industry produced no results. "Tourism" pulled up four jobs. Neither is a job title, but "tourism" worked anyway. The four jobs were not hotel reservations jobs but were vaguely related to tourism.

Articles:
> Dozens—this website relies on the editorial resources of *The Wall Street Journal*. The articles are well done and extremely informative.

Facts and figures:
> The site provides data through its extensive resources, including the *Wall Street Journal* connection.

Contacts:
> There are contacts with each job description.

Training:
> No.

Recruitment:

This isn't exactly recruiting, but for a fee you can contact many recruiters from a link on the homepage and send them a letter and your résumé. This is what the site says: "Once you've identified how many recruiters specialize in your industry and/ or job function, you will be given the option to purchase the data and download it to your computer. Cost is $1 per contact for the first 100 (minimum order of $30), and $.25 for each contact over 100."

Placement:

Yes.

Tools

Résumé posting:

Yes.

Portfolio:

No.

Skills test:

No.

Edit résumé:

Yes.

How long you will stay posted:

No data.

Automatic notice to employer if user inquires?

No.

Automatically sends your résumé?

This is what they say: "You can create a brief, confidential profile that can be searched by corporate and executive recruiters. If your qualifications match an available job, recruiters will send us an e-mail, which we will forward to you. Then, only you can decide whether to respond. We will not share your contact information with a recruiter." You can also create detailed profiles using their forms to help you remember all the important details, such as your employment history.

Notification when a matching job is available?

See above.

Perks

Every website should have a link to its site map; the bigger the site, the bigger the need for a map. This site has one. Web surfing is no different than putting a pack on your back and heading out into new territory alone. You wouldn't do that without a map, would you?

At the Job Postings station, you have lots of choices. You will see what key words you can use to locate jobs. You are offered a Briefing Book on the company offering the job and information on how it's doing on the stock market. (This website is from *The Wall Street Journal*.) You also have a link to Find Similar Jobs, but it doesn't seem to do what it claims. From "publishing jobs" we were sent to 4,070 other jobs that had nothing to do with publishing. It will also show all the jobs available with a particular company.

There is a directory of executive recruiters. You can also search the Candidate Profile database. You'll see who else is job hunting in your field (no names or contact information will be included unless you are registered as an account holder with CareerJournal).

We checked out the Future Step feature. It is free to job hunters, and is basically a thorough job application. It's available to employers and recruiters online.

Listing and Compensation Data
Number of employers offering jobs:
No data, but every search brings up ample jobs.
Good salary ranges?
Yes.

Overall Navigability
Strengths:
The Job Search button is surprisingly easy to find among the clutter.
Weaknesses:
There's a feeling that because it's *The Wall Street Journal* it may be a little too rich for everyone's blood. You may think that employers look here only for top managers, but that's wrong. You have to stick with it to find that out. When you ask for a key-word phrase, or a job title of two words, it gives you jobs that are related to only one of the words. For example, we asked for "human resources specialist" positions; the jobs that came back had the word "specialist" in the description, but none was related to human resources.
Usability:
The site is slow to load without a high-speed Internet connection.

General Review
Synopsis:
The Wall Street Journal operates this website, but there are links to many other places for information and "stuff" to buy. When

you see the jobs that are available, you know instantly that these are not fluffy jobs. The professions listed are typical, but the offerings are tremendous.

Helpfulness and value to freelancers:

This is what a search attempt brought back: "Your search for positions with freelance writer in San Francisco, California, retrieved no jobs." When "freelance" was replaced with "writer," two vacancies in San Francisco were given. When the phrase "free agent" was entered as a key word, only one job with the word "agent" in its title showed up. It wasn't, however, a job position related to the idea of "freelance" or "free agent" work—it was a ticketing agent's position.

Waste of time online?

No.

CareerWeb

www.careerweb.com

Markets Served

Employers:
> Yes.

Job seekers:
> Yes.

Fee for job seekers:
> No, unless you use their Résumé Trader service.

Type of professionals:
> All.

Information

Job listings:
> There are more job categories in this website's search form than most, and it includes a Work From Home category. On the day we visited, 158 jobs were available in this category; most were in sales and marketing and offered by the same company.

Articles:
> Their Career Advice icon gives you links to many interesting resources, bookstores, libraries, and newsgroups. When asking for career information, you may find yourself in the Google search engine, which can open up many more jobs. We viewed the results of our job search and found one for a scrap yard worker in Nova Scotia, a job we didn't expect to see on the Internet. How did we get here? We were in the Career Library and clicked on Misc Jobs.

Facts and figures:
> There's some good reading in the many short articles, with information such as fastest growing jobs for the twenty-first century, thirty jobs that have the highest rate of decline in terms of workers, and top thirteen job and career trends. Got a comfortable desk chair? You can definitely learn a lot at this site.

Contacts:

You can send the contacts an e-mail or fill out a form on the website. There are contacts for all the jobs listed.

Training:

No.

Recruitment:

No.

Placement:

They will make your résumé available to employers.

Tools

Résumé posting:

Not only can you paste your résumé into the résumé form, you can also type in a cover letter. This site gives you the option of allowing potential employers to search your résumé to find key words, a way to help them decide whether to interview you.

Portfolio:

No.

Skills test:

No.

Edit résumé:

Yes.

How long you will stay posted:

No data.

Automatic notice to employer if user inquires?

Yes.

Automatically sends your résumé?

No, a user has to inquire.

Notification when a matching job is available?

No.

Perks

Each job description has a template, which includes boldface headings for the description, skills required, general information, citizenship required, location, and in what metro areas the job was listed.

One item that looks great is actually a time-waster. They offer the chance to edit your résumé and cover letter before sending it, but after clicking on Edit, you're told that the choice is no longer available. Then you're returned to the search page to start all over.

Listing and Compensation Data
Number of employers offering jobs:
> No data.

Good salary ranges?
> Yes.

Overall Navigability
Strengths:
> The site is quite easy to read, with a minimum amount of jargon.

Weaknesses:
> The job search has to be rehighlighted for each search. This is a tedious task, scrolling down a pop-up window to find your job categories, especially when you have several categories you wish to search.

Usability:
> Loading time for this site is at a snail's pace.

General Review
Synopsis:
> The site loads slowly because it is so big. Thankfully, that time will be spent after a host of jobs appears under certain job categories.

Helpfulness and value to freelancers:
> The Work From Home job category is helpful to freelancers, although the jobs were not aimed at highly skilled people.

Waste of time online?
> No.

ComputerJobs

www.computerjobs.com

Markets Served

Employers:
> Yes.

Job seekers:
> Yes. Go to the Consultant's Corner to understand how to work this site as a freelance job seeker.

Fee for job seekers:
> No.

Type of professionals:
> IT (information technology).

Information

Job listings:
> More than 22,000 jobs.

Articles:
> There are surveys on many topics, including average hourly and annual salaries for several different job categories. Under each category, you can find Information on Definitions, Events (such as seminars), Publications, and User Groups.

Facts and figures:
> More than 4,000 companies post jobs, with 22,000 jobs available.

Contacts:
> You have the chance to get in touch with many job seekers and companies within your chosen job categories. Lots of e-mail addresses are available when you choose Consultants in the different job categories. All the consultants are listed with profiles of what they or their company does, but it isn't clear what "consultant" means. Whether they will give you advice on job searching or just try to sell you their services is unclear.

Training:
> Not exactly, unless you hook up with one of the consultants, who might take an interest in mentoring you.

Recruitment:
> Apparently not, unless an employer finds you in its listing.

Placement:
> Seems to happen when you make contact with a potential employer.

Tools

Résumé posting:
> The site posts résumés, but they don't let you post the perfect résumé that you have created (and proofread, agonized over, and redone zillions of times). You must fill out their forms online to make a résumé.

Portfolio:
> No.

Skills test:
> ComputerJobs says it will review and approve each submission to its Consultant's Corner. Your profile must pass a fairly stringent process, and if ComputerJobs chooses not to accept your submission, they will provide you with a short note explaining why. The site also claims to have a rating system, which they share with employers who show an interest in you, and a mediation process if you are unhappy with the rating system.

Edit résumé:
> Yes.

How long you will stay posted:
> From ten to ninety days. It's totally at your discretion.

Automatic notice to employer if user inquires?
> No.

Automatically sends your résumé?
> No.

Notification when a matching job is available?
> The site says this option is "coming soon." (This is promised on too many websites, only to find that "soon" has no deadline.)

Perks

> The Emerging News and Résumé Zapper ideas are great. The news articles are about Internet technology and are helpful, especially if you don't subscribe to any well-known IT publications. As for the Résumé Zapper, it's difficult to tell if the résumé on this website got zapped when the button was clicked. The address www.resumezapper.com is a different website, and the cost to use the service is $49.99. Better to go back to ComputerJobs.

Listing and Compensation Data
Number of employers offering jobs:
> More than 4,000 companies post jobs, with 22,000 jobs available.

Good salary ranges?
> The site shows salary ranges for consultants, which looked decent, but in most cases the ranges were too wide to be useful.

Overall Navigability
Strengths:
> The profile to create your résumé is easy to use.

Weaknesses:
> No jobs are listed when searched for in common categories.

Usability:
> It's a great site, but don't get caught in the My Career loop. The site says: "If we knew you a little better, this space would be filled with the newest jobs on our site that match your profile. Tell us what you want by filling out a short profile, and we'll automatically show you a list of great jobs catered to you. We'll even throw in cool facts about what's happening with your skill set in your area. You'll never think about your job search the same way again." The loop begins here, even if you've already filled out the short profile, and it's so frustrating that you wouldn't even want to hear about it.

General Review
Synopsis:
> This website genuinely wants to help you find work and uses simple language to explain how to find it. Most of the jobs seem to be hidden behind some search engine that is difficult to access.

Helpfulness and value to freelancers:
> This site is not very helpful to serious freelancers looking for hot job leads. When you conduct a job search, most of the listed career categories bounce back with the frustrating message: "At the moment there are no jobs that match your criteria. Your criteria may be too narrow. You can edit your job-matching criteria to get more results. Jobs are updated hourly, so it may be a matter of time before your dream job is posted. When it is, you'll see it here."

Waste of time online?
> For a serious freelancer, it's an 80 percent waste of time.

CoolWorks

www.coolworks.com

Markets Served
Employers:
> Yes.

Job seekers:
> Yes.

Fee for job seekers:
> No.

Type of professionals:
> Seasonal workers—from bus drivers for Gray Line in the Yukon to waiters at the Wall Drug Store in Wall, South Dakota. There's also a special category of employee titled Older and Bolder.

Information
Job listings:
> You'll arouse your wanderlust at this site. Most of the job listings come complete with links to pictures and information from the resorts/parks/cruise ships that are looking for employees at this Web location. On average, most listings gave lots of information, including room and board costs if that's necessary (for an island off the coast of Michigan, reachable only by boat, for example) and how long the tourist season lasts. The site includes listings from employers who are filled up for the current season but are accepting applications for the following year.

Articles:
> Click on Other Cool Stuff.

Facts and figures:
> Yes, in some of the articles.

Contacts:
> You can contact the human resources departments at many resorts, national parks, and companies that staff these places.

Training:
> No.

Recruitment:
> Yes.

Placement:
Yes.

Tools
Résumé posting:
You have to create a password first, but that's easy. The résumé form is quite detailed and asks if you have experience in all types of seasonal work. It also asks for what medical certifications you have. (An up-to-date CPR certificate is a plus.) You can check a box to say that you want to be notified of new postings in your areas of interest. You can also select "Types" of jobs and "Regions" when you submit your résumé, and you can have a free e-mail account with CoolWorks "to keep your job search mobile and out of your inbox at work," it says. The site claims that employers who use CoolWorks search the résumé bank and will contact you if they have something to offer.

Portfolio:
The site lets you paste your résumé into its form, so if you have a website, you can really blast your horn—although getting a seasonal job as a cook in a mountain resort probably wouldn't require a portfolio, even if it were a freelance job.

Skills test:
No.

Edit résumé:
Yes.

How long you will stay posted:
No indication was given.

Automatic notice to employer if user inquires?
No.

Automatically sends your résumé?
Yes.

Notification when a matching job is available?
No, employers will contact you.

Perks
Words of Wisdom in the profiles of the CoolWorkers section: "I went out for a walk and finally concluded to stay out till sundown, for going out, I found, was really going in." (John Muir, 1913.)

You can choose Careers to find postings for managerial positions within resorts and parks. Seasonal Professions is a place where you can find out about seasonal opportunities requiring previous experience or education.

The Message Board is a real treasure trove of information. Look at this posting: "Date: April 04, 2001, 07:14 PM. Author: mooma & poopa. Subject: National parks. We worked for Aramark in Alaska (Denali) for a summer. It was a spur of the moment thing. Just going to visit but heard about jobs applied and got them: $10 a day each for room & board. Working for Ara again in Shenandoah. We are both very senior over 65. Love to work where we would like to travel and can get in some good walks. NP [national park?] services don't pay much but the food was good and you can't beat the views. We also enjoy working with the young people, and boy do we learn a lot from them!"

Listing and Compensation Data

Number of employers offering jobs:

No data.

Good salary ranges?

No. Seasonal workers, especially those who will need room and board, make dirt for wage. One wait-staff job in Montana paid only $5.50 an hour, but there are other compensations such as adventure and new surroundings. (Hmm.)

Overall Navigability

Strengths:

It's easy to browse through the site, but be warned: If you've got even a microscopic amount of wanderlust, don't visit this site. It's good for wanderers, and for daydreamers it could be downright dangerous.

Weaknesses:

Same as above, otherwise no problems at all.

Usability:

Because this site lacks almost any commercial links, you can find your way around quite easily without getting stuck in e-commerce cyberbabble.

General Review

Synopsis:

This website is aimed at people who aren't particularly fussy about a career and mostly looking for a working vacation. It lists jobs for seasonal work in places that tourists visit and includes amusement parks, ski resorts, and national parks.

Helpfulness and value to freelancers:

The people who take these jobs are certainly independent people, so most of them qualify as freelancers.

Waste of time online?

No.

CruelWorld  +

www.cruelworld.com

Markets Served
Employers:
> Yes.

Job seekers:
> According to the site, it lists mid- to senior-level opportunities.

Fee for job seekers:
> No.

Type of professionals:
> Not a long list of job categories yet, but they ask if your profession is listed. They claim that they are expanding constantly.

Information
Job listings:
> No.

Articles:
> Yes.

Facts and figures·
> No.

Contacts:
> Only e-mail addresses.

Training:
> No.

Recruitment:
> We'll never know, because this site navigates like it's in the Twilight Zone. Maybe that's what makes this site such a cruel world. (See comment under "Waste of time online?" on the last page for this listing.)

Placement:
> They promise it, but you'll no doubt give up before this ever happens.

Tools
Résumé posting:
> Yes.

Portfolio:
> No.

Skills test:
No.
Edit résumé:
Yes.
How long you will stay posted:
No data.
Automatic notice to employer if user inquires?
No data.
Automatically sends your résumé?
No.
Notification when a matching job is available?
Yes.

Perks
You can take a quiz to determine if you should switch jobs (like most of us need help figuring out that one).

Listing and Compensation Data
Number of employers offering jobs:
No data.
Good salary ranges?
No data.

Overall Navigability
Strengths:
There is a site map. Go there first to see the whole site in outline form. All the questions are answered in the FAQ section.
Weaknesses:
There is a hesitant moment of insecurity when you may almost click off the site. (We should have.) The membership sign-up page is a "talent network," the website of another company in partnership with CruelWorld. They don't tell you until you click on Profile that you can post your own résumé. At this point there is an "ADD" button beside the résumé box. There you can add your résumé.
Usability:
This site is extremely user friendly (unless you run into the problem mentioned below under "Waste of time online?")

General Review
Synopsis:
This is actually a link to an employment agency that recently acquired CruelWorld. Once you fill out the profile/membership forms, you are taken to SpencerStuart.com for the job forms.

Helpfulness and value to freelancers:

Hard to tell.

Waste of time online?

This site is a huge waste of your precious and limited time. We spent forty-five minutes filling in the membership form, which included employment history data. When we returned to review our profile/résumé, the login site couldn't find us. (We use the same ID and password with every job-search site, so it wasn't our memory that crashed.) You have a choice: Fill out the darn thing again, or find another website among the hundreds out there. Hmm.

DreamJobs  +

www.dreamjobs.com

Markets Served
Employers:
> Yes.

Job seekers:
> Yes.

Fee for job seekers:
> If you choose the Telecommuting title, you're given several sites from which to choose. One site did charge employees a fee of 10 percent of the project's value.

Type of professionals:
> All.

Information
Job listings:
> Creativemoonlighter.com, a third-party site linked from DreamJobs, claims that it has 26,000 professionals looking for work and 3,000 firms hiring. Snagajob.com doesn't say how many listings it has. Mcfind.com (a large search engine) looks like it might have some good resources. AtoZMoonlighter.com also looks promising. There were many more resources available at DreamJobs.

Articles:
> From the links provided by DreamJobs, you'll find tons of articles. Snagajob.com, a site aimed at students looking for summer jobs, has an article on how to keep your dorm room neat and tidy.

Facts and figures:
> Go to geopolitical.com or the religion link to Christian Bible references and you've got your term paper under way. As for employment facts, you won't find much.

Contacts:
> Depending on where you land in this website, you can get contacts, other job sites, employment agencies, and employer profiles (see snagajob.com to learn all about working at McDonald's).

Training:
>No.

Recruitment:
>No.

Placement:
>Yes.

Tools

Résumé posting:
>Most of the third-party job sites offer this service.

Portfolio:
>Yes, depending on the site.

Skills test:
>No.

Edit résumé:
>The sites we linked to offered the chance to edit your profiles.

How long you will stay posted:
>Most don't say.

Automatic notice to employer if user inquires?
>No.

Automatically sends your résumé?
>No.

Notification when a matching job is available?
>Yes, for most sites.

Perks

>No real mentionables.

Listing and Compensation Data

Number of employers offering jobs:
>You'll find a large number of legitimate job-search sites branching off from DreamJobs. Most of the links are toward commercial sites.

Good salary ranges?
>No data.

Overall Navigability

Strengths:
>Each link is well defined and allows you to easily determine whether it is to a bookstore or to a true job-seeking opportunity.

Weaknesses:
>Some categories had nothing in them, such as the Mongolian Empire title. It is disappointing to think you've found a loaded site only to discover that you have encountered nothing more than fluffy pages.

Usability:
> Fairly good.

General Review
Synopsis:
> See comments under the "Job listings" heading earlier in this listing.

Helpfulness and value to freelancers:
> Not too helpful.

Waste of time online?
> For a freelancer searching for serious work, it is a waste of time.

editorandpublisher

Markets Served

Employers:
Yes.
Job seekers:
Yes.
Fee for job seekers:
No.
Type of professionals:
News media and publishing.

Information

Job listings:
Job listings are in a form like that of classified ads in a newspaper. You don't have to go through the pull-down boxes to do key-word/job/city searches. This might change.

Articles:
There are many articles, but not on the subject of job searching

Facts and figures:
If you're interested in the news media and related subjects, you can find plenty of information on this site. Here's a sample that might interest you: "John McIntyre, managing editor of Content Intelligence, a new publication put out by Lyra Research of Massachusetts, says that employment is one area where the Lyra research indicates erosion by newspapers. When given five media options for looking for employment, 32 percent of Internet-using respondents preferred to use the Web. 'That's a lot,' he says. Lyra's results echo a recent study by Greenfield Online which showed that Internet users preferred searching online for jobs over looking in the newspaper by a 'two to one margin.' "

Contacts:
There is free access to the e-mail addresses and/or telephone numbers of the employers listed in the Classified section under Help Wanted. Otherwise, you have to purchase other media contact data.

Training:
    No.
Recruitment:
    No.
Placement:
    No.

Tools

Résumé posting:
    If you buy an ad in the classified pages of *Editor & Publisher*
    magazine, it will be included in this website. To do this, go to
    the Classified section. Put your e-mail and Web address (where
    you've put your kickin' résumé) in the ad, and you've done all
    you can to get freelance work out of this site.
Portfolio:
    No.
Skills test:
    No.
Edit résumé:
    No data.
How long you will stay posted:
    No data.
Automatic notice to employer if user inquires?
    No data.
Automatically sends your résumé?
    No.
Notification when a matching job is available?
    No.

Perks

    To access the site's archives, you have to pay $5.95 for a "day
    pass" and more for a longer membership. Too bad—it would
    have been nice to read an article published in the magazine in
    June 2001 about a study that says people who use online
    career sites find that Web-based tools are more effective in job
    searching than newspaper job listings.
        There's also a Site Index. It's a great help, especially if
    you're interested in researching what's going on in this
    industry.
        The magazine sponsors conferences each year for people
    in the publishing industry. These events are listed under
    Conferences, which would be good places to go for
    networking opportunities and looking for independent
    freelance work.

Listing and Compensation Data

Number of employers offering jobs:

Less than 100.

Good salary ranges?

Salaries are probably fair. The newspaper and magazine industries have been buying the skills of writers and artists for a long time.

Overall Navigability

Strengths:

Go to the Site Index to quickly see what's available. All the site links are listed there to help you navigate.

Weaknesses:

You're apt to get excited about their online Media Directory, but all you'll probably get is a blank page (we did when we visited). In clicking around (that's doing research), you'll learn that there is a hefty charge for this information, which makes sense. *Editor & Publisher* is about the most established authority in this industry.

Usability:

Very easy and intuitive.

General Review

Synopsis:

Editor & Publisher magazine recently published this website, a sensible approach to searching for freelance writing jobs in the news media industry.

Helpfulness and value to freelancers:

You can't do a word search at this site, but at the Editorial section under the Classified section appears the word "freelance." It doesn't link to any specific jobs, but neither do the other subsections such as Graphics, Photography, Editorial, etc. As a freelancer you'll have to be creative. For example, locate a newspaper looking for a reporter in your city. Offer to cover a beat as a freelancer and accept payment by the story or piece.

Waste of time online?

If you're not a writer or publisher, this would be a waste of time. For freelance writers, it's worth some time to check it out.

4Work

www.4work.com

Markets Served
Employers:
   Yes.
Job seekers:
   Debatable.
Fee for job seekers:
   No.
Type of professionals:
   No data.

Information
Job listings:
   There are links to airlines and something called the Manufacturing Automation and Process Control Industry, a fee-based résumé-posting service, and health care jobs. The site claims to have "thousands of great jobs across the country," but how to find those jobs is the Web-burning question. The site just doesn't work.
Articles:
   Yes.
Facts and figures:
   No.
Contacts:
   E-mail the site's contacts and ask them how to get a look at the thousands of jobs they have, would you, please? If you find out, let us know. Our e-mail was never answered.
Training:
   No.
Recruitment:
   No.
Placement:
   No.

Tools
Résumé posting:
   At the Site Help page, it says that personal profiles are more helpful than a résumé. However, the site claims that it will offer

you the chance to be a Featured Job Seeker, and that you are
to use the Featured Job Seeker Wizard to post your full
résumé. If you go off to see the Wizard, you end up in the land
of cyber-Oz, and there aren't even any witches, wizards, or
little dogs.

Portfolio:
No.

Skills test:
After bumping into your first dozen or two dead ends on this
site, you'll be dizzy. It feels like they're testing your patience. If
so, you'll probably fail.

Edit résumé:
Yes.

How long you will stay posted:
No data.

Automatic notice to employer if user inquires?
No data.

Automatically sends your résumé?
No data.

Notification when a matching job is available?
The site says that this will happen and that when you fill out
the profile, you should start watching your e-mail. We're still
waiting.

Perks
On the About Us page, 4Work com claims to offer
"sophisticated search tools for job seekers and recruiters . . .
tools that help you pinpoint exactly what you are looking for.
We help you bypass the time-consuming, unsuitable matches
you typically find when searching job-posting sites." Try finding
the toolbox. When you do, let us know where it is; we never
found it.

Listing and Compensation Data
Number of employers offering jobs:
No data.

Good salary ranges?
No data.

Overall Navigability
Strengths:
None.

Weaknesses:
You'll be so disappointed in this site that you'll probably cry.
You can't search for a job throughout the country. Their
instructions say: "If you are interested in any location in the

U.S., select 'Nationwide' from the list." There is no Nationwide on the list, and there are no explanations about the page you are on. The navigation on this site works a lot like a demolition derby: Everything is crashing into everything else.

Usability:

Don't ask! You don't even want to know about it.

General Review

Synopsis:

The website claims to help you find a job, but it won't let you into the database of jobs—that is, if it has one.

Helpfulness and value to freelancers:

Come on.

Waste of time online?

Come on.

FreeAgent.com

www.freeagent.com

Markets Served

Employers:
Yes.

Job seekers:
Yes.

Fee for job seekers:
No.

Type of professionals:
All.

Information

Job listings:
Very few.

Articles:
No.

Facts and figures:
No.

Contacts:
You can fill out a comment form and submit it over the website.

Training:
No.

Recruitment:
No.

Placement:
No.

Tools

Résumé posting:
Yes.

Portfolio:
Yes, they call it an E-portfolio.

Skills test:
No.

Edit résumé:
> Yes, you can edit your E-profile. They also give you hints on how to increase the efficiency of your profile.

How long you will stay posted:
> No indication was given.

Automatic notice to employer if user inquires?
> We couldn't find any postings to test.

Automatically sends your résumé?
> No data.

Notification when a matching job is available?
> Yes, by e-mail.

Perks

You can see the number of people who view your portfolio, view the number of projects that match your portfolio, and see the number of times you came up in a search. The site offers a bartering service, but you are taken to two other websites where there is a lot of information to absorb. Remembering that you're not being paid to look for work you will find this a waste of your time.

They offer to set you up with a toll-free number, office space, a secretary, a prestigious address, and voice-mail messaging. All these come at a price, but you may be skeptical of a website that offers a prestigious address over the Internet unless the site is connected to an office rental firm. It's difficult to confirm the address as legitimate. The site also lets you bid on a job, but because we found no jobs to bid on, we weren't able to determine if this would work.

Listing and Compensation Data

Number of employers offering jobs:
> No data.

Good salary ranges?
> No data.

Overall Navigability

Strengths:
> Navigation is a breeze.

Weaknesses:
> There are tedious forms to fill out, but you can save a filled-in search form for using another day, perhaps when the site posts some jobs!

Usability:
> It's not a complicated format. The form to create your résumé is less tedious than the form to search for jobs. The form

contains "greater than" and "equals" symbols, but without any explanation of their purpose. You also have to fill out the whole form for each job classification.

General Review

Synopsis:

This website has a great name and because of its simplicity it will get many job seekers, but it can't perform under regular use and seems to have very few jobs.

Helpfulness and value to freelancers:

It promises but does not deliver.

Waste of time online?

Yes.

Freelance.com

www.freelance.com

Markets Served

Employers:

The website's Companies link says: "You pay nothing to post a project. We only charge when you book one of our freelance professionals. Even then, you pay far less than prevailing rates. Enter the types of skills you're looking for and Freelance.com will do the rest. We'll not only send you an e-mail listing of all the relevant résumés currently in our network, we'll also provide you with updates of new profiles as soon as they become available."

Job seekers:

Yes.

Fee for job seekers:

No.

Type of professionals:

It seems to be mostly IT professionals. The website says 509 types of professionals are listed.

Information

Job listings:

A few are listed on the homepage, and you can find more after joining. What happens when you finally find a link to all the projects (i.e., jobs) is . . . nothing. You get an e-mail from them that says: "Each morning you will receive the list of new projects that correspond to the profile you have provided. You can also access the complete list of our projects by using the following link: http://www.Freelance.com/C125675B0014F649/ vwMissions." What you get at this link are the two jobs listed on the homepage. The e-mail that we were promised never arrived.

Articles:

There was an article on getting IT certification through this website, a Virtual Test Center to do a free skills assessment, and training for members. However, the article promising the Test Center by March was posted February 1. At mid-June, the promise still appeared on the homepage. We couldn't find the

Virtual Test Center—not a good sign when the homepage is at least three months out of date.

Facts and figures:

They have 474 open projects, 65,000 freelance professionals, and 115 account managers, and they say that their growth rate was 200 percent in the last five years.

Contacts:

You get the e-mail address of an account manager listed with each job. The Contact button also gives you a couple of e-mail addresses for account managers. The e-mail sent to the first name bounced back undeliverable within hours. The second click on Contact received names, including one in the Pacific Northwest. A question was resent to that person, but a reply was not received.

Training:

No.

Recruitment/Placement:

Yes. The site is a resource for both job seekers and industry. Employers can look at databases by state, which have a one-line general description for each of the website's list of job seekers. They can click on each listing to get the detailed profile (no name or e-mail included). The website says: "Our network covers every industry from Agriculture & Environment and Economic & Social Development, to Energy & Infrastructure, Private Sector & Finance, and Transportation & Communications."

Tools

Résumé posting:

Yes.

Portfolio:

This may depend on the phone interview that they say they will give you. The phone call was never received, but that may be because we didn't provide a very hefty portfolio.

Skills test:

Phone interview.

Edit résumé:

Yes.

How long you will stay posted:

No data.

Automatic notice to employer if user inquires?

No.

Automatically sends your résumé?

No data.

Notification when a matching job is available?
> They say it will come by e-mail, with your account manager's name included.

Perks
> You can join by clicking on Join Our Community, but after you do that, there is no place for members to log in. The website seems aimed at employers. It's less about you finding a job than it is the employer finding you. After posting your "profile" you never see a link for members of the "community." Maybe you have to wait for the phone call from an account manager.

Listing and Compensation Data
Number of employers offering jobs:
> No data.
Good salary ranges?
> No data.

Overall Navigability
Strengths:
> This site delivers more than expected in job-searching capabilities. It lives up to its name by getting you in touch with strong potentials for specific jobs in many freelance categories.

Weaknesses:
> You have to click around to work at translating the site's jargon, that is, play a guessing game before you figure out how to work the site. The learning curve is slow. A site map would be a good idea, along with a brief paragraph or two explaining the search results categories and how to find your way around once you arrive at them.

Usability:
> This site is moderately usable. Too much extraneous stuff to wade through. Finding contract or freelance jobs is a lot of work.

General Review
Synopsis:
> When you get past the cute photos of people sitting or lounging with a laptop, you find a website that is like most others—good initially but hard to negotiate. If you peek at some of the profiles of job seekers, be ready to be intimidated unless you have an extensive IT background.

Helpfulness and value to freelancers:
> You will need a comfortable chair because this site isn't very intuitive.

Waste of time online?
> Yes and no: It tries to be helpful to job seekers, but the site is actually easier for an employer to use, which stands to reason since the website's income will come from employers when they hire one of the employees.

FreelanceWorkExchange

www.freelanceworkexchange.com

Markets Served
Employers:
> Indirectly.

Job seekers:
> Indirectly.

Fee for job seekers:
> Yes.

Type of professionals:
> Freelancers.

Information
Job listings:
> You can't view the job listings until you pay $3.75 for a trial membership.

Articles:
> There are words and more words on this website. Most have a link to someplace eager to sell you a résumé service, a book on creating websites, etc.

Facts and figures:
> No.

Contacts:
> Many.

Training:
> No.

Recruitment:
> No.

Placement:
> No.

Tools
Résumé posting:
> No.

Portfolio:
> No.

Skills test:
> No.

Edit résumé:
    No data.
How long you will stay posted:
    No data.
Automatic notice to employer if user inquires?
    No data.
Automatically sends your résumé?
    No data.
Notification when a matching job is available?
    No data.

Perks
If you have a website of your own, you might be interested in
this link. Choose Resources, and then at the bottom of that
page there is a tiny link to News. There you get a canned list of
news articles that have something to do with the word
"freelance." You can then contact a website that will sell you a
product that puts current headlines and articles about a
chosen topic on your site.

Listing and Compensation Data
Number of employers offering jobs:
    No data.
Good salary ranges?
    No data.

Overall Navigability
Strengths:
    You won't have any trouble navigating this site.
Weaknesses:
    The site designer should be up-front. If you hit the Find Work
    tab, you will be taken to the links of other job search sites, but
    not before you endure another sales pitch. You will leave here
    with the feeling that the site author has gone through lots of
    extraneous effort to sell his book.
Usability:
    Very difficult to use because you can't get anywhere until you
    sign up or buy the product. Most buttons lead to words,
    words, and more words.

General Review
Synopsis:
    This site is some dude's attempt to sell you his book about
    earning a million dollars as a freelance professional. In the
    meantime you get lost in cyberspace. When you find your way
    home, you'll resent having wasted your time.

Helpfulness and value to freelancers:
   None.
Waste of time online?
   Big time.

FreelanceWriting

www.freelancewriting.com

Markets Served

Employers:
Yes.
Job seekers:
Yes.
Fee for job seekers:
No.
Type of professionals:
Writers.

Information

Job listings:

The Freelance Jobs tab found lots of opportunities. Most intriguing was this one: "We have an immediate assignment for a writer in South Africa or Hong Kong: a profile piece of approximately 600 to 700 words about a concierge working in South Africa or Hong Kong." It was for a trade publication that serves the Southern Nevada Hotel Concierge Association members, Les Clefs d'Or USA members, concierge association presidents worldwide, and others in the hospitality industry. The job listing added that the writer would have to find the subject of the article.

There's also a link to a database of writers' conferences all over the world. If you specify where you want to go, what type of writing you want to "conference" about, and click, you've got the whole program on your screen, with an e-mail link back to the conference registration form—a very nice service.

Articles:

In the Writers' Web Events, there are many good things to read and learn.

Facts and figures:

See "Job Listings" above.

Contacts:

Throughout this site there are connections to people and publishers wanting your skills and your attention. Plan to set aside a day or two to visit this site, especially if you're a writer looking for work.

Training:

No.

Recruitment:

Yes.

Placement:

It's up to you.

Tools

Résumé posting:

Go to the Career Center, click on Freelance Job Bank, and go to Freelancers Seeking Work. Here you can post your ad with the 100-plus already onsite. The most recently posted are at the top of the list, so that's a nice bonus for a day or two. Hint: Create a dynamite headline for your ad and you'll surely attract work potential. It's all in the subject line.

Portfolio:

Put your website address in the ad we just mentioned and put samples of your writing on your website.

Skills test:

No.

Edit résumé:

No data.

How long you will stay posted:

The oldest résumés listed at the bottom were two months old.

Automatic notice to employer if user inquires?

No.

Automatically sends your résumé?

No, but an employer or anyone else can search the list of résumés by typing in a name or a subject. Seventeen résumés were found for the word "travel," seven for the word "environment," and eight for the word "Ellen," even though none of them was submitted by someone named Ellen.

Notification when a matching job is available?

No.

Perks

There's a handy tool that allows you to send the homepage to a friend, along with a personal message. This is a very collaborative site where freelancers work together well.

There's another tool that lets you "grab this newsletter content for your own website." There is a commercial or two. An ad announces an e-book for $12.95. Another offers software to help you write a personal journal for $35.

Try the Chat Room for Writers in the Networking Center. Here you will find some interesting links to other sites, a discussion forum, and classifieds. The forum had the following discussions listed when we visited: forums for book writers and screenwriters, a writers' black book of deadbeats that helps you "find out who's not paying writers," a writers' marketplace, and a listing of more than fifty writing-related forums.

The Creative Outsourcing section will lead you to several job banks where you can post for freelance opportunities as well as for full-time writing-related jobs. It is free to post paying writing jobs on this site.

The Web Events Newsletter takes awhile to load (more than two minutes without a high-speed connection), but it's good. There were articles on awards and recent achievements, new websites for writers, Web events, creative collaborations, seminars/workshops/events, new organizations, staff changes and additions, new book and script deals, new writing deals, print media news, new magazine launches, and writing contests. Somewhere in this particular issue was a link to a similar website operated by a woman in England. That led to another site that is looking for stories. This is an interesting site that will lead you to some stimulating little side junkets.

Listing and Compensation Data
Number of employers offering jobs:
No data.
Good salary ranges?
The bids listed in the eLance link, where jobs are posted and auctioned, looked low. Don't expect top dollar, benefits, and your own parking space from the jobs listed on this site.

Overall Navigability
Strengths:
The index is clear, and you get to where you expect. There are very few, if any, links that put you into a commercial site.
Weaknesses:
Some pages are slow to load. The About page is blank. The Media Kit page has only one line: "FreelanceWriting.com is not accepting any new advertising at this time. If you have any questions, please e-mail us."

Usability:
Good.

General Review

Synopsis:
This is a site that seems to have been created by and for writers looking for work, for feedback, and for connections with other writers. Getting an assignment would come only from consistent ad posting, good headlines, and lots of luck, but there's a lot of help available at this site.

Helpfulness and value to freelancers:
Very helpful.

Waste of time online?
No. Read these pages on this site: the Technical Writing FAQ section, which discusses how to become a technical writer and the primary skills required; Wake Up and Smell the Technology, about how creative writers make good technical writers; and the Tech Writing Marketplace, a linked site created by author Susan Bilheimer containing valuable links and information about the tools necessary for advanced technical writing.

FreetimeJobs

Markets Served

Employers:

Yes.

Job seekers:

Yes.

Fee for job seekers:

There is no fee to use the job-search database, but look out! One job description says "and there is no fee to begin." Another offers work from home if you first send $29.95 for access to "thousands of products from which to choose." This will remind you of those cheesy little signs nailed to battered utility poles in your town that shout "WORK FROM HOME!"

Type of professionals:

All.

Information

Job listings:

There was one job that looked promising: "Business MBA-style management writer, with background in marketing, international business management, and case-study fields, wanted for a thirty-six-page (9,000-word) project (for delivery by May 1), including some charts and tables, an academic study in business management. Must be familiar with an academic style/format, as well as having a solid command of professional writing skills. Require business-writing samples. Compensation: U.S. $720. Further details given privately to qualified applicants."

There was also this one: "Would you like to earn twelve to thirty-six dollars per hour from home with no start-up fees? Are you perceptive, intuitive, and open-minded? Then you are the one I am looking for! This job involves the use of the metaphysical skills; astrology, rune stones, I-Ching, dream interpretations, tarot cards, voice vibrations, etc., and good common sense. Experience preferred, but not necessary as some basic training is available."

Articles:
   No.
Facts and figures:
   No.
Contacts:
   No.
Training:
   No.
Recruitment:
   No.
Placement:
   Place a Bid received this message: "You are signed on as a guest member, which gives you free access to view the job postings. In order to bid, you must upgrade to our Premium membership. The cost is ten dollars for the entire year."

Tools
Résumé posting:
   No.
Portfolio:
   No.
Skills test:
   No.
Edit résumé:
   No data.
How long you will stay posted:
   No data.
Automatic notice to employer if user inquires?
   No.
Automatically sends your résumé?
   No.
Notification when a matching job is available?
   No, but they will send you e-mail when any new job postings appear.

Perks
   Thankfully, there is a place to say "NO" so that you won't receive an e-mail inbox full of nonsensical promotional offers for free cars or Viagra without a doctor's prescription.

Listing and Compensation Data
Number of employers offering jobs:
   The same few employers pop up in the job-search database.
Good salary ranges?
   No, you wouldn't even want to hear about it!

Overall Navigability
Strengths:

It's a very small site with few pages. It's easy to cruise through quickly, and you'll probably want to do it that way—that is, surf through it quickly.

Weaknesses:

This isn't a very legitimate job-search site. Too much hype, too little hope.

Usability:

Idiot-proof.

General Review
Synopsis:

This is an auction site that allows you to bid on jobs. You probably won't want to pay the ten-dollar fee; Vegas would give you better odds.

Helpfulness and value to freelancers:

Helpful, but proceed with caution.

Waste of time online?

This is almost a waste of time. Most of the jobs were in the utility-pole advertisement category. Be glad we wasted our time for you.

Guru   *www.guru.com*

Markets Served

Employers:
> Yes.

Job seekers:
> Yes.

Fee for job seekers:
> No.

Type of professionals:
> This site is aimed at freelance workers in categories such as creative, media, finance and legal, information technology, management, marketing and sales, training and advice, and Web operations and development.

Information

Job listings:
> Yes.

Articles:
> Articles offered cover topics such as how to feather your retirement nest, a profile of a freelance writer, the latest in bill-collecting technology, taxes for freelancers, and dispute resolution advice.

Facts and figures:
> More than 550,000 registered users.

Contacts:
> Their help page is loaded with contacts.

Training:
> No.

Recruitment:
> No.

Placement:
> Yes.

Tools

Résumé posting:
> You fill out their online forms to create your profile. Each page in the process has easy-to-read hints on how to improve your

profile. The process takes nearly thirty minutes. Just when you think they're going to hit you with a fee for the service, you find out that there isn't one.

Portfolio:

You can enter your website address in your Guru résumé, and if you've put pictures and details of your work history, skills, and projects on it, it's as good as lugging around your portfolio.

Skills test:

No. They do have something called Guru Talent Agency that they say "prescreens and represents top-flight IT and creative contractors and places them into projects with companies who need full-service talent placement."

Edit résumé:

Yes.

How long you will stay posted:

No data.

Automatic notice to employer if user inquires?

The user posts a bid on a project through the website. Apparently it goes right off to the company looking to hire.

Automatically sends your résumé?

No.

Notification when a matching job is available?

No.

Perks

According to the About Us page, Guru Services provides independent professionals with certain accoutrements, such as insurance to run their solo businesses. There is a link from several pages within the website to a commercial website that deals with dispute resolutions, probably a good thing to keep in mind when you're in business for yourself. Too commercial? Not at all; if you click on book titles and articles, you get exactly that—no marketing appeals.

Listing and Compensation Data

Number of employers offering jobs:

No data.

Good salary ranges?

You set your own salary range when you bid on a project.

Overall Navigability

Strengths:

There are so few commercial links that it leaves you suspect. In spite of the fact that your profile and your first bid on a project may get lost in cyberspace (like ours did), the site is fresh and clean. This is the way the Internet/Web should work.

Weaknesses:

Nothing wrong with it, except that it's not on any of the top forty lists with any of the large search engines. We asked the chat advisor of an unrelated site if he/she knew of any good sites for freelancers, and Guru.com was the first answer.

Usability:

Not one link was out of place on this site. Everything works the way that they say it will.

General Review

Synopsis:

This is a clean website, dedicated to getting work for freelancers with a minimum level of confusion.

Helpfulness and value to freelancers:

Helpful to the max.

Waste of time online?

No.

Headhunter  +

www.headhunter.net

Markets Served
Employers:
> Yes. They pay between $100 and $250 for a posting.

Job seekers:
> Yes.

Fee for job seekers:
> No.

Type of professionals:
> One would think that, with the name Headhunter, the jobs would be in the management category. They're not.

Information
Job listings:
> More than 250,000 jobs from 10,000 employers, and they claim to have 2 million résumés.

Articles:
> The Featured Employer articles were informative.

Facts and figures:
> No.

Contacts:
> Overall, the database of companies is a great resource. At the bottom of a job-description page, a link to Sologig.com, a website for freelancers, was given. With all the information on each page, it's difficult to notice the link. Sologig is owned by Headhunter and is a fee-based service. Headhunter also lists itself in the job listings, so you could contact it directly.

Training:
> No.

Recruitment:
> No data.

Placement:
> They say that they search for "YOU! Post and manage up to five résumés to target your diverse skills. Plus, posting ensures that your résumé can be read and filtered by today's hiring software." It is difficult to determine what this filtering is,

unless it's a database search available to a potential employer or employment agency. Hint: Place some good key words into your résumé for other database searches!

Tools
Résumé posting:
Yes.
Portfolio:
No.
Skills test:
No.
Edit résumé:
Yes. You can also choose to upgrade your résumé for a fee. They say that this service will list yours ahead of free postings in the search results.
How long you will stay posted:
No data.
Automatic notice to employer if user inquires?
No, you inquire on your own.
Automatically sends your résumé?
No.
Notification when a matching job is available?
Yes, by e-mail.

Perks
The Companies feature lets you browse a specific organization's list of available jobs. An Online Career Fair button takes you to company sites that Headhunter probably features. You get a website for each part of the Career Fair (six companies were featured when we clicked in) but no more data.

A cool tool is the Boss Button. It serves the sneaky employee who is looking for a job while at work. Under the Boss Button it says to click "if the boss is nearby." By clicking, it puts an article on your monitor about incorrect use of e-mail. At the end of the article appears, "Hope the boss is gone now. . . . Thanks for job searching with us; we hope that you find a position that makes you happy!!"

A list of resources is available on specific job-details pages. This is helpful information for people who want to earn an MBA online, teach online, relocate to take a new job, etc. The site also gives you a toll-free customer-service number with office hours.

Listing and Compensation Data

Number of employers offering jobs:

You can search for jobs by company, industry, or job type. If you click on Company, you will find a huge job database—10,000, the site claims. The "A" page showed listings from companies such as the well-known Amazon.com and Arrowhead Community Hospital in Phoenix. Each company listing is linked to either a short profile and/or the listed firm's website. If you're researching employers all over the country, this is a great resource.

Good salary ranges?

No data.

Overall Navigability

Strengths:

Its database of companies.

Weaknesses:

There is no freelance category, and you can't post your own résumé. You have to use the online form.

Usability:

Good.

General Review

Synopsis:

This is a good resource for patient job seekers who will take the time to figure out how to really hone their key-word search skills. The résumé form is also clear and asks the right questions.

Helpfulness and value to freelancers:

Not helpful.

Waste of time online?

It is a waste of time if you're looking only for contract/freelance work.

HotJobs

www.hotjobs.com

Markets Served

Employers:
Yes.

Job seekers:
Yes.

Fee for job seekers:
No.

Type of professionals:
The whole gamut.

Information

Job listings:
The text on the homepage says: "The site boasts hundreds of thousands of jobs."

Articles:
There is reading material available on many subjects and tied to the job category you pick. For example, if you pick Education, you'll find an article on teacher shortages.

Facts and figures:
No.

Contacts:
Clicking on Send Comments opens your e-mail program. We sent an e-mail asking for better directions to use the site and received an answer. We tried again to search for jobs, but we found zero jobs with the key-word search "freelance" in the Advertising/PR category and with the key word "reservations" in the Tourism & Hospitality category.

Training:
No.

Recruitment:
Yes.

Placement:
Yes.

Tools

Résumé posting:
Yes.

Portfolio:
    No.
Skills test:
    No.
Edit résumé:
    Yes.
How long you will stay posted:
    No data.
Automatic notice to employer if user inquires?
    No.
Automatically sends your résumé?
    No.
Notification when a matching job is available?
    No.

Perks

The Channel Discussions sound interesting. The topics are varied and give you an idea of what other people are thinking about in the job-search environment.

Listing and Compensation Data

Number of employers offering jobs:
    Hundreds of thousands.
Good salary ranges?
    There was not enough data on salaries given within the listings to determine specific salary ranges.

Overall Navigability

Strengths:
    Their tag line "Destiny Won't Find You" is like Dad's lecture every time you went looking for a summer job. This site has clean pages and not too many ads. Their Career Channel categories are well done. When you pick one, some of the items on your page are geared to that category. Here is where you can do a key-word search for jobs. They even give you examples of key words, which is most helpful when your brain is drained after hours of searching for jobs on the Internet.
Weaknesses:
    There are not enough jobs for a key-word search to give you much help. On Temp Channel, "writer job" in Los Angeles got back zero jobs. That's good because it leaves little competition.
Usability:
    This site is usable and navigates well with easily found career channels that will narrow your search into a specific category. The site has little to offer in hard leads on jobs, though.

General Review

Synopsis:

>This site was rated fourth in a top ten list by Microsoft Network. We tried to find five common jobs in large cities, including writer, housekeeper, and freelance editor, but there were none.

Helpfulness and value to freelancers:

>It promises much, giving some interesting information about job seeking in many career channels, but gives back no jobs.

Waste of time online?

>This may be a good site on which to post your résumé because you could end up the only one listed in that particular category. But if you're seriously looking for a job, it is probably a waste of time. If you're looking for education, it's not bad.

Monster

www.monster.com

Markets Served

Employers:

> This is where Monster.com gets its revenue. Posting a job costs about $295. The site says: "More than 40,000 progressive employers."

Job seekers:

> There were 14,472,702 registered users at the end of March 2001. That number has more than doubled from the year before, when there were 6.6 million registered. They had 9.3 million résumés at the end of March 2001. This has tripled from the year before. Job postings at the end of March 2001 numbered 479,004. It looks as if the door is open to everyone, and they don't seem to limit the job seekers to any one level of expertise.

Fee for job seekers:

> No.

Type of professionals:

> All

Information

Job listings:

> Yes.

Articles:

> More than you'll ever have time to read.

Facts and figures:

> More than you'll ever have time to read.

Contacts:

> There are not many ways to contact Monster.com, but you never feel alone on the site. There's a slew of links to other places for interview information, job-search tips, chat rooms, and an essay by a former Peace Corps volunteer now home from two years in Kazakhstan, where it was forty degrees below zero all winter.

Training:

> Boatloads. If you are motivated and able to learn from your research, and if you're willing to take the time to read the

articles on this site, you ought to qualify for a master's degree in human resources when you're done. Better yet, you could hang your job search consultant shingle out over the front door.

Recruitment/Placement:

It's up to you to get online, research the jobs available in your fields, and apply. You can also use something that they call an Agent, which seems a smart way to use their job bank. What it is, what it does, and how to use it are a bit confusing. You fill out another form—not too detailed—and wait for e-mails from the Agent on a daily, weekly, or monthly basis. We filled out the form on a weekend. On Tuesday morning there was an e-mail with a link back to the homepage, where there were eight jobs waiting for us.

Tools

Résumé posting:

You can create up to five résumés and post each one.

Portfolio:

No.

Skills test:

No.

Edit résumé:

Yes.

How long you will stay posted:

No data.

Automatic notice to employer if user inquires?

No data.

Automatically sends your résumé?

No.

Notification when a matching job is available?

This is where the Agent comes in handy. You'll get a list of the jobs available in your categories whenever you check out your account. You can define more than one search agent if you have more than one specialty. Each Agent works independently, scurrying around the World Wide Web looking up jobs for you.

Perks

This website is a relief. You get so many tools that you'll never find them all.

When you choose to create a new résumé, you get a pop-up page that tells you how and why you are going to do this task, answering really obvious questions that a user would ask. It also tells you that it will take about fifteen minutes to build your résumé. Another good tool: When you click on

Benefits, you get a slew of articles about this important topic. They're not all aimed at recent college grads, either.

Listing and Compensation Data
Number of employers offering jobs:

They say they have 365,485 U.S. jobs and more than 450,000 jobs in total.

Good salary ranges?

No data.

Overall Navigability
Strengths:

It is a huge site.

Weaknesses:

It is a huge site. There were a few broken links, but the site is big.

Usability:

Fairly easy, and much easier the second time around.

General Review
Synopsis:

This is an efficient, interactive job-search site with a special track for freelancers. When posting on this site, you should realize that you compete against 14 million registered users and 9 million résumés. Narrow your job criteria and be specific to improve your odds.

Helpfulness and value to freelancers:

Get comfortable; give yourself a whole day to visit. (Think of it as going to the Grand Canyon.) The site feels like you have your mom or a friendly mentor sitting beside you telling you everything you need to know.

Waste of time online?

Not unless you already know everything there is to know about getting the right job.

r144.com

www.r144.com

Markets Served

Employers:

Yes.

Job seekers:

Yes.

Fee for job seekers:

No.

Type of professionals:

Freelancers.

Information

Job listings:

Each job listing is actually the property of other websites, some of which we have already reviewed. You have to register at the site that is holding the job. Then you can return to r144.com to bid on the job.

Articles:

In the index on the left side of the homepage are links to Freelance Jobs News, Home Business News, and Careers News. There's probably some good information available. Try the Freelance Hot Links, where there's lots of information.

Facts and figures:

No.

Contacts:

With all the links and links to links, you'll have more contacts than you can handle.

Training:

No.

Recruitment:

Indirectly.

Placement:

Indirectly.

Tools

Résumé posting:

Your résumé is submitted to another job-search website that sponsors each job.

Portfolio:

Unless the sponsoring website has a place for you to enter your website address, you can't submit a portfolio. It will be removed if you try to put it in the comments that you've attached to a bid.

Skills test:

Not directly, but some of the connecting websites do test.

Edit résumé:

You can't edit your bid comments, but you can go back to the websites where you've registered and revise your profile.

How long you will stay posted:

No data.

Automatic notice to employer if user inquires?

No.

Automatically sends your résumé?

No.

Notification when a matching job is available?

No.

Perks

You can promote yourself at this site by submitting an article about yourself. If you don't toot your own horn, no one else will. If your article is accepted, it will appear in an upcoming edition of their newsletter and may even gain permanent residence on their site. When published, your article will include a link to your e-mail and website, if applicable, and a bio or summary of the services you offer.

You can view the weather report for any city, make a donation to Michael J. Fox's Parkinson's disease research foundation, learn how your stocks are doing, get an instant quote on health insurance, and buy whatever the banner ad is promoting at the time you visit the site.

Listing and Compensation Data

Number of employers offering jobs:

At the Job Bank link from the homepage, it says: "Search over 50,000 jobs. Over 4,164 jobs added this week!"

Good salary ranges?

There is quite a range of bids, from way-too-low to I-wish-I-had-the-nerve-to-ask-for-that-much.

Overall Navigability

Strengths:

It's easy to link to freelance jobs in your category.

Weaknesses:

The bidding process takes too much time. Once you're registered with each of these websites, though, you can copy and paste your bids. Hint: Put your all-purpose comments in a Word document, copy and paste it into the bidding places, and revise it a little to fit each project.

Usability:

Easy.

General Review

Synopsis:

This is a database of freelance job projects. Here's how it works for the job seeker: You 1) go to r144.com, 2) click on the Job Bank, 3) click on a job to view its summary description, 4) click on the Web address of the sponsoring site, 5) register at the third-party site (if you haven't already), and 6) go back to number 3 and click to bid on another job.

Helpfulness and value to freelancers:

Very helpful.

Waste of time online?

No.

Sologig

Markets Served

Employers:
   Yes, they can post and search for free.
Job seekers:
   They say that they have 800,000 résumés.
Fee for job seekers:
   Yes.
Type of professionals:
   Those who want freelance contract work.

Information

Job listings:
   250,000 jobs.
Articles:
   No.
Facts and figures:
   Apparently more than 7,000 profiles are read and more than
   50,000 projects are posted each month.
Contacts:
   Only e-mail addresses.
Training:
   No.
Recruitment:
   Yes.
Placement:
   Yes.

Tools

Résumé posting:
   Yes, and you can post more than one.
Portfolio:
   No, although you can list your website, which could contain
   parts of your portfolio.
Skills test:
   No.
Edit résumé:
   Yes.

How long you will stay posted:
No data.
Automatic notice to employer if user inquires?
No data.
Automatically sends your résumé?
Yes.
Notification when a matching job is available?
Nothing suggested that this was an available service.

Perks
Free business cards and (probably not free) high-speed Internet access.

Listing and Compensation Data
Number of employers offering jobs:
10,000.
Good salary ranges?
You set your own within the pull-down list.

Overall Navigability
Strengths:
This is a clean, uncluttered site.
Weaknesses:
You must pay for their service, and it seemed to have no jobs available. Under the key-word phrase "software development," with the specialty "IT" and an hourly rate of fifteen to thirty dollars in Los Angeles, their response was, "No projects matched your search criteria 'software development.' Please try again." Under "writer," for "writing," "editing," and "copy" listings in the same city, the same response was received. Hmmm . . . no writers are needed in L.A.?
Usability:
Not one link was out of place on this site. Everything works the way that they say it will.

General Review
Synopsis:
This is a for-fee website that claims to place your résumé with employers looking for freelancers. It tricks you at first—it looks free but isn't—so if you're a risk-taker, pay the seventy-five dollars for a three-month membership and let us know how it turns out.
Helpfulness and value to freelancers:
Use the service if you want to take the chance and spend the money (seventy-five dollar minimum).

Waste of time online?
> You don't have to waste much time. If you join, you fill out your profile and pray. If you don't join, you can quickly go to another site . . . click and goodbye!

Thingamajob

www.thingamajob.com

Markets Served

Employers:
Yes.
Job seekers:
Yes.
Fee for job seekers:
No.
Type of professionals:
All.

Information

Job listings:
Choose a job category. It's best not to enter a key word in the search form. To find jobs faster, don't choose a state or city, either. The site doesn't have hundreds of jobs, so you can scan down the job list quickly to see if your city is there.

Articles:
Articles are reprints from editions of newspapers across the country. You choose the topic, such as politics, and then are given eight to ten articles to read. Most aren't relevant to job-searching, but what the heck—it never hurts to be well read.

Facts and figures:
No.

Contacts:
With each job description, which is usually very extensive, is a contact e-mail address connecting you with the agency recruiter who placed the ad.

Training:
No.

Recruitment:
Yes and no. You are invited to join the individual hiring companies, and there is a short synopsis of each company's focus. We didn't go that far, but recruitment may happen at some of the hiring companies.

Placement:
Not directly. See comments under "Contact" heading.

Tools

Résumé posting:

You can paste your own résumé into their form, which is a great help. You can't edit things out once you paste them in. Make sure to strip out the formatting on your original or it will turn goofy when you paste it into the form, such as when the bullets in your original document show up as question marks.

Portfolio:

No.

Skills test:

No.

Edit résumé:

When you go to the Edit Résumé button on this site, you are asked to paste your entire résumé into a text screen for re-placement on the site. So you can't really edit your résumé; you paste in another one entirely.

How long you will stay posted:

No data.

Automatic notice to employer if user inquires?

No.

Automatically sends your résumé?

No.

Notification when a matching job is available?

Yes. This site offers a Job Alert button. You fill in the form with job categories and the locations in which you are willing to work. You will receive an e-mail automatically notifying you of each new job posting.

Perks

This site says that it has teamed up with the nation's largest health care staffing service providers, so you'll probably get some good links to jobs and employers in that industry. The homepage also has an IT Community link to more information about that industry, including a message board.

They have a Career Center that has a community message board with a Job Talk button. That's helpful if you have the time to read questions and answers. Don't let it depress you because it makes the job-search world seem bigger, though. There are a lot of people out there! You will find some good advice with good articles on changing careers, interviewing tips, writing cover letters, etc.

Listing and Compensation Data
Number of employers offering jobs:
>No data.

Good salary ranges?
>Yes.

Overall Navigability
Strengths:
>Their Virtual Interview is excellent, even for seasoned job seekers. There are ten questions with multiple-choice answers. You get the correct answer right away and statistics on how other people have answered each question. (We passed with seven out of ten correct, in case you were wondering.)
>
>Another cool tidbit is their Career Analysis Test. It will give you a list of the top ten jobs with your greatest potential for accomplishment, analyze your motivation to work with other people, and examine your work preferences. If you have recently graduated from college or have been researching a job change, the information on this site will be helpful.

Weaknesses:
>A bigger job list is needed.

Usability:
>Good.

General Review
Synopsis:
>This is a network of about nine hiring companies or employment agencies. There are jobs listed, but you must go to the agency directly to apply.

Helpfulness and value to freelancers:
>When the key word "freelance" was entered, no results came up. Leaving out the key word gives you more jobs. When "free agent" was used, it was changed to "free and agent," which brought up no results. Leave out key words to find jobs, but good luck on getting anything.

Waste of time online?
>It is not helpful if you are looking for freelance or home-based work. If you want contract work, you might be able to find something, especially if you're looking in a major city.

Tripod

www.tripod.com

Markets Served

Employers:
   Yes.
Job seekers:
   Yes.
Fee for job seekers:
   No.
Type of professionals:
   All.

Information

Job listings:
   The big numbers are here. The site starts with 149,700 jobs. A narrowed search got 94,600 part-time jobs, with no location specified. Legal jobs got 345; the Management choice gave 1,540 jobs. Narrowing further, South Carolina and Education/Training jobs got none. Wisconsin and Marketing jobs got one listing. All-states and Marketing got 74. Some were Work at Home ads that promise $5,000 of personal income in one week. Nonetheless, the advantage of using this site to find freelance work is its large job database.

Articles:
   The standard stuff is here to help you write a better cover letter and résumé, but nothing extraordinary.

Facts and figures:
   No.

Contacts:
   There were lots of contacts such as the e-mail addresses of recruiting firms posting jobs. You might be better off returning to the Tripod site at www.Tripod.lycos.com/member_spotlight and contacting some of the folks who have put up real résumé-type websites.

Training:
   No.

Recruitment:

No. The Recruitment tab at the top of the homepage is directed at employers. It looks as though you could peek at other people's résumés, but you can't unless you sign up first.

Placement:

Yes.

Tools

Résumé posting:

When you post your résumé or portfolio here, it goes to Headhunter, not to Lycos. This is really weird, and there is no explanation as to why.

Portfolio:

Because you can create your own website with Tripod, you can have a portfolio online.

Skills test:

No.

Edit résumé:

You can edit both your website and your résumé.

How long you will stay posted:

No data.

Automatic notice to employer if user inquires?

No.

Automatically sends your résumé?

Probably, but you'll need to complete the member sign-up form and post your résumé before you can find out. This routine takes you through a maze of marketing offers for CDs and other impulse-purchase products. If you mistype a field, you'll be rerouted back to the sign-up page, where you'll have to start completely over again. After a couple of loop-de-endless-loops through this frustrating routine, we gave up trying to find out about the auto-send possibility.

Notification when a matching job is available?

There is an e-mail notification service somewhere in the Lycos site, although you'll have a hard time finding it.

Perks

There is a career coaching chat room, a sneaky Boss Button (to click if the boss is near so that your monitor will suddenly project a long text article about work performance or some other goofy topic), and a Company Profiles section, which is good if you have the time to conduct research.

The site contains the usual, run-of-the-mill material such as career fair information, which is not very helpful, especially to freelancers. There is a link to a newsletter for job seekers, and we found a good article about how to question an employer who didn't hire you, a different angle toward the work-searching task that may be insightful for both you and the employer.

The link to Contract Jobs is fairly useful. There are lots of jobs here, but you'll have a déjà vu experience on this site, especially if you've seen a lot of freelance job-search sites. After you've seen enough of these larger sites, you'll start to believe that the same staffing agencies are mastering them, with savvy Webmasters who are adept at placing the same job and projects in multiple locations throughout the Web. That's why Internet job hunting can be so tricky and why you should use this book as your map along the job-searching part of the information superhighway.

Listing and Compensation Data

Number of employers offering jobs:
No data.

Good salary ranges?
There is a salary comparison service at Lycos. It's thorough, and you'll be pleasantly surprised if you decide to try the service. It's a great way to discover the minimum, middle, and top range of fees being charged for a wide range of freelance jobs. For example, within the large category Printing/Publishing, you can check salaries of Artists; Copy Writers I, II, and III; Editors; Grants/Proposal Writers; Graphic Design Specialists; Photofinishing Technicians; Platemakers; Proofreaders; Speech Writers; Technical Illustrators; and Technical Writers I, II, and III. You have a choice of location and you can compare one location to another.

Overall Navigability

Strengths:
The site is maintained well, i.e., it has no broken links.

Weaknesses:
You will be disappointed by where the links will take you. In the Contract Work category are these postings: "Pegasus Modeling Service (Outreach Office), an International Modeling/ Talent Agency, is now accepting applications for models between the ages of eighteen to thirty years of age. Those with little or no experience are encouraged to apply." Here's another kind of post you'll get very tired of: "Make BIG MONEY! Easy & Simple. WE SHOW YOU HOW. GUARANTEED! We'll show you how you will make $5,000, at least, a week! IT'S FREE! Go to Web site for more information."

Usability:
> Go to the site map from Tripod first to get directions to the job-search area. The link is at the top in small letters on the right side of the homepage.

General Review
Synopsis:
> The irreverent and silly tone of this site is sometimes frustrating. Looking for freelance work, or any work for that matter, is serious business. The link Elvis Spotted on Lycos is not helpful in finding freelance or contract work and gets in the way. Because there's a lot of these senseless, stupid, and inane links and banners on this site, you may at first feel a little skeptical. Hang with it, though, because there are lots of project jobs and freelance work posted. You can always check out Elvis if you get bored.

Helpfulness and value to freelancers:
> Helpful.

Waste of time online?
> It's not a waste of time, but you'll spend a lot of it here.

WorldOpinion

www.worldopinion.com

Markets Served
Employers:
> Yes.

Job seekers:
> Yes.

Fee for job seekers:
> No.

Type of professionals:
> If you're a freelance job hunter, you should be interested in the marketing field. This can encompass Web writers, IT engineers, marketing directors, vice presidents of marketing and strategic development, and technical marketing managers.

Information
Job listings:
> On a Saturday, there were 5,550 jobs listed; the next day 5,341 jobs were available. Staffing services sponsored some of these positions, but most were placed directly by the employer.

Articles:
> The site is sponsored by approximately twenty marketing and social research associations, both national and international in scope, so there are links that will keep you occupied for days. This site will survey you for everything, and much of it seems highly reliable and scientific.

Facts and figures:
> This is a good place for salary data, but plan to run into some dead ends while researching. You may get distracted and learn, for example, that the starting salary for teachers in a private school system in Baker, Oregon, is $19,500. (Ouch!) A good link to this salary data is http://jobstar.org/tools/salary/sal-prof.htm#Technical.

Contacts:
> The sponsors of this website don't push themselves on you, but there are links to every association you can imagine. If you're looking for work as an independent agent, it seems sensible to belong to one or two of these groups.

Training:
> Even training for job hunters is covered here. You can enter the Job Hunters Career Center and find Résumé Writing 101, among many other related topics. From here you can be taken to a long list of articles on the same subject, each linked to the actual article or to the publication that printed the article. We did find commercial solicitations, but not until the end of the article list, where several companies offered products.

Recruitment:
> The employers and staffing agencies that are listed under the Classified section put their best foot forward in describing their companies by recruiting you through their "help wanted" ads.

Placement:
> No.

Tools

Résumé posting:
> You'll want to create a login password first, then go to the Site Map, then to Classified Ads, then to login, then to Résumé.

Portfolio:
> When you write your ad for your résumé, list your website address. The viewer is then informed of a location at which he or she can look at your work, your portfolio, and your picture—whatever you want to share.

Skills test:
> No.

Edit résumé:
> Yes.

How long you will stay posted:
> Sixty days.

Automatic notice to employer if user inquires?
> No.

Automatically sends your résumé?
> No.

Notification when a matching job is available?
> No data.

Perks

> The Calendar furnishes details about hundreds of research events, seminars, and academic meetings worldwide. The News provides the latest breaking research news and dozens of photos from major meetings and conferences. The Newsstand offers access to fifty research publications. Stock Watch monitors twenty-one research organizations, including several

that trade on the Toronto and London exchanges. The Reference section includes links to research associations, a glossary of terms, and many other useful research-related topics. The Bookstore gives you access to dozens of the latest research and marketing publications that can easily be ordered online. That's just the index. Go deeper and you'll get lost. It's like spending a day in your favorite library, bookstore, or museum.

Listing and Compensation Data
Number of employers offering jobs:

There are more than 5,000 jobs offered, some from the same employer, but it looks as if many employers are represented.

Good salary ranges?

Yes.

Overall Navigability
Strengths:

Because the commercial emphasis of the site is low-key, you can find your way around quite easily without bumping into ads that take you away from your focus.

Weaknesses:

Where is the site's copy editor? There appeared on the site this hastily composed sentence: "Complete the following information to add or update *you firms* information in the WorldOpinion directory."

Usability:

In a word, awesome.

General Review
Synopsis:

As the name of the website implies, this is opinion. The jobs offered through the site are related to the opinion industry, probably because the site is sponsored by some of the most respected opinion groups in the world. You can do job hunting here, but of equal importance, you can carry on your own research to become a more rounded freelancer. Both tasks are covered.

Helpfulness and value to freelancers:

Very helpful.

Waste of time online?

Not at all.

Index

Abbreviations 167
About.com 11, 24
Academic preparation 82
Account manager 261-262
Accredited university 31
Accrediting agency 118
Active employment 40
Active firewalls 94
Ad posting 270
Adobe Acrobat 158, 166, 191-192, 214
Adobe GoLive 163
Adobe Illustrator 191
Adobe Photoshop 188, 191, 195
Adobe 158, 163, 166, 171, 188, 191-192, 195, 214
ADSL 129, 143
Adult education courses 118
Advertisement 168
Advertising/PR category 280
AFP 110
Agency recruiter 292
Aggressive marketing techniques 156
Agricultural economy 27
Agriculture & Environment 261
Airline flights, booking 49
Alt link 203
AltaVista 65
Alternative Web browsers 156
Amateur programmers 162
Amazon.com 126, 226, 279
American Demographics magazine 11
American Institute of Architects 29, 31-32
American Society of Association Executives 55
American Society of Magazine Editors 93
Amusement parks 244
Analog telephone fax machine 35
Analog video capture card 188-189
Analytical skills 39
Anarchic Internet 126
Andreesen, Marc 125
Animators 8, 12

Annual report 41, 80
Annual salaries 239
AOL 55, 110, 145, 147
Apple Computer 4, 37, 138, 158, 192
Application programs 61, 77
Applications folder 175
Appointment scheduling 78
Aquent 213-215
Aramark 244
Architects 29-32, 49
Archives of news stories 211
ARPANET 52, 124
Art 54, 62, 217
ArtHire 216-217
Artificial intelligence 106
Artists 7, 71, 217
ASCII 165-166
Asian Americans 223
Asian companies 55
ASP 77-78, 147, 158
Associated Press Managing Editors Association 93
AT&T 36, 154, 205
Atkinson, Robert D. 112
ATMs 49
AtoZMoonlighter.com 248
Attachment feature 161
Attachment size limit 150
Auction site 273
Audio 49, 127, 158, 189, 192
Audio/video 158
Audio-editing software 189
Australia 111
Authenticity certificates 98
Author 7-8, 10, 22, 68-69, 89-90, 106, 125, 162, 244, 265, 270
Auto Notify 217
Automated e-mail message 65
Average length of workweek 11, 44
Bachelor of Architecture degree 31
Bachelor's degree 31, 40, 62, 70

Bandwidth 61, 127
Bank accounts 49, 95, 105
Banner ads 221
Basic HTML tags 169
Basic Internet Software 7, 155
Basic Web page 163
Bell 103 modem 36
Benefits 14-15, 19, 33-34, 47, 73, 78, 215, 269, 285
Bergen, Jack 82
Best Buy 96
BestJobsUSA 219
Bidding 82, 100, 126, 258, 272-273, 275, 286-288
Bilheimer, Susan 270
Bill-collecting technology 274
Billing service 214
Black Collegian magazine, *The* 223-224
Blacksburg Electronic Village 145
Blank lines 176
Blank page 253, 269
Boldface headings 237
Bookkeeping 103
Bookmarking 156
Border sizes 173
Boss Button 278, 296
Boss 9, 11, 13, 32, 46, 69, 95, 102, 278, 296
Brick-and-mortar history 89
Broadband 97, 141, 145, 147
Broadcast 8, 231
Brochures 13
Broken links 285
Browser 24, 156, 171, 177
Building material 29
Bulk e-mail 159
Bulleted list 170
Bulletin boards 80, 85, 89, 93, 119, 125, 197
Bullets 166
Bureau of Labor Statistics 7, 11, 30, 39, 41, 60, 70, 74, 81, 91
Business applications 51
Business articles 71
Business cards 13, 87, 183, 198, 200, 290
Business consultants 8

Business correspondence 150, 159, 160
Business degree 82
Business management 54
Business operations 6, 8-9, 17, 41, 43, 56-58, 77, 86, 186
Business-to-business 7, 57, 86
Business-writing samples 271
Cable modem 142-144, 147-148
Cable-free Ethernet network 138
CAD 50
California 17, 75, 231, 235
Calzada, Alicia Wagner 110-111
CampusCareerCenter Worldwide 64
Canada 4, 85
Candidate profile database 234
Capitalism 28
Capture card 188-189
Career analysis test 294
Career center 11, 268, 293, 300
Career development 22-23, 62, 87, 230, 236, 296
Career Fair 220, 278, 296
Career profile 29, 38, 59, 68, 79, 90
CareerBuilder 201, 226-227
CareerCity 229
CareerJournal 232, 234
CareerWeb 236
Cartoonists 8
CD-ROM 130, 139, 152
CDs 145, 189, 192, 194, 189, 296
Cell phone 55, 144
Censis Research Centre of Italy 106
Certification of computing professionals 40
Chat room 213, 269, 276, 296
Childcare 44, 49
Children's books 198
Chinese 24, 27
Christian 219, 248
CIM 50
Cisco Systems Inc. 15, 77
Citizen of the Internet 162
Civil engineer 30
Civil service job 76
Classified section 59, 251-253, 300

Clean Air Act 45

Clerical support 102

Climate Magazine 77

CNC 50

Coded computer language 38

Coding tags 172

Cold calls 13, 18

Cold War 123

Collaboration 7-8, 85-86, 127

College 5, 64, 70, 82, 92, 225, 285

Color printer 134

Commercial servers 127, 180

Commercial Web space 180, 193, 196, 275

Commodities of trade 52

Communication devices 78

Communication skills 39, 61, 80

Communications 35-36, 41, 45, 52, 54, 68, 78, 81, 92, 97, 107, 124-125, 138, 160, 221, 261

Community centers 118

Community message board 293

Community relations 81

Compact Disc-Read Only Memory 130, 139, 152

Compensation 98, 211, 215, 217, 221, 225, 228, 230, 234, 238, 241, 244, 246, 249, 253, 255, 258, 262, 265, 269, 271-272, 275, 279, 281, 285, 287, 290, 294, 297, 301

Composer 169

Compressed formats 191

CompUSA 96

Computer acronyms 137

Computer application capacity 77

Computer chip makers 139

Computer controlled devices 50

Computer course 118

Computer desktop 177

Computer editing 188

Computer engineer 38

Computer equipment 61, 76, 135

Computer graphics–oriented industries 166

Computer industry 5, 58, 130, 133-134, 141

Computer instruction 118-119

Computer language 38, 59, 163, 169

Computer manufacturer 131

Computer market 37

Computer model number 131

Computer monitor 16, 146, 191

Computer processor speed 139

Computer programming 9, 38-40, 59-60, 62

Computer science 62, 75

Computer security professional 39

Computer settings 132

Computer specs 133, 136

Computer stores 119, 132, 135, 190

Computer systems analyst 38

Computer typesetter 75-76

Computer video-instruction series 119

Computer viruses 96

Computer-aided design 50

Computerized workstations 50, 77

ComputerJobs 64, 239-240

Computer-related jobs 40, 125, 203

Condition of payment 29

Conferences 80, 252, 267, 300

Confidential profile 233

Congress 44

Connection type 142, 149, 151

Connectivity 4, 17, 56, 72

Consensus decision-making 54

Conservation librarian 231

Constructing Web pages 59

Construction 29-30, 34

Consultant 8, 86, 239-241, 284

Contact employers 159, 184, 201, 243

Contact information 100, 110, 233-234

Content writer 70

Contract jobs 15-16, 19, 40, 57, 66-67, 77, 86, 93, 102, 202, 221, 297

Cookies 97

CoolWorks 242-243

Copy editor 70, 75, 301

Copy machine 36

Copy writer 70

Copyright 20, 195

Copyright, freelancer's 20

Copywriters 8

Corporate client 19, 79

Corrected version of text 90

Cost efficiency 54

Cost of a new computer 131

Cost-saving tips 136

Council of Public Relations Firms 82

Court reporter 8, 91

Cover letter 237, 295

CPR certificate 243

Create documents 162, 166, 169

Create folders 160

Creative work 10, 29, 59, 62, 68, 124, 192, 216, 269-270, 275

Creativemoonlighter.com 62, 248

Credit card 42, 77, 95, 97-98, 105, 125, 212

Credit-checking service 215

CruelWorld 245-246

Curricula 31, 40, 82, 93

Customer satisfaction 103

Customer service 146, 149, 151

Cyber Detective 95

CyberAtlas.com 5

Cyberbusiness 56

Daily responsibilities of employment 41

Damsen, Fred 75

DAT player 189

Data communication units 36

Data entry 91, 93

Database developers 15

Database management 77

Database of jobs/companies 225, 256, 277, 279, 288

Database 15, 17-18, 20, 65, 77-78, 93, 100, 166, 199, 211, 221, 225, 228-229, 232, 234, 256, 261, 267, 271-272, 277-279, 288, 295

Day care 19

Dcpubs 76

Deadline 240

Dealership 50, 99

Decentralized workforce 6-7, 19, 41-42

Dedicated phone line 124, 145

Definition of freelance 72

Degree course 118

Deleted text 190

Denali 244

Department of Defense's Advanced Research Projects Agency 124

Description meta tag 198

Design rules 194

Design software 59

Design 4, 12, 29-31, 49-50, 59-62, 76-77, 86, 124, 140, 156, 163, 165-166, 168, 179-182, 186, 192-195, 209, 212, 216, 221, 265, 297

Designing websites 120

Desktop 50, 77, 85-86, 161, 177, 213

Diamond, Gregory 68-69, 71

Dictaphones 4

Digital age 8, 17, 78, 107, 111

Digital camera 111, 134

Digital communications 36

Digital economy 8, 15

Digital format 3, 89, 189

Digital music 141

Digital networks 107

Digital photograph 188

Digital video 140, 189

Diplomacy 80

DirecPC 148

Direct marketing 212

Directmarketingcareers.com 64

Disability insurance 107

Disabilty 45

Disbursement of products 28

Discussion forum 103, 269

Disk space 156

Distribution of résumés 87

Distribution systems 43, 112

Diversity page 230

Doctor's prescription 272

Domain registration 181

Domain 6, 45, 151, 157, 181

DOS 37

Dot-com 125-126, 146

Downloading 79, 95, 97, 142, 144, 157-158, 160-162, 180, 189, 191, 193, 214, 233

Downsizing 10, 41-42, 112

Drafter 30

DreamJobs 248-249

Dreamweaver 163, 169

Drive Size A 137
Driver's Seat For 112
Driving directions 227
Drop-down menu 169
DSL consumers 151
DSL installations 143
DSL 143-144, 148, 151
DVDs 139
Earthlink Web 147
eBay 126, 135
Ebbing Tide, The 68
E-book 269
E-commerce 6-7, 55-56, 86, 107, 244
Economic downturns 15, 18
Economic growth 28, 54, 113, 127
Editor & Publisher 252-253
Editor 4, 8-9, 16, 54, 61-62, 68-70, 72, 75, 85-86,
    91, 93, 100, 153, 163, 169, 175-176, 181, 213,
    251-253, 282, 297, 301
Editorial careers 93
Editor's DeskTop 85-86
Educated workers 29, 33-34, 54
Education 10, 22-23, 31-32, 40, 44, 51, 61, 82,
    92, 106-107, 109, 118, 223, 230-231, 243, 280,
    282, 295
Education/Training jobs 295
Educational requirement 92
EduPro Systems 119
Edwards, Sarah 5
E-lance 17, 19, 98
ELance.com 17, 82, 193, 202, 269
Electronic commerce 56-57
Electronic Recruiting Index 58, 64-65
Electronically composed music 192
E-mail attachments 75, 96, 150, 165, 209, 260
E-mail résumés 88, 165
E-mail service 78, 97, 149-150, 153, 156, 158,
    160, 243, 280, 284, 296
E-mail software 46, 129, 150
E-mail, effective use of 17, 65, 76, 90, 100, 158-
    159, 165, 210-211, 218, 227, 267, 272
Embossed-looking image 195
Emerald Coast Jobs, Inc. 77
Emerging News, The 240

E-messaging 56
Employee benefit 41
Employee relations 81
Employer articles 277
Employer data 230
Employer websites 65
Employment agencies 215, 219, 228, 246, 248,
    278, 294
Employment history 233, 247
Employment opportunities 225
Employment Outlook 30, 39, 60, 70, 81, 91
Encyclopedia Britannica 219
Engine sites 64, 198-199
Engineering department 50
England 70, 76, 90, 92, 269
English skills 90, 92
Entertainment industry 7
Entrepreneurs 9-10, 125
Entry-level salary 225
E-portfolio 257
E-recruitment 63, 66
E-Spiders 65
Essential plug-ins 157
Ethernet 130, 138, 145
Etiquette 159
Eudora 149, 158
European 27, 55
Europemedia 55
E-village 7, 85
Examination requirement 31
Executive recruitment 232-234
Expansion cards 140
Expansion of the Internet 7, 126
Expense account 14, 42
Expense of wiring 103
Expertise 17, 21, 38, 58, 185, 283
Explorer 145, 153, 155-157, 177
External communication 56
External drives 51, 140
External port 78
Extra e-mail accounts 150
Extra money 9, 194
Face-to-face communication 87
Facsimile machine 35-36

Fair wages 33
Family 44, 47, 69, 97, 102, 110, 113, 119, 130, 133, 135, 159
FAQ section 227, 230, 246, 270
FastCompany.com 67
Fastest-growing career fields 82
Fastest-growing freelance fields 59
Fax machines 35-36
Fax 19, 35-36, 43, 50, 78, 198
Features, built-in 187
Federal Aid Highway Act of 1956 34
Federal government 29, 142, 221
Fee-based service 254, 277
Fell, Diana 11
Feudal system of economics 27
Feudalistic agricultural age 53
Fiber-optic lines 3, 51
Fiction story 218
Fifth Discipline, The 54
File sizes 189, 191-192
File Transfer Protocol 125, 161, 180
Financial planning 9, 12
Firewalls 94, 97-98
FireWire 140, 189
First Industrial Revolution 105
Fitzpatrick, Dolores 90-92
Floor-covering installers 99
Floppy disk 139
Florida 76
Font size 170, 175
For-fee website 290
Formatting features 166
For-sale ads 135
Fossil fuel emissions 45
Free access 251, 272
Free ads 211
Free agent 5, 10-12, 16, 67, 74, 85, 102, 106-107, 111, 209
Free e-mail account 243
Free ISPs 146
Free software 158, 180
Free tech support 135
Free Web hosting 180, 196
Free Web space 151

Free-labor movement 28
Freelance business 13-14, 17, 110
Freelance career 5, 21-23, 29-30, 35, 38, 55, 62, 68-70, 79, 90-91, 106, 110-111
Freelance commerce 57
Freelance experts 85
Freelance market 12, 18, 49, 89-90, 260
Freelance résumé 89, 94, 221
Freelance.com 17, 71, 260
FreelanceWorkExchange.com 89, 264
FreelanceWriting.com 72, 267, 269
FreetimeJobs 271
Freeware 158, 162
Frequency modulation 36
FTP 61, 125, 153, 161-162, 180
Full-time 9, 16, 33, 71, 76, 90, 102, 202, 219, 269
Functionality of websites 59
Fund-raising 81
G3 processor 130
Gallup poll 11
Gates, Bill 3, 37, 117, 138
General management 232
Generation One 108-109, 113-114
Generation X 108
Generation Y 108
Geopolitical.com 248
GIF 188, 191
Gilder, George 112
Globalization 4-5, 90, 109, 112
Glossary of terms 301
Google 120, 202-203, 236
Gottlieb, Paul 112
Government research computers 124
Government Technology magazine 54, 108
Government 7, 30, 51, 81, 221
Graduate/Professional school 224
Grammar 70, 92, 159, 167
Grant/Proposal writers 297
Graphic Artists Guild 62
Graphic arts/design 8-9, 12, 49, 59-60, 62, 140, 168, 179, 182, 192, 195, 209, 213, 221, 297
Graphical environment 125
Graphical user interface 37, 52

Graphics cards 130, 140-141

Graphics 59, 62, 123, 125, 130, 137, 140-141, 166, 181, 187-188, 191-193, 202, 213, 253

Grappo, Gary Joseph 22

Greenfield Online 251

Greenhouse gases 45

Grove, Dan 86

GUI 37

Guru.com 17, 202, 274, 276

Hard drive 37, 95-97, 130-131, 137, 161, 175, 184

Harris, Blake 54, 108

Harvard 109, 231

Hawks, Carrie Rathbun 80

Headhunter 167, 201, 277-278, 296

Health care 44, 79, 107, 221, 254, 293

Health insurance 14-15, 287

Hebrew 24

Heinrichs, Jay 16

HEL 145

Help tutorials, built-in 119

Help Wanted 201, 251, 300

High school 31, 40, 62, 225

Higher education 106-107, 118

High-speed communication 36, 54, 106-107, 112

High-speed computer connectivity 17

High-speed Internet access 72, 85, 141, 144-145, 234, 269, 290

High-speed modem 61

High-tech expertise 58

Hiring companies 46, 226, 292, 294

Hispanic Americans 223

History feature 156

HMO/PPO 14

Hobbyists 87

Home-based businesses 41, 43, 57, 74, 77, 106, 111

Home-based freelance workers 74

Homework 24, 88

Hospitality industry 267

Hotel reservations 232

HotJobs 90, 167-168, 201, 280

Hotmail 150

HTML code 171-172

HTML programmer 12

HTML 4-5, 12, 59-61, 69, 96, 145, 151, 158, 163, 166-172, 174-181, 190, 193, 199-200

Http 5, 7, 32, 52, 61, 98, 172, 174, 260, 299

Human resources 54, 166, 221, 234, 242, 284

Hyperlinks 59, 178

Hypertext 52, 59, 163, 169

IBM 3, 37, 77

ICab 156

IEEE 140, 189

Illustrator files 191

Illustrators 8

Image quality 188

Image-editing software 188

IMAP 149-150

IMHO 160

Inbox 160, 243, 272

Independence 16, 28, 102

Independent Home Workers Alliance 93

Index every page 198

Industrialization 32, 41, 43, 53, 55, 108, 112-113

Information age 53, 55, 58, 108

Information systems manager 39

Information Technology Association of America 15

Information technology 15, 46, 55, 57-58, 111-112, 239, 274

Innovation 107

Installation cost 144

Instant messaging 4, 144

Insurance 14-15, 36-37, 42, 68, 98, 107, 215, 275, 287

Intel 37

Interactive job-search site 285

Interactive online portfolio 183

Interface 37, 52, 163

Intern Development Program of the American Institute of Architects 31

Internal memory 37

Internal network 54

Internal Revenue Service 43

International Business Machines 37

International perspectives 41
International telegraph 35
International Telework Association 73
International 4, 16, 35, 37, 41, 69, 73, 271, 297, 299
Internet confidentiality 93
Internet connection 121, 129, 138, 141-143, 145, 149, 155, 234
Internet Explorer 153, 155-157, 177
Internet software 7, 129, 153, 155-157
Internet spider services 93
Internet startup companies 126
Internet-navigating experience 130
Internet-related business operations 56
Internet-related entrepreneurial innovation 106
Internetrepreneurial 106-107
Internship 31, 64
Interpreters 8
Interviews 5, 16, 18, 68, 127, 194, 201, 215, 230, 283, 293
Introduction of the IBM PC 37
IP 52, 61, 95, 124, 129, 151-153
Ireland 76
IRS 223
Isolation 47
ISPs 141, 143-146, 148-151, 180
IT background 262
IT certification 260
IT Community link 293
IT publications 240
IT 72, 118, 133, 212, 221, 275
Italy 27, 106
Jackson, Paul J. 41
Jackson, Scott 77
Japanese 27
Jesse, Jack 10
JIB List 110
Job-hunting tips 201
JobLink 210-211
Jobsonline.com 7, 201
Journalism 70, 79-80, 82-83, 92, 210, 212
JPEG 188, 191
Kazakhstan 283

Keets, Kristen 17-18
Kelsey Group 56
Kenrick, Pat 37
Key word 65, 171, 198, 210, 220-221, 227-228, 234-235, 237, 251, 278-281, 290, 292, 294
Key words, examples 281
Keypunch machines 3
Kinko's 226
Kirsch, Sylvia 38-40
Klein, Steve 106-107
Knowledge economy 8
Korn, Arthur 35
L.A. 290
Labor economics 34
Labor markets 58
Labor unions 33
LAN 51-52, 54, 107
Landscape architect 30
Language instruction pages 24
Language translation 69
LANs 46, 51
Laptop 69, 144, 218, 262
Large businesses 125
Large calculators 37
Large cities 112, 282
Large classes 118
Large corporation 63, 145, 107
Large dot-coms 18
Lawler, Jennifer 100
Layoffs 126
Layout 49, 76, 137, 167, 172
Legal jobs 295
Les Clefs d'Or USA 267
Liability 14
Library technician 91
Life insurance 68
Lifestyle 10, 12, 14, 22-23, 90, 102, 111
Like millions of Americans 129
Line breaks 176
Link 87, 293, 299
Linux 133
Lisbon 110
Local Area Network 46, 51
Local commerce monitor 56

Local File feature 177
Local newspaper 119, 135, 201
Login site 247
London exchanges 301
Long Island 76
Los Angeles 281, 290
Lot of Internet entrepreneurs 125
Lotus 1-2-3 software 37
Lycos 295-298
Lyra Research of Massachusetts 251
Ma Bell 124
Mac OS 133
Macintosh 130, 133, 151, 153, 157, 162, 175, 192
Macromedia Dreamweaver 163
Magazine writer 70
Mainframe 51, 125
Management 42-43, 53-55, 77, 80, 232, 243, 271, 274, 277, 295
Manufacturing 36, 42, 49-50, 254
Marine engineer 30
Marketing consultants 8
Marketing professional Employment Outlook 60
Marketing 8, 17, 29, 56, 59-62, 64, 75, 77-78, 81-82, 89, 156, 210, 212, 218, 232, 236, 271, 274-275, 295-296, 299, 301
Mass communication 82, 108
Master of Architecture 31
Master's degree 31, 284
Maximum size of a file 150
MBA online 278
McAfee VirusScan 96
McDonnough, Katie 30
McIntyre, John 251
McKinsey & Company 15
McNealy, Scott
Mechanical engineer 30
Media drive 139
Media Kit page 269
Media Player 158
Media relations services 81
Median annual income 71
Mediation process 240

Medical Leave Act 44
Meta tags 171, 198-200
Metropolitan New Economy Index 112
Michigan 5, 18, 30, 63-64, 80, 109, 124, 242
Microcomputer specialist 39
Microsoft Corporation 3, 15
Microsoft Explorer 145, 153, 177
Microsoft Network 282
Microsoft Outlook Express 158
Microsoft Windows 151, 158
Microsoft Word 162-163, 165, 190
Microsoft 3, 15, 77, 119, 138, 145, 151, 153, 155-156, 158, 162-163, 165, 177, 190, 282
Microsoft.com Note 138
MIDI format 192
Midwest 75
Military 27, 52
Minidisc player 189
Ministereo jack 189
Minority issues 223
Miracles Unlimited Counseling Center 10
Mississippi 71
Missouri 220
MITS 37
Modem 17, 19-20, 36, 43, 52, 61, 113, 130, 138, 141-145, 147-149
Monster.com 18, 167-168, 201, 203, 283
Montana 244
Moore, Cathy 100
Morino Institute 106
Mosaic 4, 52, 125
MP3 format 192
MPEG 192
MRPA 63-64
MSN Web 147
Muir, John 243
Multimedia 60, 62, 123, 128, 184, 202
Music 157
National Architectural Registration Board 31
National Book Award 211
National defense 36
National flooring company 99
National Labor Union 33
National parks 242, 244

National Press Photographers Association site 110
National Public Radio 68
National Writers Union 68
Native Americans 223
Netiquette 126, 159
Netizen 162
Netpreneurial 106-107
Netscape 125, 145, 149, 153, 155-157, 169, 177
Network administrators 15
Networking hardware 138
New Jersey 56
New York Times, The 20, 76, 114
New York 3-4, 20, 76, 114, 160
Newsday 20, 76
Newsgroups 4, 19, 85, 89, 93, 97, 125, 236
Newsletter 17, 68, 210, 269, 287, 296
Newspaper advertisements 18
Newspaper 18, 212, 218, 221, 253
Newspapers' employment sections 221
NFO WorldGroup 49
Noncomputer-based graphics 188
Non-Pentium processors 134
Nonprofit ventures 126
Norton Antivirus 96
Notepad 169, 175
Nova Scotia 236
Novell 51, 119
Number-crunching 123
OCR software 187
Oech, Robert von 21
Office environment 46, 50, 102
Office of Advocacy 56-57
Office space 14, 19, 77, 103, 258
Online forum discussion group 103
Online portfolios 195
Online résumé services 88
Online Résumés 7, 65-66, 87-90, 94, 151, 155, 161, 163, 165-168, 178, 177-183, 186, 196-197, 210, 214
Online Theft 7, 95
Ontario 85
Operating System 3, 37, 132, 137
Opinion groups 301

Oracle 15, 77
Oregon 220, 231, 299
OS 3, 37, 132, 137
Outlook Express 158
Outside magazine 16
Outside recruiters 18
Outsourcing firms 16
Pacific Northwest 261
Page designer/layout artist 76
Page width 167
PageSucker 193
PBS Career Center 11
PCDs 78
PCI cards 140
PDA 12, 78
PDF 158, 166, 191-192
Pegasus Modeling Service 297
Pentium II processor 130
People of color 223
PepsiCo 109
Periodical publisher 75
Peripheral devices 50-51
Personal communication device 78
Personal contact 87
Phone interview 261
Phone jack connector 138
Phone line 3, 14, 43, 124, 138, 141, 143-145
Photofinishing technicians 297
Photography 9, 12, 62, 75, 121, 185, 188, 196, 253, 300
Photoshop 188, 191, 195
Physical portfolios 184, 194, 196
Physical science 31
Pink, Daniel 67, 106
Pixel height 217
Political parties 106
Political science 79
Polochek, Neal 56
Population demographics 113
Portable disks 139
Portable document format 158, 166, 191-192
Portfolio 7, 121, 127, 183-184, 186, 189, 190-196, 217-218, 243, 252, 261, 296
Ports 140

Portugal 109
Post office box 97
Prepress production manager 216
Previous employer 76
Previous experience 243
Printer 194
Printing/Publishing 297
Printouts 183, 194
Private school system 299
Private Sector & Finance 261
Private tutors 119
Process Control Industry 254
Processor speed 139
Production manager 76, 216
Production process 214
Productivity of offsite personnel 46
Professional fees 17
Professional societies 29
Professional-looking résumé 121, 168
Profession-related site 200
Programming 8, 12, 15, 38-39, 52, 59-61, 162-163, 169, 183
Progressive employers 283
Progressive Policy Institute 112
Project postings 72, 87, 100, 248
Proofreaders 8, 75, 90-93, 213, 297
Prospecting letters 13
PRSA 80, 82
PSAs 227
Psychological barriers of communication 46
Public domain 157
Public libraries 136
Public Relations Society of America 80, 82
Public relations 8-9, 70, 75, 78-83, 102
Public sector 107
Public-access computers 136
Publications 20, 68-69, 239-240, 300-301
Publishable work 89
Publishing industry 252
Pull-down boxes 251
Pull-down list 290
Pull-down menus 37, 163
Purchasing 55, 133, 135
Quark 171

QuickTime 4, 158, 192
R144.com 286, 288
Radio Shack 37
RAM 137-138
Random access memory 137-138
RealPlayer 158
Real-time interviews 201
Recruitment/Placement 18, 42, 63-66, 88, 210, 214, 216, 229, 233-234, 237, 242, 249, 252, 254, 255, 257, 261, 264, 268, 272, 274, 280, 284, 286, 289, 292
Recycle bin 68
Reference section 301
Referral service 40
Refurbished computer 135
Religion link 248
Removable-media drives 139
Rent 43
Reporters 80
Research opportunities 80
Research publications 300
Researchers 100
Resource communications 221
Reston 227
Résumés online 7, 65-66, 87-90, 94, 151, 155, 161, 163, 165-168, 178, 177-183, 186, 196-197, 210, 214
Retail sales worker 225
Retirement plans 107
Risi, Deborah 68
Risks 10, 14, 73, 96, 290
RJ-45 connector 138
Robinson, David 59, 61
Robotics 49, 106
Rodriguez, Joseph 36
Royal Institute of British Architects 29
Rural areas 34, 111, 113-114, 143-144
Salaries of artists 297
Salary comparison service 297
Salary data 211, 215, 217, 221, 228, 230, 238, 244, 246, 255, 258, 262, 265, 269, 275, 294, 297, 299
Salary.com 15
Sales analysis 50

Sales pitches 141, 265

Sales professional 60

Sample online résumé 177-179

San Diego 220

San Francisco 235

Satellite Internet 144

Satellite 3, 41, 51, 144, 146-149

Scam artists 100, 127

Scanner 50, 121, 134, 140, 187-188

Screenwriters 269

Sculptor 30

Seagull management 42

Search engine 32, 64-65, 196, 198-199, 202, 236, 241, 248

Seasonal workers 67, 242-244

Second income 74

Second Industrial Revolution 105

Second phone line 141, 144

Secondhand machine 135

Sector of the economy 41

Selenium photocell transmitter 35

Self-deducted 14

Self-employed 5, 9, 11-12, 39, 43, 60-61, 67, 69, 73-74

Senge, Peter M. 54

Shareware 97, 158, 162

Shockwave 157

Shortage of qualified workers 58

Silicon 124

SimpleText 175

Skydiving 71

Slavery 105

Small business 56-58, 63, 74, 114

Small office/home office 57, 60, 103

SmarterWork.com 100

Snagajob.com 248

Snail mail 7, 111

Social research associations 299

Social security 14, 95, 97, 105, 223

Soft employment market 16

Software applications 77

Software development 15, 290

Software industry 40, 77

Software Information Industry Association 40

Software programs 7, 37, 39, 62, 65, 69, 91, 95-97, 105, 155, 157, 162

SOHOs 57, 103

Sologig.com 277, 289

Sound cards 130, 141

Sound input 141

Sound technicians 8

South Africa 267

South Carolina 295

South Dakota 242

Southern Nevada Hotel Concierge Association 267

Space constraints 201

Spanish 24, 27

Speech impediments 46

Speech writer 70, 218, 297

SpencerStuart.com 246

Spiders, resume 65, 93

Spreadsheet applications 37

Spreadsheet calculations 77

Staffing agencies 215, 230, 297, 299-300

Start-up fees 271

Statistics 11

Stock market 80, 126, 234, 300

Student/instructor ratio 118

Stuffit Expander 157

Summer jobs 248, 281

Sun Microsystems 96

Sweatshops 33

Switch careers 23

Switzerland 125

Sygate 97

T1 lines 61, 145

Tapscott, Don 8

Taxes 102, 107

TCP/IP 52, 61, 95, 124, 129, 151-153

Tech support 15, 131, 135, 145-146, 149, 196

Tech Writing Marketplace 270

Technical careers 32

Technical illustrators 297

Technical marketing managers 299

Technical support 15, 131, 135, 145-146, 149, 196

Technical writer 12, 70-71, 270

Technological revolution 10
Technology workers 15
Technology, new 58
Telecommunications 38, 40, 73-74
Telecommuting 20, 43, 45, 47, 73, 87, 248
Teleconferencing 41, 85
Telegraph 35-36
Telephone interviews 68
Telephone lines 36, 51, 124
Telephone number 94, 95, 110, 251
Telephotography equipment 36
Teletype-style printers 124
Television 3-4, 49, 55, 119, 127, 142
Telework 6, 40-42, 42-43, 45-47, 72-75
Teleworking: International Perspectives 41
Telnet 125
Temp 16, 67, 213, 216, 281
Text documents 175, 187, 190
Text editor 175-176
Text-only areas of the Internet 126
Text-only copyright notice 195
Thingamajob 292
Third-party computerized database 20
Third-party e-mail account 97
Third-party site 90, 248, 288
Thompson, Hunter S. 88
Thoreau, Henry David 12, 23
Tiano, Steve 75
Time magazine 20
Time Warner Cable 148
Toastmasters 218
Toll-free number 258, 278
Top-producing freelance markets 89
Top-ranked pages 199
Toronto 4, 301
Tourism 232, 280
Transmission Control Protocol/Internet
    Protocol 52, 61, 95, 124, 129, 151-153
Trojan Horse programs 95, 97
Trucking personnel 42
Twenty-four-hour service 63, 77, 145
U.K. 100
U.S. Department of Energy 45
U.S. Department of Labor 11, 44, 58, 91

U.S. Small Business Administration 56-57
UCLA 124
United Nations 45
Universal resource locator 24, 168, 172, 174,
    197, 220
University of Michigan 124
University of North Carolina 3
University of Utah 124
UNIX 61
Upgrades 130-131, 135, 137, 272, 278
Uploading 160
Urban areas 20, 34, 112-113
URL 24, 168, 172, 174, 197, 220
USB 140
Usenet 4, 19, 97, 125-126, 156, 202-203
User names 196
Vatican City 24
Vegas 273
Verbal communication skills 80
Verizon Web 147
Vesely, Rebecca 64
Video 38, 119, 127, 140, 157-158, 183, 186, 188-
    189, 192, 194-196
Videoconference 86, 109
Video-editing software 188
Virginia 68, 98, 145, 227
Virtual business environments 85, 111
Virtual freelancer 19
Virtual interview 294
Virtual recruitment 7, 63
Virtual test center 260-261
Virus protection software 96
Viruses 97
Visual artists 7, 217
Visual impairments 46
Visual presentation 59
Vocational programs 6, 40, 62, 93
Voice recognition 69
Wages 29, 35
Wait-staff job 244
Wall Drug Store 242
Wall Street Journal 232, 234
Wall Street 125-127, 232, 234
Wallace, Delores 35

Wallinski, Joseph 79-80

WAN 43, 46, 51-52, 54, 77, 107

Warranties 135-136

Watermark image 195

Web browsers 4, 52, 59, 96, 125, 149, 155-156, 161, 169, 188, 199

Web design 8, 59, 59-62, 77, 86, 156, 163, 168-169, 180-182, 193, 209, 213, 216

Web editors 163

Web page creation 59, 77

Web page templates 181

Web servers 52, 96, 98, 127, 133, 161, 180

Web surfing 125-126, 144, 156, 233

Web writers 267, 269, 299

Web-based e-mail service 150

Website designer 59-62

Website recruitment 67

Webtechniques Magazine 5

Wedding planning 9

Weekend classes 118

Weekly newsletters 68

Westover, Lance Jeff 67

Wheelchairs 46

While e-commerce 56

Wide Area Network 43, 46, 51-52, 54, 77, 107

Wilson, Dan 85-86, 88-89

Windows 51, 61, 132-133, 138, 151-153, 157-158, 162, 175, 192

Wireless communications 107

Wireless Ethernet 138

Wireless Internet access 3, 144

Wireless Web Connect 148

Wisconsin 295

Woodford, Katherine 68, 98

Word document 166, 187, 190, 288

Word processing 8, 37, 49-50, 69, 91-92, 150, 153, 162-163, 165, 187, 190

Work hours 13, 32-33, 102

World cultures 223

World economy 16

WorldOpinion 299, 301

Writer 8-9, 12, 16, 18, 20, 59, 61-62, 68-72, 75, 80, 85, 87, 91, 93, 98, 100, 185, 196, 198, 209-210, 213, 217-218, 235, 253, 267-271, 274, 281-282, 290, 297, 299

Writers' conferences 267

Writing-related forums 269

Yellow Pages 118, 146, 199

Yukon 242

Site Address	Markets Served
	1=Employers
	2=Employees
	3=General Public
	4=All
		# Employers Offering Jobs
		1=Excellent
		2= Very Good
		3=Okay
		4=Could Use
		Improvement
		5=Poor

Ajr.newslink.org	1, 2	5
Aquent.com	4	5
ArtHire.com	4	5
BestJobsUSA.com	4	5
Black-Collegian.com	4	4
CareerBuilder.com	4	5
CareerCity.com	4	5
CareerJournal.com	4	2
CareerWeb.com	4	5
ComputerJobs.com	4	2
CoolWorks.com	4	5
CruelWorld.com	4	5
DreamJobs.com	4	4
editorandpublisher.com	4	4
4Work.com	1	5
FreeAgent.com	4	5
Freelance.com	1, 2	5
FreelanceWorkExchange.com	4	5
FreelanceWriting.com	4	5
FreetimeJobs.com	4	5
Guru.com	4	5
Headhunter.net	4	1
HotJobs.com	4	1
Monster.com	4	2
r144.com	4	1
Sologig.com	4	1
Thingamajob.com	4	5
Tripod.com	4	5
WorldOpinion.com	4	2

Compensation Data	Homepage	Usability	Helpfulness to Freelancers
1=Excellent 2=Very Good 3=Okay 4=Could Use Improvement 5=Poor	1=Excellent 2=Very Good 3=Okay 4=Could Use Improvement 5=Poor	1=Excellent 2=Very Good 3=Okay 4=Could Use Improvement 5=Poor	A=Highly Recommended B=May Be Helpful C=Probably Not Worth the Time D=Don't Waste the Time
5	2	1	A
2	2	2	B
5	2	2	A
3	2	1	B
3	1	1	B
5	2	3	B
3	2	2	B
2	3	3	B-C
3	3	4	C
3	2	3	B
5	2	2	B
5	1	2	B
5	3	3	C
2	2	1	B
5	4	5	D
5	2	2	C
5	4	4	B
5	3	3	D
3	3	3	A
5	5	4	C
1	2	1	A
5	2	3	C
5	2	2	D
5	3	2	B
1	2	1	A
1	2	5	C
2	2	2	C
2	4	3	B
2	1	1	A

About the Authors

Robert Anthony has been a visual artist and a freelance writer for more than twenty years and has worked online exclusively since 1998. He serves as the *Web Work* columnist for the nationally distributed print publication, *Writers' Journal Magazine,* and has worked on a multitude of high-end professional writing, communications, and marketing projects, including Web content development, technical writing, magazine writing, and e-mail marketing design. His Web writings have been published at www.review.com (The Princeton Review), www.corvus.com (American Amateur Astronomy Association), www.rockler.com (Rockler Woodworking and Hardware), www.govtjob.net/CMcareerprofile.htm (Government Job.net), and www.mrpaonline.org (Michigan Recreation and Park Association). As a pioneering project manager for one of the nation's first Web-based magazine publications, *Profiles Online;* staff writer for The Princeton Review Publishing; and communications/marketing manager for the Michigan Recreation and Park Association, he has helped pioneer structured approaches to Web-based commerce and editorial content and design since 1994. From 1994 to 1999 he served as executive editor for *Profiles Magazine* and *Profiles Online.* From 1988 to 1994 he served as communications director for Employee Compensation Advisors, Incorporated. He lives with his wife and children in Lansing, Michigan, a town he claims is one of America's biggest small towns. You can reach him anytime, day or night, at his personal website located at www.profilesonline.com, or via his personal e-mail address at editor@profilesonline.com.

Jim Blau is a freelance writer, copyeditor, Mac tech support guy, database designer, and all-'round technogeeky wordsmith. He is 32 years old and lives in New York City with Greta, Partial, and Shovel, two of whom are cats.

Notes

Notes

Notes

Notes

Notes

Notes